Fuzzy Logic, Neural Network and Genetic Algorithms Handbook

Fuzzy Logic, Neural Network and Genetic Algorithms Handbook

Jan Bundschuh

Oxford Book Company
Jaipur ▪ New Delhi

Published By

Oxford Book Company

Regd. Off. "Bony Residency", Gate No. 2
Opp. Tilak Public School, Vishweswariya Nagar,
Gopalpura Road, Jaipur - 302018, India
Ph: 0141 - 2761280, Telefax: 2761381
email - oxfordbookjpr@gmail.com
website - oxfordbookcompany.com

Delhi Office: 102, 1st Floor, Satyam House,
4327/3, Ansari Road, Darya Ganj,
New Delhi - 110002, India
Ph: 011-45652440

Distributed by
KEYA INTERNATIONAL PRESS LLP
E-mail: keyainternationalpressllp@gmail.com

Published in India, 2026

ISBN : 9789350305577

Typeset by Shivangi Computers, Jaipur

Printed and bound in India by Replika Press Pvt. Ltd.

Contents

Preface

Fuzzy logic and probabilistic logic are mathematically similar – both have truth values ranging between 0 and 1 – but conceptually distinct, due to different interpretations. Fuzzy logic corresponds to "degrees of truth", while probabilistic logic corresponds to "probability, likelihood"; as these differ, fuzzy logic and probabilistic logic yield different models of the same real-world situations. Both degrees of truth and probabilities range between 0 and 1 and hence may seem similar at first. For example, let a 100 ml glass contain 30 ml of water. Then we may consider two concepts: Empty and Full. The meaning of each of them can be represented by a certain fuzzy set. Then one might define the glass as being 0.7 empty and 0.3 full. Note that the concept of emptiness would be subjective and thus would depend on the observer or designer. Another designer might equally well design a set membership function where the glass would be considered full for all values down to 50 ml. It is essential to realize that fuzzy logic uses truth degrees as a mathematical model of the vagueness phenomenon while probability is a mathematical model of ignorance.

Fuzzy logic is a form of many-valued logic; it deals with reasoning that is approximate rather than fixed and exact. In contrast with traditional logic theory, where binary sets have two-valued logic: true or false, fuzzy logic variables may have a truth value that ranges in degree between 0 and 1. Fuzzy logic has been extended to handle the concept of partial truth, where the truth value may range between completely true and completely false. Furthermore, when linguistic variables are used, these degrees may be managed by specific functions. Fuzzy logic began with the 1965 proposal of fuzzy set theory by Lotfi Zadeh. Fuzzy logic has been applied to many fields, from control theory to artificial intelligence. The reasoning in fuzzy logic is similar to human reasoning. It allows for approximate values and inferences as well as incomplete or ambiguous data (fuzzy data) as opposed to only relying on crisp data (binary yes/no choices). Fuzzy logic is able to process incomplete data and provide approximate solutions to problems other methods find difficult to solve. Terminology used in fuzzy logic not used in other methods are: very high, increasing, somewhat decreased, reasonable and very low.

Hope, this Handbook provides a useful addition to the readers and the neural network community.

— Jan Bundschuh

Chapter 1

Introduction

Fuzzy Logic

Fuzzy logic is a form of many-valued logic; it deals with reasoning that is approximate rather than fixed and exact. In contrast with traditional logic theory, where binary sets have two-valued logic: true or false, fuzzy logic variables may have a truth value that ranges in degree between 0 and 1. Fuzzy logic has been extended to handle the concept of partial truth, where the truth value may range between completely true and completely false. Furthermore, when linguistic variables are used, these degrees may be managed by specific functions.

Fuzzy logic began with the 1965 proposal of fuzzy set theory by Lotfi Zadeh. Fuzzy logic has been applied to many fields, from control theory to artificial intelligence.

Overview

The reasoning in fuzzy logic is similar to human reasoning. It allows for approximate values and inferences as well as incomplete or ambiguous data (fuzzy data) as opposed to only relying on crisp data (binary yes/no choices). Fuzzy logic is able to process incomplete data and provide approximate solutions to problems other methods find difficult to solve. Terminology used in fuzzy logic not used in other methods are: very high, increasing, somewhat decreased, reasonable and very low.

Degrees of Truth

Fuzzy logic and probabilistic logic are mathematically similar – both have truth values ranging between 0 and 1 – but conceptually distinct, due to different interpretations. Fuzzy logic corresponds to "degrees of truth", while probabilistic logic corresponds to "probability, likelihood"; as these differ, fuzzy logic and probabilistic logic yield different models of the same real-world situations. Both degrees of truth and probabilities range between 0 and 1 and hence may seem similar at first.

For example, let a 100 ml glass contain 30 ml of water. Then we may consider two concepts: Empty and Full. The meaning of each of them can be represented by a certain fuzzy set. Then one might define the glass as being 0.7 empty and 0.3 full. Note that the concept of emptiness would be subjective and thus would depend on the observer or designer.

Another designer might equally well design a set membership function where the glass would be considered full for all values down to 50 ml. It is essential to realize that fuzzy logic uses truth degrees as a mathematical model of the vagueness phenomenon while probability is a mathematical model of ignorance.

Applying Truth Values

A basic application might characterize subranges of a continuous variable. For instance, a temperature measurement for anti-lock brakes might have several separate membership functions defining particular temperature ranges needed to control the brakes properly. Each function maps the same temperature value to a truth value in the 0 to 1 range. These truth values can then be used to determine how the brakes should be controlled.

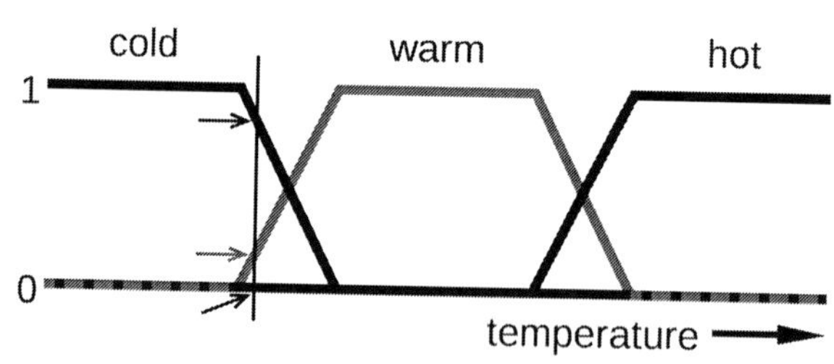

Figure: Fuzzy logic temperature

In this image, the meaning of the expressions cold, warm, and hot is represented by functions mapping a temperature scale. A point on that scale has three "truth values"—one for each of the three functions. The vertical line in the image represents a particular temperature that the three arrows (truth values) gauge. Since the red arrow points to zero, this temperature may be interpreted as "not hot". The orange arrow (pointing at 0.2) may describe it as "slightly warm" and the blue arrow (pointing at 0.8) "fairly cold".

Linguistic Variables

While variables in mathematics usually take numerical values, in fuzzy logic applications, the non-numeric linguistic variables are often used to facilitate the expression of rules and facts.

A linguistic variable such as age may have a value such as young or its antonym old. However, the great utility of linguistic variables is that they can be modified via linguistic hedges applied to primary terms. The linguistic hedges can be associated with certain functions.

Example

Fuzzy set theory defines fuzzy operators on fuzzy sets. The problem in applying this is that the appropriate fuzzy operator may not be known. For this reason, fuzzy logic usually uses IF-THEN rules, or constructs that are equivalent, such as fuzzy associative matrices.

Rules are usually expressed in the form:

IF variable IS property THEN action

For example, a simple temperature regulator that uses a fan might look like this:

IF temperature IS very cold THEN stop fan

IF temperature IS cold THEN turn down fan

IF temperature IS normal THEN maintain level

IF temperature IS hot THEN speed up fan.

There is no "ELSE" – all of the rules are evaluated, because the temperature might be "cold" and "normal" at the same time to different degrees.

The AND, OR, and NOT operators of boolean logic exist in fuzzy logic, usually defined as the minimum, maximum, and complement; when they are defined this way, they are called the Zadeh operators. So for the fuzzy variables x and y:

NOT x = (1 - truth(x))

x AND y = minimum(truth(x), truth(y))

x OR y = maximum(truth(x), truth(y)).

There are also other operators, more linguistic in nature, called hedges that can be applied. These are generally adverbs such as "very", or "somewhat", which modify the meaning of a set using a mathematical formula.

Logical Analysis

In mathematical logic, there are several formal systems of "fuzzy logic"; most of them belong among so-called t-norm fuzzy logics.

Propositional Fuzzy Lkogics

The most important propositional fuzzy logics are:

- Monoidal t-norm-based propositional fuzzy logic MTL is an axiomatisation of logic where conjunction is defined by a left continuous t-norm, and implication is defined as the residuum of the t-norm. Its models correspond to MTL-algebras that are prelinear commutative bounded integral residuated lattices.
- Basic propositional fuzzy logic BL is an extension of MTL logic where conjunction is defined by a continuous t-norm, and implication is also defined as the residuum of the t-norm. Its models correspond to BL-algebras.
- £ukasiewicz fuzzy logic is the extension of basic fuzzy logic BL where standard conjunction is the £ukasiewicz t-norm. It has the axioms of basic fuzzy logic plus an axiom of double negation, and its models correspond to MV-algebras.
- Gödel fuzzy logic is the extension of basic fuzzy logic BL where conjunction is Gödel t-norm. It has the axioms of BL plus an axiom of idempotence of conjunction, and its models are called G-algebras.
- Product fuzzy logic is the extension of basic fuzzy logic BL where conjunction is product t-norm. It has the axioms of BL plus another axiom for cancellativity of conjunction, and its models are called product algebras.
- Fuzzy logic with evaluated syntax (sometimes also called Pavelka's logic), denoted by EV£, is a further generalisation of mathematical fuzzy logic. While the above kinds of fuzzy logic have traditional syntax and many-valued semantics, in EV£ is evaluated also syntax. This means that each formula has an evaluation. Axiomatisation of EV£ stems from £ukasziewicz fuzzy logic. A generalisation of classical Gödel completeness theorem is provable in EV£.

Predicate Fuzzy Logics

These extend the above-mentioned fuzzy logics by adding universal and existential quantifiers in a manner similar to the way that predicate logic is created from propositional logic. The semantics of the universal (resp. existential) quantifier in t-norm fuzzy logics is the infimum (resp. supremum) of the truth degrees of the instances of the quantified subformula.

Decidability Issues for Fuzzy Logic

The notions of a "decidable subset" and "recursively enumerable subset" are basic ones for classical mathematics and classical logic. Then, the question of a suitable extension of such concepts to fuzzy set theory arises.

A first proposal in such a direction was made by E.S. Santos by the notions of fuzzy Turing machine, Markov normal fuzzy algorithm and fuzzy program. Successively, L. Biacino and G. Gerla showed that such a definition is not adequate and therefore proposed the following one. Ü denotes the set of rational numbers in [0,1].

A fuzzy subset s : S → [0,1] of a set S is recursively enumerable if a recursive map h : S×N → Ü exists such that, for every xin S, the function h(x,n) is increasing with respect to n and s(x) = lim h(x,n). We say that s is decidable if both s and its complement –s are recursively enumerable. An extension of such a theory to the general case of the L-subsets is proposed in Gerla 2006. The proposed definitions are well related with fuzzy logic. Indeed, the following theorem holds true (provided that the deduction apparatus of the fuzzy logic satisfies some obvious effectiveness property).

Theorem. Any axiomatisable fuzzy theory is recursively enumerable. In particular, the fuzzy set of logically true formulas is recursively enumerable in spite of the fact that the crisp set of valid formulas is not recursively enumerable, in general. Moreover, any axiomatisable and complete theory is decidable.

It is an open question to give supports for a Church thesis for fuzzy logic claiming that the proposed notion of recursive enumerability for fuzzy subsets is the adequate one. To this aim, further investigations on the notions of fuzzy grammar and fuzzy Turing machine should be necessary. Another open question is to start from this notion to find an extension of Gödel's theorems to fuzzy logic.

Fuzzy Databases

Once fuzzy relations are defined, it is possible to develop fuzzy relational databases. The first fuzzy relational database, FRDB, appeared in Maria Zemankova's dissertation. Later, some other models arose like the Buckles-Petry model, the Prade-Testemale Model, the Umano-Fukami model or the GEFRED model by J.M. Medina, M.A. Vila et al. In the context of fuzzy databases, some fuzzy querying languages have been defined, highlighting the SQLf by P. Bosc et al. and the FSQL by J. Galindo et al. These languages define some structures in order to include fuzzy aspects in the SQL statements, like fuzzy conditions, fuzzy comparators, fuzzy constants, fuzzy constraints, fuzzy thresholds, linguistic labels and so on.

Comparison to Probability

Fuzzy logic and probability are different ways of expressing uncertainty. While both fuzzy logic and probability theory can be used to represent subjective belief, fuzzy set theory uses the concept of fuzzy set membership (i.e., how much a variable is in a set), and probability theory uses the concept of subjective probability (i.e., how probable do I think that a variable is in a set).

While this distinction is mostly philosophical, the fuzzy-logic-derived possibility measure is inherently different from the probability measure, hence they are not directly equivalent. However, many statisticians are persuaded by the work of Bruno de Finetti that only one kind of mathematical uncertainty is needed and thus fuzzy logic is unnecessary.

On the other hand, Bart Kosko argues that probability is a subtheory of fuzzy logic, as probability only handles one kind of uncertainty. He also claims to have proven a derivation of Bayes' theorem from the concept of fuzzy subsethood. Lotfi Zadeh argues that fuzzy logic is different in character from probability, and is not a replacement for it. He fuzzified probability to fuzzy probability and also generalised it to what is called possibility theory. (cf.)

Neural Network

The term neural network was traditionally used to refer to a network or circuit of biological neurons. The modern usage of the term often refers to artificial neural networks, which are composed of artificial neurons or nodes. Thus the term has two distinct usages:

1. Biological neural networks are made up of real biological neurons that are connected or functionally related in a nervous system. In the field of neuroscience, they are often identified as groups of neurons that perform a specific physiological function in laboratory analysis.

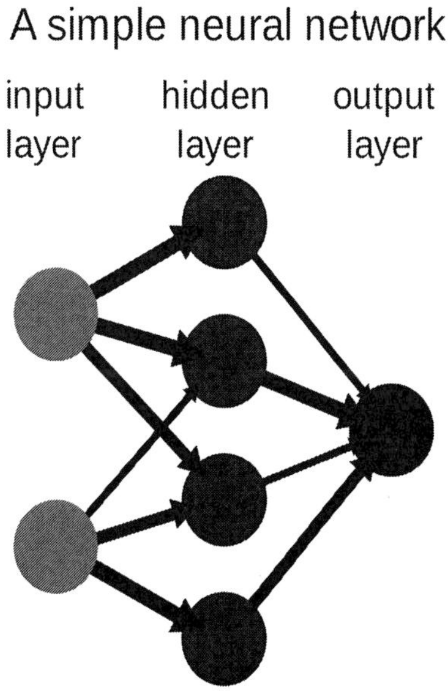

Figure: Simplified view of a feedforward artificial neural network

2. Artificial neural networks are composed of interconnecting artificial neurons (programming constructs that mimic the properties of biological neurons). Artificial neural networks may either be used to gain an understanding of biological neural networks, or for solving artificial intelligence problems without necessarily creating a model of a real biological system. The real, biological nervous system is highly complex: artificial neural network algorithms attempt to abstract this complexity and focus on what may hypothetically matter most from an information processing point of view. Good performance (e.g. as measured by good predictive ability, low generalisation error), or performance mimicking animal or human error patterns, can then be used as one source of evidence towards supporting the hypothesis that the abstraction really captured something important from the point of view of information processing in the brain. Another incentive for these abstractions

is to reduce the amount of computation required to simulate artificial neural networks, so as to allow one to experiment with larger networks and train them on larger data sets.

This article focuses on the relationship between the two concepts; for detailed coverage of the two different concepts refer to the separate articles: biological neural network and artificial neural network.

A biological neural network is composed of a group or groups of chemically connected or functionally associated neurons. A single neuron may be connected to many other neurons and the total number of neurons and connections in a network may be extensive. Connections, called synapses, are usually formed from axons to dendrites, though dendrodendritic microcircuits and other connections are possible. Apart from the electrical signaling, there are other forms of signaling that arise from neurotransmitter diffusion, which have an effect on electrical signaling. As such, neural networks are extremely complex. Artificial intelligence and cognitive modeling try to simulate some properties of biological neural networks. While similar in their techniques, the former has the aim of solving particular tasks, while the latter aims to build mathematical models of biological neural systems.

In the artificial intelligence field, artificial neural networks have been applied successfully to speech recognition, image analysis and adaptive control, in order to construct software agents (in computer and video games) or autonomous robots. Most of the currently employed artificial neural networks for artificial intelligence are based on statistical estimations, Classification optimisation and control theory.

The cognitive modelling field involves the physical or mathematical modeling of the behaviour of neural systems; ranging from the individual neural level (e.g. modelling the spike response curves of neurons to a stimulus), through the neural cluster level (e.g. modelling the release and effects of dopamine in the basal ganglia) to the complete organism (e.g. behavioural modelling of the organism's response to stimuli). Artificial intelligence, cognitive modelling, and neural networks are information processing paradigms inspired by the way biological neural systems process data.

History of the Neural Network Analogy

In the brain, spontaneous order appears to arise out of decentralized networks of simple units (neurons). Neural network theory has served both to better identify how the neurons in the brain function and to provide the basis for efforts to create artificial intelligence. The preliminary theoretical base for contemporary neural networks was independently proposed by Alexander Bain (1873) and William James (1890). In their work, both thoughts and body activity resulted from interactions among neurons within the brain.

For Bain, every activity led to the firing of a certain set of neurons. When activities were repeated, the connections between those neurons strengthened. According to his theory, this repetition was what led to the formation of memory. The general scientific community at the time was skeptical of Bain's theory because it required what appeared to be an inordinate number of neural connections within the brain. It is now apparent that the brain is exceedingly complex and that the same brain "wiring" can handle multiple problems and inputs.

James's theory was similar to Bain's, however, he suggested that memories and actions resulted from electrical currents flowing among the neurons in the brain. His model, by focusing on the flow of electrical currents, did not require individual neural connections for each memory or action.

C. S. Sherrington (1898) conducted experiments to test James's theory. He ran electrical currents down the spinal cords of rats. However, instead of the demonstrating an increase in electrical current as projected by James, Sherrington found that the electrical current strength decreased as the testing continued over time. Importantly, this work led to the discovery of the concept of habituation.

McCullouch and Pitts (1943) created a computational model for neural networks based on mathematics and algorithms. They called this model threshold logic. The model paved the way for neural network research to split into two distinct approaches. One approach focused on biological processes in the brain and the other focused on the application of neural networks to artificial intelligence.

In the late 1940s psychologist Donald Hebb created a hypothesis of learning based on the mechanism of neural plasticity that is now known as Hebbian learning. Hebbian learning is considered to be a 'typical' unsupervised learning rule and its later variants were early models for long term potentiation. These ideas started being applied to computational models in 1948 with Turing's B-type machines. Farley and Clark (1954) first used computational machines, then called calculators, to simulate a Hebbian network at MIT. Other neural network computational machines were created by Rochester, Holland, Habit, and Duda (1956).

Rosenblatt (1958) created the perceptron, an algorithm for pattern recognition based on a two-layer learning computer network using simple addition and subtraction. With mathematical notation, Rosenblatt also described circuitry not in the basic perceptron, such as the exclusive-or circuit, a circuit whose mathematical computation could not be processed until after the back propogation algorithm was created by Werbos (1975).

The perceptron is essentially a linear classifier for classifying data specified by parameters and an output function f = w'x + b. Its parameters are adapted with an ad-hoc rule similar to stochastic steepest gradient descent. Because the inner product is a linear operator in the input space, the perceptron can only perfectly classify a set of data for which different classes are linearly separable in the input space, while it often fails completely for non-separable data. While the development of the algorithm initially generated some enthusiasm, partly because of its apparent relation to biological mechanisms, the later discovery of this inadequacy caused such models to be abandoned until the introduction of non-linear models into the field.

Neural network research stagnated after the publication of research of machine learning research by Minsky and Papert (1969). They discovered two key issues with the computational machines that processed neural networks. The first issue was that single-layer neural networks were incapable of processing the exclusive-or circuit. The second significant issue was that computers were not sophisticated enough to effectively handle the long run time required by large neural networks. Neural network research slowed until computers achieved greater processing power. Also key in later advances was the backpropogation algorithm which effectively solved the exclusive-or problem (Werbos 1975).

The cognitron (1975) designed by Kunihiko Fukushima was an early multilayered neural network with a training algorithm. The actual structure of the network and the methods used to set the interconnection weights change from one neural strategy to another, each with its advantages and disadvantages. Networks can propagate information in one direction only, or they can bounce back and forth until self-activation at a node occurs and the network settles on a final state. The ability for bi-directional flow of inputs between neurons/ nodes was produced with the Hopfield's network (1982), and specialization of these node layers for specific purposes was introduced through the first hybrid network.

The parallel distributed processing of the mid-1980s became popular under the name connectionism. The text by Rummelhart and McClelland (1986) provided a full exposition of the use connectionism in computers to simulate neural processes.

The rediscovery of the backpropagation algorithm was probably the main reason behind the repopularisation of neural networks after the publication of "Learning Internal Representations by Error Propagation" in 1986 (Though backpropagation itself dates from 1969). The original network utilized multiple layers of weight-sum units of the type f = g(w'x + b), where g was a sigmoid function or logistic function such as used in logistic regression.

Training was done by a form of stochastic gradient descent. The employment of the chain rule of differentiation in deriving the appropriate parameter updates results in an algorithm that seems to 'backpropagate errors', hence the nomenclature.

However it is essentially a form of gradient descent. Determining the optimal parameters in a model of this type is not trivial, and local numerical optimisation methods such as gradient descent can be sensitive to initialization because of the presence of local minima of the training criterion. In recent times, networks with the same architecture as the backpropagation network are referred to as multilayer perceptrons. This name does not impose any limitations on the type of algorithm used for learning.

The backpropagation network generated much enthusiasm at the time and there was much controversy about whether such learning could be implemented in the brain or not, partly because a mechanism for reverse signaling was not obvious at the time, but most importantly because there was no plausible source for the 'teaching' or 'target' signal. However, since 2006, several unsupervised learning procedures have been proposed for neural networks with one or more layers, using so-called deep learning algorithms. These algorithms can be used to learn intermediate representations, with or without a target signal, that capture the salient features of the distribution of sensory signals arriving at each layer of the neural network.

The Brain, Neural Networks and Computers

Neural networks, as used in artificial intelligence, have traditionally been viewed as simplified models of neural processing in the brain, even though the relation between this model and brain biological architecture is debated, as little is known about how the brain actually works.

A subject of current research in theoretical neuroscience is the question surrounding the degree of complexity and the properties that individual neural elements should have to reproduce something resembling animal intelligence.

Historically, computers evolved from the von Neumann architecture, which is based on sequential processing and execution of explicit instructions. On the other hand, the origins of neural networks are based on efforts to model information processing in biological systems, which may rely largely on parallel processing as well as implicit instructions based on recognition of patterns of 'sensory' input from external sources. In other words, at its very heart a neural network is a complex statistical processor (as opposed to being tasked to sequentially process and execute).

Neural coding is concerned with how sensory and other information is represented in the brain by neurons. The main goal of studying neural coding is to characterize the relationship between the stimulus and the individual or ensemble neuronal responses and the relationship among electrical activity of the neurons in the ensemble. It is thought that neurons can encode both digital and analogue information.

Neural Networks and Artificial Intelligence

A neural network (NN), in the case of artificial neurons called artificial neural network (ANN) or simulated neural network (SNN), is an interconnected group of natural or artificial neurons that uses a mathematical or computational model for information processing based on a connectionistic approach to computation. In most cases an ANN is an adaptive system that changes its structure based on external or internal information that flows through the network.

In more practical terms neural networks are non-linear statistical data modeling or decision making tools. They can be used to model complex relationships between inputs and outputs or to find patterns in data.

However, the paradigm of neural networks - i.e., implicit, not explicit , learning is stressed - seems more to correspond to some kind of natural intelligence than to the traditional symbol-based Artificial Intelligence, which would stress, instead, rule-based learning.

Background

An artificial neural network involves a network of simple processing elements (artificial neurons) which can exhibit complex global behaviour, determined by the connections between the processing elements and element parameters. Artificial neurons were first proposed in 1943 by Warren McCulloch, a neurophysiologist, and Walter Pitts, a logician, who first collaborated at the University of Chicago.

One classical type of artificial neural network is the recurrent Hopfield net.

In a neural network model simple nodes (which can be called by a number of names, including "neurons", "neurodes", "Processing Elements" (PE) and "units"), are connected together to form a network of nodes — hence the term "neural network". While a neural network does not have to be adaptive per se, its practical use comes with algorithms designed to alter the strength (weights) of the connections in the network to produce a desired signal flow.

In modern software implementations of artificial neural networks the approach inspired by biology has more or less been abandoned for a more practical approach based on statistics and signal processing. In some of these systems, neural networks, or parts of neural networks (such as artificial neurons), are used as components in larger systems that combine both adaptive and non-adaptive elements.

The concept of a neural network appears to have first been proposed by Alan Turing in his 1948 paper "Intelligent Machinery".

Applications of Natural and of Artificial Neural Networks

The utility of artificial neural network models lies in the fact that they can be used to infer a function from observations and also to use it. Unsupervised neural networks can also be used to learn representations of the input that capture the salient characteristics of the input distribution, and more recently, deep learning algorithms, which can implicitly learn the distribution function of the observed data. Learning in neural networks is particularly useful in applications where the complexity of the data or task makes the design of such functions by hand impractical.

The tasks to which artificial neural networks are applied tend to fall within the following broad categories:

- Function approximation, or regression analysis, including time series prediction and modeling.
- Classification, including pattern and sequence recognition, novelty detection and sequential decision making.
- Data processing, including filtering, clustering, blind signal separation and compression.

Application areas of ANNs include system identification and control (vehicle control, process control), game-playing and decision making (backgammon, chess, racing), pattern recognition (radar systems, face identification, object recognition), sequence recognition (gesture, speech, handwritten text recognition), medical diagnosis, financial applications, data mining (or knowledge discovery in databases, "KDD"), visualization and e-mail spam filtering.

Neural Networks and Neuroscience

Theoretical and computational neuroscience is the field concerned with the theoretical analysis and computational modeling of biological neural systems. Since neural systems are intimately related to cognitive processes and behaviour, the field is closely related to cognitive and behavioural modeling.

The aim of the field is to create models of biological neural systems in order to understand how biological systems work. To gain this understanding, neuroscientists strive to make a link between observed biological processes (data), biologically plausible mechanisms for neural processing and learning (biological neural network models) and theory (statistical learning theory and information theory).

Types of Models

Many models are used in the field, each defined at a different level of abstraction and trying to model different aspects of neural systems. They range from models of the short-term behaviour of individual neurons, through models of how the dynamics of neural circuitry arise from interactions between individual neurons, to models of how behaviour can arise from abstract neural modules that represent complete subsystems. These include models of the long-term and short-term plasticity of neural systems and its relation to learning and memory, from the individual neuron to the system level.

Current Research

While initially research had been concerned mostly with the electrical characteristics of neurons, a particularly important part of the investigation in recent years has been the exploration of the role of neuromodulators such as dopamine, acetylcholine, and serotonin on behaviour and learning.

Biophysical models, such as BCM theory, have been important in understanding mechanisms for synaptic plasticity, and have had applications in both computer science and neuroscience. Research is ongoing in understanding the computational algorithms used in the brain, with some recent biological evidence for radial basis networks and neural backpropagation as mechanisms for processing data.

Computational devices have been created in CMOS for both biophysical simulation and neuromorphic computing. More recent efforts show promise for creating nanodevices for very large scale principal components analyses and convolution. If successful, these efforts could usher in a new era of neural computing that is a step beyond digital computing, because it depends on learning rather than programming and because it is fundamentally analogue rather than digital even though the first instantiations may in fact be with CMOS digital devices.

Architecture

The basic architecture consists of three types of neuron layers: input, hidden, and output. In feed-forward networks, the signal flow is from input to output units, strictly in a feed-forward direction. The data processing can extend over multiple layers of units, but no feedback connections are present. Recurrent networks contain feedback connections. Contrary to feed-forward networks, the dynamical properties of the network are important. In some cases, the activation values of the units undergo a relaxation process such that the network will evolve to a stable state in which these activations do not change anymore.

In other applications, the changes of the activation values of the output neurons are significant, such that the dynamical behaviour constitutes the output of the network. Other neural network architectures include adaptive resonance theory maps and competitive networks.

Criticism

A common criticism of neural networks, particularly in robotics, is that they require a large diversity of training for real-world operation. This is not surprising, since any learning machine needs sufficient representative examples in order to capture the underlying structure that allows it to generalise to new cases. Dean Pomerleau, in his research presented in the paper "Knowledge-based Training of Artificial Neural Networks for Autonomous Robot Driving," uses a neural network to train a robotic vehicle to drive on multiple types of roads (single lane, multi-lane, dirt, etc.).

A large amount of his research is devoted to (1) extrapolating multiple training scenarios from a single training experience, and (2) preserving past training diversity so that the system does not become overtrained (if, for example, it is presented with a series of right turns – it should not learn to always turn right). These issues are common in neural networks that must decide from amongst a wide variety of responses, but can be dealt with in several ways, for example by randomly shuffling the training examples, by using a numerical optimisation algorithm that does not take too large steps when changing the network connections following an example, or by grouping examples in so-called mini-batches.

A. K. Dewdney, a former Scientific American columnist, wrote in 1997, "Although neural nets do solve a few toy problems, their powers of computation are so limited that I am surprised anyone takes them seriously as a general problem-solving tool." (Dewdney, p. 82)

Arguments for Dewdney's position are that to implement large and effective software neural networks, much processing and storage resources need to be committed. While the brain has hardware tailored to the task of processing signals through a graph of neurons, simulating even a most simplified form on Von Neumann technology may compel a NN designer to fill many millions of database rows for its connections - which can consume vast amounts of computer memory and hard disk space. Furthermore, the designer of NN systems will often need to simulate the transmission of signals through many of these connections and their associated neurons - which must often be matched with incredible amounts of CPU processing power and time. While neural networks often yield effective programs, they too often do so at the cost of efficiency (they tend to consume considerable amounts of time and money).

Arguments against Dewdney's position are that neural nets have been successfully used to solve many complex and diverse tasks, ranging from autonomously flying aircraft to detecting credit card fraud .

Technology writer Roger Bridgman commented on Dewdney's statements about neural nets:

Neural networks, for instance, are in the dock not only because they have been hyped to high heaven, (what hasn't?) but also because you could create a successful net without understanding how it worked: the bunch of numbers that captures its behaviour would in all probability be "an opaque, unreadable table...valueless as a scientific resource". In spite of his emphatic declaration that science is not technology, Dewdney seems here to pillory neural nets as bad science when most of those devising them are just trying to be good engineers. An unreadable table that a useful machine could read would still be well worth having.

In response to this kind of criticism, one should note that although it is true that analysing what has been learned by an artificial neural network is difficult, it is much easier to do so than to analyse what has been learned by a biological neural network. Furthermore, researchers involved in exploring learning algorithms for neural networks are gradually uncovering generic principles which allow a learning machine to be successful. For example, Bengio and LeCun (2007) wrote an article regarding local vs non-local learning, as well as shallow vs deep architecture .

Some other criticisms came from believers of hybrid models (combining neural networks and symbolic approaches). They advocate the intermix of these two approaches and believe that hybrid models can better capture the mechanisms of the human mind (Sun and Bookman 1990).

Genetic Algorithm

A genetic algorithm (GA) is a search heuristic that mimics the process of natural evolution. This heuristic is routinely used to generate useful solutions to optimisation and search problems. Genetic algorithms belong to the larger class of evolutionary algorithms (EA), which generate solutions to optimisation problems using techniques inspired by natural evolution, such as inheritance, mutation, selection, and crossover.

Methodology

In a genetic algorithm, a population of strings (called chromosomes or the genotype of the genome), which encode candidate solutions (called individuals, creatures, or phenotypes) to an optimisation problem, evolves toward better solutions. Traditionally, solutions are represented in binary as strings of 0s and 1s, but other encodings are also possible. The evolution usually starts from a population of randomly generated individuals and happens in generations. In each generation, the fitness of every individual in the population is evaluated, multiple individuals are stochastically selected from the current population (based on their fitness), and modified (recombined and possibly randomly mutated) to form a new population. The new population is then used in the next iteration of the algorithm. Commonly, the algorithm terminates when either a maximum number of generations has been produced, or a satisfactory fitness level has been reached for the population. If the algorithm has terminated due to a maximum number of generations, a satisfactory solution may or may not have been reached.

Genetic algorithms find application in bioinformatics, phylogenetics, computational science, engineering, economics, chemistry, manufacturing, mathematics, physics and other fields.

A typical genetic algorithm requires:

1. a genetic representation of the solution domain,
2. a fitness function to evaluate the solution domain.

A standard representation of the solution is as an array of bits. Arrays of other types and structures can be used in essentially the same way. The main property that makes these genetic representations convenient is that their parts are easily aligned due to their fixed size, which facilitates simple crossover operations. Variable length representations may also be used, but crossover implementation is more complex in this case. Tree-like representations are explored in genetic programming and graph-form representations are explored in evolutionary programming.

The fitness function is defined over the genetic representation and measures the quality of the represented solution. The fitness function is always problem dependent. For instance, in the knapsack problem one wants to maximize the total value of objects that can be put in a knapsack of some fixed capacity. A representation of a solution might be an array of bits, where each bit represents a different object, and the value of the bit (0 or 1) represents whether or not the object is in the knapsack. Not every such representation is valid, as the size of objects may exceed the capacity of the knapsack. The fitness of the solution is the sum of values of all objects in the knapsack if the representation is valid, or 0 otherwise. In some problems, it is hard or even impossible to define the fitness expression; in these cases, interactive genetic algorithms are used.

Once the genetic representation and the fitness function are defined, a GA proceeds to initialize a population of solutions (usually randomly) and then to improve it through repetitive application of the mutation, crossover, inversion and selection operators.

Initialization

Initially many individual solutions are (usually) randomly generated to form an initial population. The population size depends on the nature of the problem, but typically contains several hundreds or thousands of possible solutions. Traditionally, the population is generated randomly, allowing the entire range of possible solutions (the search space). Occasionally, the solutions may be "seeded" in areas where optimal solutions are likely to be found.

Selection

During each successive generation, a proportion of the existing population is selected to breed a new generation. Individual solutions are selected through a fitness-based process, where fitter solutions (as measured by a fitness function) are typically more likely to be selected. Certain selection methods rate the fitness of each solution and preferentially select the best solutions. Other methods rate only a random sample of the population, as the latter process may be very time-consuming.

Reproduction

The next step is to generate a second generation population of solutions from those selected through genetic operators: crossover (also called recombination), and/or mutation. For each new solution to be produced, a pair of "parent" solutions is selected for breeding from the pool selected previously. By producing a "child" solution using the above methods of crossover and mutation, a new solution is created which typically shares many of the characteristics of its "parents". New parents are selected for each new child, and the process continues until a new population of solutions of appropriate size is generated. Although reproduction methods that are based on the use of two parents are more "biology inspired", some research suggests more than two "parents" are better to be used to reproduce a good quality chromosome.

These processes ultimately result in the next generation population of chromosomes that is different from the initial generation. Generally the average fitness will have increased by this procedure for the population, since only the best organisms from the first generation are selected for breeding, along with a small proportion of less fit solutions, for reasons already mentioned above.

Although Crossover and Mutation are known as the main genetic operators, it is possible to use other operators such as regrouping, colonization-extinction, or migration in genetic algorithms.

Termination

This generational process is repeated until a termination condition has been reached. Common terminating conditions are:

- A solution is found that satisfies minimum criteria
- Fixed number of generations reached
- Allocated budget (computation time/money) reached
- The highest ranking solution's fitness is reaching or has reached a plateau such that successive iterations no longer produce better results
- Manual inspection
- Combinations of the above

Simple generational genetic algorithm procedure:

1. Choose the initial population of individuals
2. Evaluate the fitness of each individual in that population
3. Repeat on this generation until termination (time limit, sufficient fitness achieved, etc.):

1. Select the best-fit individuals for reproduction
2. Breed new individuals through crossover and mutation operations to give birth to offspring
3. Evaluate the individual fitness of new individuals
4. Replace least-fit population with new individuals

The Building Block Hypothesis

Genetic algorithms are simple to implement, but their behaviour is difficult to understand. In particular it is difficult to understand why these algorithms frequently succeed at generating solutions of high fitness when applied to practical problems. The building block hypothesis (BBH) consists of:

1. A description of a heuristic that performs adaptation by identifying and recombining "building blocks", i.e. low order, low defining-length schemata with above average fitness.
2. A hypothesis that a genetic algorithm performs adaptation by implicitly and efficiently implementing this heuristic.

Goldberg describes the heuristic as follows:

"Short, low order, and highly fit schemata are sampled, recombined [crossed over], and resampled to form strings of potentially higher fitness. In a way, by working with these particular schemata [the building blocks], we have reduced the complexity of our problem; instead of building high-performance strings by trying every conceivable combination, we construct better and better strings from the best partial solutions of past samplings.

"Because highly fit schemata of low defining length and low order play such an important role in the action of genetic algorithms, we have already given them a special name: building blocks. Just as a child creates magnificent fortresses through the arrangement of simple blocks of wood, so does a genetic algorithm seek near optimal performance through the juxtaposition of short, low-order, high-performance schemata, or building blocks."

Observations

There are several general observations about the generation of solutions specifically via a genetic algorithm:

- Selection is clearly an important genetic operator, but opinion is divided over the importance of crossover versus mutation.

Some argue that crossover is the most important, while mutation is only necessary to ensure that potential solutions are not lost. Others argue that crossover in a largely uniform population only serves to propagate innovations originally found by mutation, and in a non-uniform population crossover is nearly always equivalent to a very large mutation (which is likely to be catastrophic). There are many references in Fogel (2006) that support the importance of mutation-based search.

- As with all current machine learning problems it is worth tuning the parameters such as mutation probability, crossover probability and population size to find reasonable settings for the problem class being worked on. A very small mutation rate may lead to genetic drift (which is non-ergodic in nature). A recombination rate that is too high may lead to premature convergence of the genetic algorithm. A mutation rate that is too high may lead to loss of good solutions unless there is elitist selection. There are theoretical but not yet practical upper and lower bounds for these parameters that can help guide selection.
- Often, GAs can rapidly locate good solutions, even for large search spaces. The same is of course also true for evolution strategies and evolutionary programming.

Criticisms

There are several criticisms of the use of a genetic algorithm compared to alternative optimisation algorithms:

- Repeated fitness function evaluation for complex problems is often the most prohibitive and limiting segment of artificial evolutionary algorithms. Finding the optimal solution to complex high dimensional, multimodal problems often requires very expensive fitness function evaluations. In real world problems such as structural optimisation problems, one single function evaluation may require several hours to several days of complete simulation. Typical optimisation methods can not deal with such types of problem. In this case, it may be necessary to forgo an exact evaluation and use an approximated fitness that is computationally efficient. It is apparent that amalgamation of approximate models may be one of the most promising approaches to convincingly use GA to solve complex real life problems.

- The "better" solution is only in comparison to other solutions. As a result, the stop criterion is not clear in every problem.
- In many problems, GAs may have a tendency to converge towards local optima or even arbitrary points rather than the global optimum of the problem. This means that it does not "know how" to sacrifice short-term fitness to gain longer-term fitness. The likelihood of this occurring depends on the shape of the fitness landscape: certain problems may provide an easy ascent towards a global optimum, others may make it easier for the function to find the local optima. This problem may be alleviated by using a different fitness function, increasing the rate of mutation, or by using selection techniques that maintain a diverse population of solutions, although the No Free Lunch theoremproves that there is no general solution to this problem. A common technique to maintain diversity is to impose a "niche penalty", wherein, any group of individuals of sufficient similarity (niche radius) have a penalty added, which will reduce the representation of that group in subsequent generations, permitting other (less similar) individuals to be maintained in the population. This trick, however, may not be effective, depending on the landscape of the problem. Another possible technique would be to simply replace part of the population with randomly generated individuals, when most of the population is too similar to each other. Diversity is important in genetic algorithms (and genetic programming) because crossing over a homogeneous population does not yield new solutions. In evolution strategies and evolutionary programming, diversity is not essential because of a greater reliance on mutation.
- Operating on dynamic data sets is difficult, as genomes begin to converge early on towards solutions which may no longer be valid for later data. Several methods have been proposed to remedy this by increasing genetic diversity somehow and preventing early convergence, either by increasing the probability of mutation when the solution quality drops (called triggered hypermutation), or by occasionally introducing entirely new, randomly generated elements into the gene pool (called random immigrants). Again, evolution strategies and evolutionary programming can be implemented with a so-

called "comma strategy" in which parents are not maintained and new parents are selected only from offspring. This can be more effective on dynamic problems.

- GAs cannot effectively solve problems in which the only fitness measure is a single right/wrong measure (like decision problems), as there is no way to converge on the solution (no hill to climb). In these cases, a random search may find a solution as quickly as a GA. However, if the situation allows the success/failure trial to be repeated giving (possibly) different results, then the ratio of successes to failures provides a suitable fitness measure.
- For specific optimisation problems and problem instances, other optimisation algorithms may find better solutions than genetic algorithms (given the same amount of computation time). Alternative and complementary algorithms include evolution strategies, evolutionary programming, simulated annealing, Gaussian adaptation, hill climbing, and swarm intelligence (e.g.: ant colony optimisation, particle swarm optimisation) and methods based on integer linear programming. The question of which, if any, problems are suited to genetic algorithms (in the sense that such algorithms are better than others) is open and controversial.

Variants

The simplest algorithm represents each chromosome as a bit string. Typically, numeric parameters can be represented by integers, though it is possible to use floating point representations. The floating point representation is natural to evolution strategies and evolutionary programming. The notion of real-valued genetic algorithms has been offered but is really a misnomer because it does not really represent the building block theory that was proposed by John Henry Holland in the 1970s. This theory is not without support though, based on theoretical and experimental results. The basic algorithm performs crossover and mutation at the bit level. Other variants treat the chromosome as a list of numbers which are indexes into an instruction table, nodes in a linked list, hashes, objects, or any other imaginable data structure. Crossover and mutation are performed so as to respect data element boundaries. For most data types, specific variation operators can be designed. Different chromosomal data types seem to work better or worse for different specific problem domains.

When bit-string representations of integers are used, Gray coding is often employed. In this way, small changes in the integer can be readily effected through mutations or crossovers. This has been found to help prevent premature convergence at so called Hamming walls, in which too many simultaneous mutations (or crossover events) must occur in order to change the chromosome to a better solution.

Other approaches involve using arrays of real-valued numbers instead of bit strings to represent chromosomes. Theoretically, the smaller the alphabet, the better the performance, but paradoxically, good results have been obtained from using real-valued chromosomes.

A very successful (slight) variant of the general process of constructing a new population is to allow some of the better organisms from the current generation to carry over to the next, unaltered. This strategy is known as elitist selection.

Parallel implementations of genetic algorithms come in two flavours. Coarse-grained parallel genetic algorithms assume a population on each of the computer nodes and migration of individuals among the nodes. Fine-grained parallel genetic algorithms assume an individual on each processor node which acts with neighbouring individuals for selection and reproduction. Other variants, like genetic algorithms for online optimisation problems, introduce time-dependence or noise in the fitness function.

Genetic algorithms with adaptive parameters (adaptive genetic algorithms, AGAs) is another significant and promising variant of genetic algorithms. The probabilities of crossover (pc) and mutation (pm) greatly determine the degree of solution accuracy and the convergence speed that genetic algorithms can obtain. Instead of using fixed values of pc and pm, AGAs utilize the population information in each generation and adaptively adjust the pc and pm in order to maintain the population diversity as well as to sustain the convergence capacity. In AGA (adaptive genetic algorithm), the adjustment of pc and pm depends on the fitness values of the solutions. In CAGA (clustering-based adaptive genetic algorithm), through the use of clustering analysis to judge the optimisation states of the population, the adjustment of pc and pm depends on these optimisation states. The GEGA program is an ab initiogradient embedded GA, a program for finding the global minima of clusters developed by Anastassia Alexandrova at Utah State University. GEGA employs geometry-cuts for the GA, ab initio level of computation for geometry optimisation and vibrational frequency analysis, with local minima only, and a specific mutational procedure based on the so called "kick technique".

It can be quite effective to combine GA with other optimisation methods. GA tends to be quite good at finding generally good global solutions, but quite inefficient at finding the last few mutations to find the absolute optimum. Other techniques (such as simple hill climbing) are quite efficient at finding absolute optimum in a limited region. Alternating GA and hill climbing can improve the efficiency of GA while overcoming the lack of robustness of hill climbing.

This means that the rules of genetic variation may have a different meaning in the natural case. For instance – provided that steps are stored in consecutive order – crossing over may sum a number of steps from maternal DNA adding a number of steps from paternal DNA and so on. This is like adding vectors that more probably may follow a ridge in the phenotypic landscape. Thus, the efficiency of the process may be increased by many orders of magnitude. Moreover, the inversion operator has the opportunity to place steps in consecutive order or any other suitable order in favour of survival or efficiency.

A variation, where the population as a whole is evolved rather than its individual members, is known as gene pool recombination.

Linkage-learning

A number of variations have been developed to attempt to improve performance of GAs on problems with a high degree of fitness epistasis, i.e. where the fitness of a solution consists of interacting subsets of its variables. Such algorithms aim to learn (before exploiting) these beneficial phenotypic interactions. As such, they are aligned with the Building Block Hypothesis in adaptively reducing disruptive recombination. Prominent examples of this approach include the mGA, GEMGA and LLGA.

Problem Domains

Problems which appear to be particularly appropriate for solution by genetic algorithms include timetabling and scheduling problems, and many scheduling software packages are based on GAs. GAs have also been applied to engineering. Genetic algorithms are often applied as an approach to solve global optimisation problems.

As a general rule of thumb genetic algorithms might be useful in problem domains that have a complex fitness landscape as mixing, i.e., mutation in combination with crossover, is designed to move the population away from local optima that a traditional hill climbing algorithm might get stuck in. Observe that commonly used crossover operators cannot change any uniform population. Mutation alone can provide ergodicity of the overall genetic algorithm process.

Examples of problems solved by genetic algorithms include: mirrors designed to funnel sunlight to a solar collector, antennae designed to pick up radio signals in space, and walking methods for computer figures. Many of their solutions have been highly effective, unlike anything a human engineer would have produced, and inscrutable as to how they arrived at that solution.

History

Computer simulations of evolution started as early as in 1954 with the work of Nils Aall Barricelli, who was using the computer at the Institute for Advanced Study in Princeton, New Jersey. His 1954 publication was not widely noticed. Starting in 1957, the Australian quantitative geneticist Alex Fraser published a series of papers on simulation of artificial selection of organisms with multiple loci controlling a measurable trait. From these beginnings, computer simulation of evolution by biologists became more common in the early 1960s, and the methods were described in books by Fraser and Burnell (1970) and Crosby (1973). Fraser's simulations included all of the essential elements of modern genetic algorithms. In addition, Hans-Joachim Bremermann published a series of papers in the 1960s that also adopted a population of solution to optimisation problems, undergoing recombination, mutation, and selection. Bremermann's research also included the elements of modern genetic algorithms. Other noteworthy early pioneers include Richard Friedberg, George Friedman, and Michael Conrad. Many early papers are reprinted by Fogel (1998).

Although Barricelli, in work he reported in 1963, had simulated the evolution of ability to play a simple game, artificial evolution became a widely recognized optimisation method as a result of the work of Ingo Rechenberg and Hans-Paul Schwefel in the 1960s and early 1970s – Rechenberg's group was able to solve complex engineering problems through evolution strategies. Another approach was the evolutionary programming technique of Lawrence J. Fogel, which was proposed for generating artificial intelligence. Evolutionary programming originally used finite state machines for predicting environments, and used variation and selection to optimise the predictive logics. Genetic algorithms in particular became popular through the work of John Holland in the early 1970s, and particularly his book Adaptation in Natural and Artificial Systems (1975). His work originated with studies of cellular automata, conducted by Holland and his students at the University of Michigan. Holland introduced a formalized framework for predicting the quality of the next generation, known as Holland's Schema Theorem. Research in GAs remained largely theoretical until the mid-1980s, when The First International Conference on Genetic Algorithms was held in Pittsburgh, Pennsylvania.

As academic interest grew, the dramatic increase in desktop computational power allowed for practical application of the new technique. In the late 1980s, General Electric started selling the world's first genetic algorithm product, a mainframe-based toolkit designed for industrial processes. In 1989, Axcelis, Inc. released Evolver, the world's first commercial GA product for desktop computers. The New York Times technology writer John Markoff wrote about Evolver in 1990.

Related Techniques

Parent Fields

Genetic algorithms are a sub-field of:

- Evolutionary algorithms
- Evolutionary computing
- Metaheuristics
- Stochastic optimisation
- Optimisation.

Related Fields

Evolutionary Algorithms

Evolutionary algorithms is a sub-field of evolutionary computing.

- Evolution strategies (ES, see Rechenberg, 1994) evolve individuals by means of mutation and intermediate or discrete recombination. ES algorithms are designed particularly to solve problems in the real-value domain. They use self-adaptation to adjust control parameters of the search. Derandomization of self-adaptation has led to the contemporary Covariance Matrix Adaptation Evolution Strategy (CMA-ES).

- Evolutionary programming (EP) involves populations of solutions with primarily mutation and selection and arbitrary representations. They use self-adaptation to adjust parameters, and can include other variation operations such as combining information from multiple parents.
- Genetic programming (GP) is a related technique popularized by John Koza in which computer programs, rather than function parameters, are optimised. Genetic programming often uses tree-based internal data structures to represent the computer programs for adaptation instead of the list structures typical of genetic algorithms.
- Grouping genetic algorithm (GGA) is an evolution of the GA where the focus is shifted from individual items, like in classical GAs, to groups or subset of items. The idea behind this GA evolution proposed by Emanuel Falkenauer is that solving some complex problems, a.k.a. clustering or partitioning problems where a set of items must be split into disjoint group of items in an optimal way, would better be achieved by making characteristics of the groups of items equivalent to genes. These kind of problems include bin packing, line balancing, clustering with respect to a distance measure, equal piles, etc., on which classic GAs proved to perform poorly. Making genes equivalent to groups implies chromosomes that are in general of variable length, and special genetic operators that manipulate whole groups of items. For bin packing in particular, a GGA hybridized with the Dominance Criterion of Martello and Toth, is arguably the best technique to date.
- Interactive evolutionary algorithms are evolutionary algorithms that use human evaluation. They are usually applied to domains where it is hard to design a computational fitness function, for example, evolving images, music, artistic designs and forms to fit users' aesthetic preference.

Swarm Intelligence

Swarm intelligence is a sub-field of evolutionary computing.

- Ant colony optimisation (ACO) uses many ants (or agents) to traverse the solution space and find locally productive areas.

While usually inferior to genetic algorithms and other forms of local search, it is able to produce results in problems where no global or up-to-date perspective can be obtained, and thus the other methods cannot be applied.

- Particle swarm optimisation (PSO) is a computational method for multi-parameter optimisation which also uses population-based approach. A population (swarm) of candidate solutions (particles) moves in the search space, and the movement of the particles is influenced both by their own best known position and swarm's global best known position. Like genetic algorithms, the PSO method depends on information sharing among population members. In some problems the PSO is often more computationally efficient than the GAs, especially in unconstrained problems with continuous variables.
- Intelligent Water Drops or the IWD algorithm is a nature-inspired optimisation algorithm inspired from natural water drops which change their environment to find the near optimal or optimal path to their destination. The memory is the river's bed and what is modified by the water drops is the amount of soil on the river's bed.

Other Evolutionary Computing Algorithms

Evolutionary computation is a sub-field of the metaheuristic methods.

- Harmony search (HS) is an algorithm mimicking musicians behaviours in improvisation process.
- Memetic algorithm (MA), also called hybrid genetic algorithm among others, is a relatively new evolutionary method where local search is applied during the evolutionary cycle. The idea of memetic algorithms comes from memes, which unlike genes, can adapt themselves. In some problem areas they are shown to be more efficient than traditional evolutionary algorithms.
- Bacteriologic algorithms (BA) inspired by evolutionary ecology and, more particularly, bacteriologic adaptation. Evolutionary ecology is the study of living organisms in the context of their environment, with the aim of discovering how they adapt. Its basic concept is that in a heterogeneous environment, you can't find one individual that fits the whole environment. So, you need to reason at the population level. It is also believed

BAs could be successfully applied to complex positioning problems (antennas for cell phones, urban planning, and so on) or data mining.

- Cultural algorithm (CA) consists of the population component almost identical to that of the genetic algorithm and, in addition, a knowledge component called the belief space.
- Gaussian adaptation (normal or natural adaptation, abbreviated NA to avoid confusion with GA) is intended for the maximisation of manufacturing yield of signal processing systems. It may also be used for ordinary parametric optimisation. It relies on a certain theorem valid for all regions of acceptability and all Gaussian distributions. The efficiency of NA relies on information theory and a certain theorem of efficiency. Its efficiency is defined as information divided by the work needed to get the information. Because NA maximises mean fitness rather than the fitness of the individual, the landscape is smoothed such that valleys between peaks may disappear. Therefore it has a certain "ambition" to avoid local peaks in the fitness landscape. NA is also good at climbing sharp crests by adaptation of the moment matrix, because NA may maximise the disorder (average information) of the Gaussian simultaneously keeping the mean fitness constant.

Other Metaheuristic Methods

Metaheuristic methods broadly fall within stochastic optimisation methods.

- Simulated annealing (SA) is a related global optimisation technique that traverses the search space by testing random mutations on an individual solution. A mutation that increases fitness is always accepted. A mutation that lowers fitness is accepted probabilistically based on the difference in fitness and a decreasing temperature parameter. In SA parlance, one speaks of seeking the lowest energy instead of the maximum fitness. SA can also be used within a standard GA algorithm by starting with a relatively high rate of mutation and decreasing it over time along a given schedule.
- Tabu search (TS) is similar to simulated annealing in that both traverse the solution space by testing mutations of an individual solution. While simulated annealing generates only one mutated

solution, tabu search generates many mutated solutions and moves to the solution with the lowest energy of those generated. In order to prevent cycling and encourage greater movement through the solution space, a tabu list is maintained of partial or complete solutions. It is forbidden to move to a solution that contains elements of the tabu list, which is updated as the solution traverses the solution space.

- Extremal optimisation (EO) Unlike GAs, which work with a population of candidate solutions, EO evolves a single solution and makes local modifications to the worst components. This requires that a suitable representation be selected which permits individual solution components to be assigned a quality measure ("fitness"). The governing principle behind this algorithm is that of emergent improvement through selectively removing low-quality components and replacing them with a randomly selected component. This is decidedly at odds with a GA that selects good solutions in an attempt to make better solutions.

Other Stochastic Optimisation Methods

- The cross-entropy (CE) method generates candidates solutions via a parameterized probability distribution. The parameters are updated via cross-entropy minimization, so as to generate better samples in the next iteration.
- Reactive search optimisation (RSO) advocates the integration of sub-symbolic machine learning techniques into search heuristics for solving complex optimisation problems. The word reactive hints at a ready response to events during the search through an internal online feedback loop for the self-tuning of critical parameters. Methodologies of interest for Reactive Search include machine learning and statistics, in particular reinforcement learning, active or query learning, neural networks, and meta-heuristics.

Chapter 2

Fuzzy Logic

Many-valued Logic

In logic, a many-valued logic (also multi- or multiple-valued logic) is a propositional calculus in which there are more than two truth values. Traditionally, in Aristotle's logical calculus, there were only two possible values (i.e., "true" and "false") for any proposition. An obvious extension to classical two-valued logic is an n-valued logic for n greater than 2. Those most popular in the literature are three-valued (e.g., £ukasiewicz's and Kleene's, which accept the values "true", "false", and "unknown"), the finite-valued with more than three values, and the infinite-valued, such as fuzzy logic and probability logic.

History

The first known classical logician who didn't fully accept the law of excluded middle was Aristotle(who, ironically, is also generally considered to be the first classical logician and the "father of logic"). Aristotle admitted that his laws did not all apply to future events (De Interpretatione, ch. IX), but he didn't create a system of multi-valued logic to explain this isolated remark. Until the coming of the 20th century, later logicians followed Aristotelian logic, which includes or assumes the law of the excluded middle.

The 20th century brought back the idea of multi-valued logic. The Polish logician and philosopher, Jan £ukasiewicz, began to create systems of many-valued logic in 1920, using a third value, "possible", to deal with Aristotle's paradox of the sea battle. Meanwhile, the American mathematician, Emil L. Post(1921), also introduced the formulation of additional truth degrees with n e" 2, where n are the truth values. Later, Jan £ukasiewicz and Alfred Tarski together formulated a logic on n truth values where ne" 2. In 1932 Hans

Reichenbach formulated a logic of many truth values where n'!infinity. Kurt Gödel in 1932 showed that intuitionistic logic is not a finitely-many valued logic, and defined a system of Gödel logics intermediate between classical and intuitionistic logic; such logics are known as intermediate logics.

Examples of Relation to Classical Logic

Logics are usually systems intended to codify rules for preserving some semantic property of propositions across transformations. In classical logic, this property is "truth." In a valid argument, the truth of the derived proposition is guaranteed if the premises are jointly true, because the application of valid steps preserves the property. However, that property doesn't have to be that of "truth"; instead, it can be some other concept.

Multi-valued logics are intended to preserve the property of designationhood (or being designated). Since there are more than two truth values, rules of inference may be intended to preserve more than just whichever corresponds (in the relevant sense) to truth.

For example, in a three-valued logic, sometimes the two greatest truth-values (when they are represented as e.g. positive integers) are designated and the rules of inference preserve these values. Precisely, a valid argument will be such that the value of the premises taken jointly will always be less than or equal to the conclusion.

For example, the preserved property could be justification, the foundational concept of intuitionistic logic.

Thus, a proposition is not true or false; instead, it is justified or flawed. A key difference between justification and truth, in this case, is that the law of excluded middle doesn't hold: a proposition that is not flawed is not necessarily justified; instead, it's only not proven that it's flawed.

The key difference is the determinacy of the preserved property: One may prove that P is justified, that P is flawed, or be unable to prove either.

A valid argument preserves justification across transformations, so a proposition derived from justified propositions is still justified. However, there are proofs in classical logic that depend upon the law of excluded middle; since that law is not usable under this scheme, there are propositions that cannot be proven that way.

Relation to Fuzzy Logic

Multi-valued logic is closely related to fuzzy set theory and fuzzy logic. The notion of fuzzy subset was introduced by Lotfi Zadeh as a formalization of vagueness; i.e., the phenomenon that a predicate may apply to an object not absolutely, but to a certain degree, and that there may be borderline cases. Indeed, as in multi-valued logic, fuzzy logic admits truth values different from "true" and "false". As an example, usually the set of possible truth values is the whole interval [0,1]. Nevertheless, the main difference between fuzzy logic and multi-valued logic is in the aims. In fact, in spite of its philosophical interest (it can be used to deal with the Sorites paradox), fuzzy logic is devoted mainly to the applications. More precisely, there are two approaches to fuzzy logic. The first one is very closely linked with multi-valued logic tradition (Hajek school). So a set of designed values is fixed and this enables us to define an entailment relation. The deduction apparatus is defined by a suitable set of logical axioms and suitable inference rules. Another approach (Goguen, Pavelka and others) is devoted to defining a deduction apparatus in which approximate reasonings are admitted. Such an apparatus is defined by a suitable fuzzy subset of logical axioms and by a suitable set of fuzzy inference rules. In the first case the logical consequence operator gives the set of logical consequence of a given set of axioms. In the latter the logical consequence operator gives the fuzzy subset of logical consequence of a given fuzzy subset of hypotheses.

Research Venues

An IEEE International Symposium on Multiple-Valued Logic (ISMVL) has been held annually since 1970. It mostly caters to applications in digital design and verification. The exists the Journal of Multiple-Valued Logic and Soft Computing.

Reason

Reason is a term that refers to the capacity human beings have to make sense of things, to establish and verify facts, and to change or justify practices, institutions, and beliefs. It is closely associated with such characteristically human activities as philosophy, science, language, mathematics, and art, and is normally considered to be a definitive characteristic of human nature. The concept of reason is sometimes referred to as rationality and sometimes as discursive reason, in opposition to "intuitive reason".

Reason or "reasoning" is associated with thinking, cognition, and intellect. Reason, like habit or intuition, is one of the ways by which thinking comes from one idea to a related idea. For example, it is the means by which rational beings understand themselves to think about cause and effect, truth and falsehood, and what is good or bad.

In contrast to reason as an abstract noun, a reason is a consideration which explains or justifies some event, phenomenon or behaviour. The ways in which human beings reason through argument are the subject of inquiries in the field of logic.

Reason is closely identified with the ability to self-consciously change beliefs, attitudes, traditions, and institutions, and therefore with the capacity for freedom and self-determination.

Psychologists and cognitive scientists have attempted to study and explain how people reason, e.g. which cognitive and neural processes are engaged, and how cultural factors affect the inferences that people draw. The field of automated reasoning studies how reasoning may or may not be modeled computationally. Animal psychology considers the controversial question of whether animals can reason.

Etymology and Related Words

In the English language and other modern European languages, "reason", and related words, represent words which have always been used to translate Latin and classical Greek terms in the sense of their philosophical usage.

- The original Greek term was logos, the root of the modern English word "logic" but also a word which could mean for example "language" or "explanation" or an "account" (of money handled).
- As a philosophical term logos was translated in its non-linguistic senses in Latin as ratio. This was originally not just a translation used for philosophy, but was also commonly a translation for logos in the sense of an account of money.
- French .raison is derived directly from Latin, and this is the direct source of the English word "reason".

The earliest major philosophers to publish in English, such as Francis Bacon, Thomas Hobbes, and John Locke also routinely wrote in Latin and French, and compared their terms to Greek, treating the words "logos", "ratio", "raison" and "reason" as inter-changeable. The meaning of the word "reason" in senses such as "human reason" also overlaps to a large extent with "rationality" and the adjective of "reason" in philosophical contexts is normally "rational", rather than "reasoned" or "reasonable". Some philosophers such as Thomas Hobbes, for example, also used the word ratiocination as a synonym for "reasoning".

Philosophical History

Philosophy can be described as a way of life based upon reason, and in the other direction reason has been one of the major subjects of philosophical discussion since ancient times. Reason is often said to be reflexive, or "self-correcting," and the critique of reason has been a persistent theme in philosophy. It has been defined in different ways, at different times, by different thinkers.

Classical Philosophy

For many classical philosophers, nature was understood teleologically, meaning that every type of thing had a definitive purpose which fit within a natural order that was itself understood to have aims. Perhaps starting with Pythagoras or Heraclitus, the cosmos is even said to have reason. Reason, by this account, is not just one characteristic that humans happen to have, and that influences happiness amongst other characteristics. Reason was considered to be of higher stature than other characteristics of human nature, such as sociability, because it is something humans share with nature itself, linking an apparently immortal part of the human mind with the divine order of the cosmos itself. Within the human mind or soul (psyche), reason was described by Plato as being the natural monarch which should rule over the other parts, such as spiritedness (thumos) and the emotions. Aristotle, Plato's student, defined human beings as rational animals, emphasizing reason as a characteristic of human nature. He defined the highest human happiness or well being (eudaimonia) as a life which is lived consistently, excellently and completely in accordance with reason.

The conclusions to be drawn from the discussions of Aristotle and Plato on this matter are amongst the most debated in the history of philosophy. But teleological accounts such as Aristotle's were highly influential for those who attempt to explain reason in a way which is consistent with monotheism and the immortality and divinity of the human soul. For example, in the neo-platonist account of Plotinus, the cosmos has one soul, which is the seat of all reason, and the souls of all individual humans are part of this soul. Reason is for Plotinus both the provider of form to material things, and the light which brings individuals souls back into line with their source. Such neo-Platonist accounts of the rational part of the human soul were standard amongst medieval Islamic philosophers, and under this influence, mainly via Averroes, came to be debated seriously in Europe until well into the renaissance, and they remain important in Iranian philosophy.

Subject-centred Reason in Early Modern Philosophy

The early modern era was marked by a number of significant changes in the understanding of reason, starting in Europe. One of the most important of these changes involved a change in the metaphysical understanding of human beings. Scientists and philosophers began to question the teleological understanding of the world. Nature was no longer assumed to be human-like, with its own aims or reason, and human nature was no longer assumed to work according to anything other than the same "laws of nature" which affect inanimate things. This new understanding eventually displaced the previous world view that derived from a spiritual understanding of the universe.

Accordingly, in the 17th century, René Descartes explicitly rejected the traditional notion of humans as "rational animals," suggesting instead that they are nothing more than "thinking things" along the lines of other "things" in nature. Any grounds of knowledge outside that understanding was, therefore, subject to doubt.

In his search for a foundation of all possible knowledge, Descartes deliberately decided to throw into doubt all knowledge – except that of the mind itself in the process of thinking:

At this time I admit nothing that is not necessarily true. I am therefore precisely nothing but a thinking thing; that is a mind, or intellect, or understanding, or reason – words of whose meanings I was previously ignorant.

This eventually became known as epistemological or "subject-centred" reason, because it is based on the "knowing subject", who perceives the rest of the world and itself as a set of objects to be studied, and successfully mastered by applying the knowledge accumulated through such study. Breaking with tradition and many thinkers after him, Descartes explicitly did not divide the incorporeal soul into parts, such as reason and intellect, describing them as one indivisible incorporeal entity.

A contemporary of Descartes, Thomas Hobbes described reason as a broader version of "addition and subtraction" which is not limited to numbers. This understanding of reason is sometimes termed "calculative" reason. Similar to Descartes, Hobbes asserted that "No discourse whatsoever, can end in absolute knowledge of fact, past, or to come" but that "sense and memory" is absolute knowledge.

In the late 17th century, through the 18th century, John Locke and David Hume developed Descartes' line of thought still further. Hume took it in an especially skeptical direction, proposing that there could be no possibility of deducing relationships of cause and effect, and therefore no knowledge is based on reasoning alone, even if it seems otherwise.

Hume famously remarked that, "We speak not strictly and philosophically when we talk of the combat of passion and of reason. Reason is, and ought only to be the slave of the passions, and can never pretend to any other office than to serve and obey them." Hume also took his definition of reason to unorthodox extremes by arguing, unlike his predecessors, that human reason is not qualitatively different from either simply conceiving individual ideas, or from judgments associating two ideas, and that "reason is nothing but a wonderful and unintelligible instinct in our souls, which carries us along a certain train of ideas, and endows them with particular qualities, according to their particular situations and relations." It followed from this that animals have reason, only much less complex than human reason.

In the 18th century, Immanuel Kant attempted to show that Hume was wrong by demonstrating that a "transcendental" self, or "I", was a necessary condition of all experience. Therefore, suggested Kant, on the basis of such a self, it is in fact possible to reason both about the conditions and limits of human knowledge. And so long as these limits are respected, reason can be the vehicle of morality, justice and understanding.

Substantive and Formal Reason

In the formulation of Kant, who wrote some of the most influential modern treatises on the subject, the great achievement of reason is that it is able to exercise a kind of universal law-making. Kant was able therefore to re-formulate the basis of moral-practical, theoretical and aesthetic reasoning, on "universal" laws.

Here practical reasoning is the self-legislating or self-governing formulation of universal norms, and theoretical reasoning the way humans posit universal laws of nature.

Under practical reason, the moral autonomy or freedom of human beings depends on their ability to behave according to laws that are given to them by the proper exercise of that reason. This contrasted with earlier forms of morality, which depended on religious understanding and interpretation, or nature for their substance.

According to Kant, in a free society each individual must be able to pursue their goals however they see fit, so long as their actions conform to principles given by reason. He formulated such a principle, called the "categorical imperative", which would justify an action only if it could be universalized:

Act only according to that maxim whereby you can, at the same time, will that it should become a universal law.

In contrast to Hume then, Kant insists that reason itself (German Vernunft) has natural ends itself, the solution to the metaphysical problems, especially the discovery of the foundations of morality. Kant claimed that this problem could be solved with his "transcendental logic" which unlike normal logic is not just an instrument, which can be used indifferently, as it was for Aristotle, but a theoretical science in its own right and the basis of all the others.

According to Jürgen Habermas, the "substantive unity" of reason has dissolved in modern times, such that it can no longer answer the question "How should I live?" Instead, the unity of reason has to be strictly formal, or "procedural." He thus described reason as a group of three autonomous spheres (on the model of Kant's three critiques):

1. Cognitive-instrumental reason is the kind of reason employed by the sciences. It is used to observe events, to predict and control outcomes, and to intervene in the world on the basis of its hypotheses;
2. Moral-practical reason is what we use to deliberate and discuss issues in the moral and political realm, according to universalizable procedures (similar to Kant's categorical imperative); and

3. Aesthetic reason is typically found in works of art and literature, and encompasses the novel ways of seeing the world and interpreting things that those practices embody.

For Habermas, these three spheres are the domain of experts, and therefore need to be mediated with the "lifeworld" by philosophers. In drawing such a picture of reason, Habermas hoped to demonstrate that the substantive unity of reason, which in pre-modern societies had been able to answer questions about the good life, could be made up for by the unity of reason's formalizable procedures.

The Critique of Reason

Kant, Hegel, Kierkegaard, Nietzsche, Heidegger, Foucault, Rorty, and a number of other philosophers have contributed to a debate about what reason means, or ought to mean. Some, like Kierkegaard, Nietzsche, and Rorty, are skeptical about subject-centred, universal, or instrumental reason, and even skeptical toward reason as a whole. Others, including Hegel, believe that it has obscured the importance of intersubjectivity, or "spirit" in human life, and attempt to reconstruct a model of what reason should be.

Some thinkers, e.g. Foucault, believe there are other forms of reason, neglected but essential to modern life, and to our understanding of what it means to live a life according to reason.

In the last several decades, a number of proposals have been made to "re-orient" this critique of reason, or to recognize the "other voices" or "new departments" of reason:

For example, in opposition to subject-centred reason, Habermas has proposed a model of communicative reason that sees it as an essentially cooperative activity, based on the fact of linguistic intersubjectivity.

Nikolas Kompridis has proposed a widely encompassing view of reason as "that ensemble of practices that contributes to the opening and preserving of openness" in human affairs, and a focus on reason's possibilities for social change.

The philosopher Charles Taylor, influenced by the 20th century German philosopher Martin Heidegger, has proposed that reason ought to include the faculty of disclosure, which is tied to the way we make sense of things in everyday life, as a new "department" of reason.

In the essay “What is Enlightenment?”, Michel Foucault proposed a concept of critique based on Kant’s distinction between “private” and “public” uses of reason. This distinction, as suggested, has two dimensions:

- Private reason is the reason that is used when an individual is “a cog in a machine” or when one “has a role to play in society and jobs to do: to be a soldier, to have taxes to pay, to be in charge of a parish, to be a civil servant.”
- Public reason is the reason used “when one is reasoning as a reasonable being (and not as a cog in a machine), when one is reasoning as a member of reasonable humanity.” In these circumstances, “the use of reason must be free and public.”

Reason Compared to Related Concepts

Reason Compared to Logic

The terms “logic” or “logical” are sometimes used as if they were identical with the term “reason” or with the concept of being “rational”, or sometimes logic is seen as the most pure or the defining form of reason. For example in modern economics, rational choice is assumed to equate to logically consistent choice.

Reason and logic can however be thought of as distinct, although logic is one important aspect of reason. Author Douglas Hofstadter, in Gödel, Escher, Bach, characterizes the distinction in this way. Logic is done inside a system while reason is done outside the system by such methods as skipping steps, working backward, drawing diagrams, looking at examples, or seeing what happens if you change the rules of the system.

Reason is a type of thought, and the word “logic” involves the attempt to describe rules or norms by which reasoning operates, so that orderly reasoning can be taught. The oldest surviving writing to explicitly consider the rules by which reason operates are the works of the Greek philosopher Aristotle, especially Prior Analysis and Posterior Analysis.

Although the Ancient Greeks had no separate word for logic as distinct from language and reason, Aristotle’s newly coined word ”syllogism” (syllogismos) identified logic clearly for the first time as a distinct field of study. When Aristotle referred to “the logical” (hç logikç), he was referring more broadly to rational thought.

Reason Compared to Cause-and-effect thinking, and Symbolic Thinking

As pointed out by philosophers such as Hobbes, Locke and Hume, some animals are also clearly capable of a type of "associative thinking", even to the extent of associating causes and effects. A dog once kicked, can learn how to recognize the warning signs and avoid being kicked in the future, but this does not mean the dog has reason in any strict sense of the word. It also does not mean that humans acting on the basis of experience or habit are using their reason.

Human reason requires more than being able to associate two ideas, even if those two ideas might be described by a reasoning human as a cause and an effect, perceptions of smoke, for example, and memories of fire. For reason to be involved, the association of smoke and the fire would have to be thought through in a way which can be explained, for example as cause and effect. In the explanation of Locke, for example, reason requires the mental use of a third idea in order to make this comparison by use of syllogism.

More generally, reason in the strict sense requires the ability to create and manipulate a system of symbols, as well as indices and icons, according to Charles Sanders Peirce, the symbols having only a nominal, though habitual, connection to either smoke or fire. One example of such a system of artificial symbols and signs is language.

The connection of reason to symbolic thinking has been expressed in different ways by philosophers. Thomas Hobbes described the creation of "Markes, or Notes of remembrance" (Leviathan Ch.4) as "speech". He used the word "speech" as an English version of the Greek word logos so that speech did not need to be communicated. When communicated, such speech becomes language, and the marks or notes or remembrance are called "Signes" by Hobbes.

Reason, Imagination, Mimesis, and Memory

Reason and imagination rely on similar mental processes. Imagination is not only found in humans. Aristotle, for example, stated that phantasia (imagination: that which can hold images or phantasmata) and phronein (a type of thinking which can judge and understand in some sense) also exist in some animals. According to him, both are related to the primary perceptive ability of animals, which gathers the perceptions of different senses and defines the order of the things that are perceived without distinguishing universals, and without deliberation or logos. But this is not yet reason, because human imagination is different.

The recent modern writings of Terrence Deacon and Merlin Donald, writing about the origin of language, also connect reason connected to not only language, but also mimesis, More specifically they describe the ability to create language as part of an internal modeling of reality which is specific to humankind. Other results are consciousness, and imagination or fantasy. In contrast, modern proponents of a genetic pre-disposition to language itself include Noam Chomsky and Steven Pinker, to whom Donald and Deacon can be contrasted.

As reason is symbolic thinking, and peculiarly human, then this implies that humans have a special ability to maintain a clear consciousness of the distinctness of "icons" or images and the real things they represent. Starting with a modern author, Merlin Donald writes

A dog might perceive the "meaning" of a fight that was realistically play-acted by humans, but it could not reconstruct the message or distinguish the representation from its referent (a real fight). [...] Trained apes are able to make this distinction; young children make this distinction early – hence, their effortless distinction between play-acting an event and the event itself

In classical descriptions, an equivalent description of this mental faculty is eikasia, in the philosophy of Plato. This is the ability to perceive whether a perception is an image of something else, related somehow but not the same, and which therefore allows humans to perceive that a dream or memory or a reflection in a mirror is not reality as such. What Klein refers to as dianoetic eikasia is the eikasia concerned specifically with thinking and mental images, such as those mental symbols, icons, "signes" and marks which are discussed above as definitive of reason. Explaining reason from this direction: human thinking is special in the way that we often understand visible things as if they were themselves images of our intelligible "objects of thought" as "foundations" (hypothçses in Ancient Greek). This thinking (dianoia) is "an activity which consists in making the vast and diffuse jungle of the visible world depend on a plurality of more 'precise' noçta".

Both Merlin Donald and the Socratic authors such Plato and Aristotle emphasize the importance of mimesis, often translated as "imitation" or "representation". Donald writes

Imitation is found especially in monkeys and apes [... but...] Mimesis is fundamentally different from imitation and mimicry in that it involves the invention of intentional representations. [...] Mimesis is not absolutely tied to external communication.

Mimçsis is a concept, now popular again in academic discussion, which was particularly prevalent in Plato's works, and within Aristotle, it is discussed mainly in the Poetics. In Michael Davis's account of the theory of man in this work.

It is the distinctive feature of human action, that whenever we choose what we do, we imagine an action for ourselves as though we were inspecting it from the outside. Intentions are nothing more than imagined actions, internalizings of the external. All action is therefore imitation of action; it is poetic...

Donald like Plato (and Aristotle, especially in On Memory and Recollection), emphasizes the peculiarity in humans of voluntary initiation of a search through one's mental world. The ancient Greekanamnçsis, normally translated as "recollection" was opposed to mneme or "memory". Memory, shared with some animals, requires a consciousness not only of what happened in the past, but also that something happened in the past, which is in other words a kind of eikasia "but nothing except man is able to recollect". Recollection is a deliberate effort to search for and recapture something which was once known. Klein writes that, to "become aware of our having forgotten something means to begin recollecting". Donald calls the same thing "autocueing", which he explains as follows: "Mimetic acts are reproducible on the basis of internal, self-generated cues. This permits voluntary recall of mimetic representations, without the aid of external cues – probably the earliest form of representational "thinking"."

In a celebrated paper in modern times, the fantasy author and philologist J.R.R. Tolkien wrote in his essay "On Fairy Stories" that the terms "fantasy" and "enchantment" are connected to not only "the satisfaction of certain primordial human desires" but also "the origin of language and of the mind".

Logical Reasoning Methods and Argumentation

Looking at logical categorizations of different types of reasoning the traditional main division made in philosophy is between deductive reasoning and inductive reasoning. Formal logic has been described as "the science of deduction". The study of inductive reasoning is generally carried out within the field known as informal logic or critical thinking.

Deductive Reasoning

Reasoning in an argument is valid if the argument's conclusion must be true when the premises (the reasons given to support that conclusion) are true. One classic example of deductive reasoning is that found in syllogisms like the following:

Premise 1: All humans are mortal.

Premise 2: Socrates is a human.

Conclusion: Socrates is mortal.

The reasoning in this argument is valid, because there is no way in which the premises, 1 and 2, could be true and the conclusion, 3, be false.

Inductive Reasoning

Induction is a form of inference producing propositions about unobserved objects or types, either specifically or generally, based on previous observation. It is used to ascribe properties or relations to objects or types based on previous observations or experiences, or to formulate general statements or laws based on limited observations of recurring phenomenal patterns.

Inductive reasoning contrasts strongly with deductive reasoning in that, even in the best, or strongest, cases of inductive reasoning, the truth of the premises does not guarantee the truth of the conclusion. Instead, the conclusion of an inductive argument follows with some degree of probability. Relatedly, the conclusion of an inductive argument contains more information than is already contained in the premises. Thus, this method of reasoning is ampliative.

A classic example of inductive reasoning comes from the empiricist David Hume:

Premise: The sun has risen in the east every morning up until now.

Conclusion: The sun will also rise in the east tomorrow.

Abductive Reasoning

Abductive reasoning, or argument to the best explanation, is a form of inductive reasoning, since the conclusion in an abductive argument does not follow with certainty from its premises and concerns something unobserved. What distinguishes abduction from the other forms of reasoning is an attempt to favour one conclusion above others, by attempting to falsify alternative explanations or by demonstrating the likelihood of the favoured conclusion, given a set of more or less disputable assumptions. For example, when a patient displays certain symptoms, there might be various possible causes, but one of these is preferred above others as being more probable.

Analogical Reasoning

Analogical reasoning is reasoning from the particular to the particular. An example follows:

Premise 1: Socrates is human and Socrates died.

Premise 2: Plato is human.

Conclusion: Plato will die.

Analogical reasoning can be viewed as a form of inductive reasoning, since the truth of the premises does not guarantee the truth of the conclusion. However, the traditional view is that inductive reasoning is reasoning from the particular to the general, and thus analogical reasoning is distinct from inductive reasoning.

Fallacious Reasoning

Flawed reasoning in arguments is known as fallacious reasoning. Reasoning within arguments can be bad because it commits either a formal fallacy or an informal fallacy.

Formal fallacies occur when there is a problem with the form, or structure, of the argument. The word "formal" refers to this link to the form of the argument. An argument that contains a formal fallacy will always be invalid. Consider, for example, the following argument:

1. If a drink is made with cocoa, it will be hot.
2. This drink was not made with boiling water.
3. This drink is not hot.

An informal fallacy is an error in reasoning that occurs due to a problem with the content, rather than mere structure, of the argument.

Traditional Problems Raised Concerning Reason

Philosophy is sometimes described as a life of reason, with normal human reason pursued in a more consistent and dedicated way than usual. Two categories of problem concerning reason have long been discussed by philosophers concerning reason, essentially being reasonings about reasoning itself as a human aim, or philosophizing about philosophizing. The first question is concerning whether we can be confident that reason can achieve knowledge of truth better than other ways of trying to achieve such knowledge. The other question is whether a life of reason, a life which aims to be guided by reason, is a good aim which can be expected to achieve a happy life more so than other ways of life (whether such a life of reason results in knowledge or not).

Reason Versus Truth, and "First Principles"

Since classical times a question has remained constant in philosophical debate (which is sometimes seen as a conflict between movements called Platonism and Aristotelianism) concerning the role of reason in confirming truth. People use logic, deduction, and induction, to reach conclusions they think are true. Conclusions reached in this way are considered more certain than sense perceptions on their own. On the other hand, if such reasoned conclusions are only built originally upon a foundation of sense perceptions, then, the argument being considered goes, our most logical conclusions can never be said to be certain because they are built upon the very same fallible perceptions they seek to better.

This leads to the question of what types of first principles, or starting points of reasoning, are available for someone seeking to come to true conclusions. In Greek, "first principles" are archai, "starting points", and the faculty used to perceive them is sometimes referred to in Aristotle and Platoas nous which was close in meaning to "awareness" or "consciousness".

Empiricism (sometimes associated with Aristotle but more correctly associated with British philosophers such as John Locke and David Hume, as well as their ancient equivalents such as Democritus) asserts that sensory impressions are the only available starting points for reasoning and attempting to attain truth. This approach always leads to the controversial conclusion that absolute knowledge is not attainable. Idealism, (associated with Plato and his school), claims that there is a "higher" reality, from which certain people can directly arrive at truth without needing to rely only upon the senses, and that this higher reality is therefore the primary source of truth.

Philosophers such as Plato, Aristotle, Al-Farabi, Avicenna, Averroes, Maimonides, Aquinas and Hegelare sometimes said to have argued that reason must be fixed and discoverable—perhaps by dialectic, analysis, or study. In the vision of these thinkers, reason is divine or at least has divine attributes. Such an approach allowed religious philosophers such as Thomas Aquinas and Étienne Gilson to try to show that reason and revelation are compatible. According to Hegel, "...the only thought which Philosophy brings with it to the contemplation of History, is the simple conception of reason; that reason is the Sovereign of the World; that the history of the world, therefore, presents us with a rational process."

Since the 17th century rationalists, reason has often been taken to be a subjective faculty, or rather the unaided ability (pure reason) to form concepts. For Descartes, Spinoza and Leibniz, this was associated with mathematics. Kant attempted to show that pure reason could form concepts (timeand space) that are the conditions of experience. Kant made his argument in opposition to Hume, who denied that reason had any role to play in experience.

Reason versus Emotion or Passion

Starting with the description of the rational and irrational soul found in Plato and Aristotle, which is explained above, western literature often treats reason as being opposed to emotions or feelings—desires, fears, hates, drives, or passions. This was an understanding of human nature which was developed for example by Stoic philosophy in Roman times. For example people might say their passions made them behave contrary to reason, or that their reason kept the passions under control (often expressed in colloquial terms as the dilemma between following "the head" (reason) "or the heart" (emotions)).

It has however also become common, already since David Hume, and more recently since the writings of Freud, to describe reason as actually being a slave to the passions, or at best an arbiter of conflicting desires, rather than their natural monarch. Reasoning which allows someone to pretend to that the object of their desire is demanded by logic alone is called "rationalization".

Rousseau is notable as the philosopher who first proposed, in his second Discourse, that reason (along with political life) is not natural to mankind, and not even good for mankind. In order to discover what can really be said about what is natural to mankind, and what, other than reason and civil society, "best suits his constitution", Rousseau saw "two principles prior to reason" in human nature, one is an intense interest in our own well-being, and the other is a natural repugnance of seeing any sentient being, especially one like ourselves, perish and suffer. It is from these two passions that humans began to desire more than they could achieve, became dependent upon each other, and started to establish relationships of authority and obedience, effecting putting the human race into slavery. Rousseau says that he almost dares to assert that nature does not destine men to be healthy. Concerning the practical implications, according to Velkley, "Rousseau outlines certain programs of rational self-correction, most notably the political legislation of the Contrat Social and the moral education in Émile. All the same, Rousseau understands such corrections to be only ameliorations of an essentially unsatisfactory condition, that of socially and intellectually corrupted humanity".

This quandary presented by Rousseau was the inspiration of Kant's new way of justifying reason as freedom to create good and evil, which are therefore not to be blamed on nature or God. "In various ways, German Idealism after Kant, and major later figures such Nietzsche, Bergson, Husserl, Scheler, and Heidegger, remain pre-occupied with this problem of the justice of the metaphysical demands or "urges" of reason". The influence of Rousseau and these later writers is also large upon art and politics. Many writers (such as Nikos Kazantzakis) extol passion and disparage reason; while in politics modern nationalism is a direct result of Rousseau's argument that rationalist cosmopolitanism brings man ever further from his natural state.

Reason versus Faith or Tradition

Though theologies and religions typically do not claim to be irrational, there is often a perceived conflict or tension between faith and tradition on the one hand, and reason on the other, as potentially competing sources of wisdom, law and truth. Defenders of traditions and faiths from claims that they are irrationalist for ignoring or even attempting to forbid reason and argument concerning some subjects, typically maintain that there is no real conflict with reason, because reason itself is not enough to explain such things as the origins of the universe, or right and wrong, and so reason can and should be complemented by other sources of knowledge, or in other words "first principles". The counter claim to this is that such a defence does not logically explain why some arguments from reason would be forbidden or ignored, while others are favoured, which tends to be a property of all religion and traditional wisdom.

There are enormously wide differences between different faiths, or even schools within different faiths, concerning this matter.

Some commentators have claimed that Western civilization can be almost defined by its serious testing of the limits of tension between "unaided" reason and faith in "revealed" truths—figuratively summarized as Athens and Jerusalem, respectively. Leo Strauss spoke of a "Greater West" which included all areas under the influence of the tension between Greek rationalism and Abrahamicrevelation, including the Muslim lands. He was particularly influenced by the great Muslim philosopher Al-Farabi. In order to consider to what extent Eastern philosophy might have partaken of these important tensions, Strauss thought it best to consider whether dharma or tao may be equivalent to Nature (by which we mean physis in Greek). According to Strauss the beginning of philosophy involved the "discovery or invention of nature" and the "pre-philosophical equivalent of nature" was supplied by "such notions as 'custom' or 'ways'" which appear to be "really universal" "in all times and places". The philosophical concept of nature or natures as a way of understanding archai (first principles of knowledge) brought about a peculiar tension between reasoning on the one hand, and tradition or faith on the other.

Although there is this special history of debate concerning reason and faith in the Islamic, Christian and Jewish traditions, the pursuit of reason is sometimes argued to be compatible with the other practice of other religions of a different nature, such as Hinduism, because they do not define their tenets in such an absolute way.

Reason in Particular Fields of Study

Reason in Political Philosophy and Ethics

Aristotle famously described reason (with language) as a part of human nature which means that it is best for humans to live "politically" meaning in communities of about the size and type of a small city state (polis in Greek). For example...

It is clear, then, that a human being is more of a political [politikon = of the polis] animal [zôion] than is any bee or than any of those animals that live in herds. For nature, as we say, makes nothing in vain, and humans are the only animals who possess reasoned speech [logos]. Voice, of course, serves to indicate what is painful and pleasant; that is why it is also found in other animals, because their nature has reached the point where they can perceive what is painful and pleasant and express these to each other. But speech [logos] serves to make plain what is advantageous and harmful and so also what is just and unjust. For it is a peculiarity of humans, in contrast to the other animals, to have perception of good and bad, just and unjust, and the like; and the community in these things makes a household or city [polis]. [...] By nature, then, the drive for such a community exists in everyone, but the first to set one up is responsible for things of very great goodness. For as humans are the best of all animals when perfected, so they are the worst when divorced from law and right. The reason is that injustice is most difficult to deal with when furnished with weapons, and the weapons a human being has are meant by nature to go along with prudence and virtue, but it is only too possible to turn them to contrary uses. Consequently, if a human being lacks virtue, he is the most unholy and savage thing, and when it comes to sex and food, the worst. But justice is something political [to do with the polis], for right is the arrangement of the political community, and right is discrimination of what is just. (Aristotle's Politics 1253a 1.2. Peter Simpson's translation, with Greek terms inserted in square brackets.)

The concept of human nature being fixed in this way, implied, in other words, that we can define what type of community is always best for people. This argument has remained a central argument in all political, ethical and moral thinking since then, and has become especially controversial since firstly Rousseau's Second Discourse, and secondly, the Theory of Evolution. Already in Aristotle there was an awareness that the polis had not always existed and had needed to be invented or developed by humans themselves. The household came first, and the first villages and cities were just extensions of that, with the first cities being run as if they were still families with Kings acting like fathers.

Friendship [philia] seems to prevail [in] man and woman according to nature [kata phusin]; for people are by nature [tçi phusei] pairing [sunduastikon] more than political [politikon = of the polis], inasmuch as the household [oikos] is prior [proteron = earlier] and more necessary than the polis and making children is more common [koinoteron] with the animals. In the other animals, community [koinônia] goes no further than this, but people live together [sumoikousin] not only for the sake of making children, but also for the things for life; for from the start the functions [erga] are divided, and are different [for] man and woman. Thus they supply each other, putting their own into the common [eis to koinon]. It is for these [reasons] that both utility [chrçsimon] and pleasure [hçdu] seem to be found in this kind of friendship. (Nicomachean Ethics, VIII.12.1162a. Rough literal translation with Greek terms shown in square brackets.)

Rousseau in his Second Discourse finally took the shocking step of claiming that this traditional account has things in reverse: with reason, language and rationally organized communities all having developed over a long period of time merely as a result of the fact that some habits of cooperation were found to solve certain types of problems, and that once such cooperation became more important, it forced people to develop increasingly complex cooperation—often only in order to defend themselves from each other.

In other words, according to Rousseau, reason, language and rational community did not arise because of any conscious decision or plan by humans or gods, nor because of any pre-existing human nature. As a result, he claimed, living together in rationally organized communities like modern humans is a development which has many negative aspects compared to the original state of man as an ape. If there be anything specifically human in this theory, it is the flexibility and adaptability of humans. This view of the animal origins of distinctive human characteristics later received support from Charles Darwin's Theory of Evolution.

The two competing theories concerning the origins of reason are relevant to political and ethical thought because according to the Aristotelian theory, there is a best way of living together which exists independently of historical circumstances. According to Rousseau, we should even doubt that reason, language and politics are a good thing, as opposed to being simply the best option given the particular course of events which lead to today. Rousseau's theory, that human nature is malleable rather than fixed, is often taken to imply, for example by Karl Marx, a wider range of possible ways of living together than traditionally known.

However, while Rousseau's initial impact encouraged bloody revolutions against traditional politics, including both the French

Revolution and the Russian Revolution, his own conclusions about the best forms of community seem to have been remarkably classical, in favour of city-states such as Geneva, and rural living.

Psychology

Scientific research into reasoning is carried out within the fields of psychology and cognitive science. Psychologists attempt to determine whether or not people are capable of rational thought in a number of different circumstances.

Assessing how well someone engages in reasoning is the project of determining the extent to which the person is rational or acts rationally. It is a key research question in the psychology of reasoning. Rationality is often divided into its respective theoretical and practical counterparts.

Behavioural Experiments on Human Reasoning

Experimental cognitive psychologists carry out research on reasoning behaviour. Such research may focus, for example, on how people perform on tests of reasoning such as intelligence or IQ tests, or on how well people's reasoning matches ideals set by logic. Experiments examine how people make inferences from conditionals e.g., If A then B and how they make inferences about alternatives, e.g., A or else B. They test whether people can make valid deductions about spatial and temporal relations, e.g., A is to the left of B, or A happens after B, and about quantified assertions, e.g., All the A are B. Experiments investigate how people make inferences about factual situations, hypothetical possibilities, probabilities, and counterfactual situations.

Developmental Studies of Children's Reasoning

Developmental psychologists investigate the development of reasoning from birth to adulthood. Piaget's theory of cognitive development was the first complete theory of reasoning development. Subsequently, several alternative theories were proposed, including the neo-Piagetian theories of cognitive development.

Neuroscience of Reasoning

The biological functioning of the brain is studied by neurophysiologists and neuropsychologists. Research in this area includes research into the structure and function of normally functioning brains, and of damaged or otherwise unusual brains. In addition to carrying out research into reasoning, some psychologists, for example, clinical psychologists and psychotherapists work to alter people's reasoning habits when they are unhelpful.

Computer Science

Automated Reasoning

In artificial intelligence and computer science, scientists study and use automated reasoning for diverse applications including automated theorem proving the formal semantics of programming languages, and formal specification in software engineering.

Meta-Reasoning

Meta-reasoning is reasoning about reasoning. In computer science, a system performs meta-reasoning when it is reasoning about its own operation. This requires a programming language capable of reflection, the ability to observe and modify its own structure and behaviour.

Principle of Bivalence

In logic, the semantic principle (or law) of bivalence states that every declarative sentence expressing a proposition (of a theory under inspection) has exactly one truth value, either true or false. A logic satisfying this principle is called a two-valued logic or bivalent logic.

In formal logic, the principle of bivalence becomes a property that a semantics may or may not possess. It is not the same as the law of excluded middle, however, and a semantics may satisfy that law without being bivalent.

The principle of bivalence is studied in philosophical logic to address the question of which natural-language statements have a well-defined truth value.

Sentences which predict events in the future, and sentences which seem open to interpretation, are particularly difficult for philosophers who hold that the principle of bivalence applies to all declarative natural-language statements. Many-valued logics formalize ideas that a realistic characterization of the notion of consequence requires the admissibility of premises which, owing to vagueness, temporal or quantum indeterminacy, or reference-failure, cannot be considered classically bivalent. Reference failures can also be addressed by free logics.

Relationship with the Law of the Excluded Middle

The principle of bivalence is related to the law of excluded middle though the latter is a syntactic expression of the language of a logic of the form "P ∨ ¬P". The difference between the principle and the law is important because there are logics which validate the law but which do not validate the principle.

For example, the three-valued Logic of Paradox (LP) validates the law of excluded middle, but not the law of non-contradiction, ¬(P ¬P), and its intended semantics is not bivalent. In classical two-valued logic both the law of excluded middle and the law of non-contradiction hold.

Many modern logic programming systems replace the law of the excluded middle with the concept of negation as failure. The programmer may wish to add the law of the excluded middle by explicitly asserting it as true; however, it is not assumed a priori.

Classical Logic

The intended semantics of classical logic is bivalent, but this is not true of every semantics for classical logic. In Boolean-valued semantics (for classical propositional logic), the truth values are the elements of an arbitrary Boolean algebra, "true" corresponds to the maximal element of the algebra, and "false" corresponds to the minimal element. Intermediate elements of the algebra correspond to truth values other than "true" and "false". The principle of bivalence holds only when the Boolean algebra is taken to be the two-element algebra, which has no intermediate elements.

Assign Boolean semantics to classical predicate calculus requires that the model be a complete Boolean algebra because the universal quantifier maps to the infimum operation, and the existential quantifier maps to the supremum; this is called a Boolean-valued model. All finite Boolean algebras are complete.

Criticisms

Future Contingents

A famous example is the contingent sea battle case found in Aristotle's work, De Interpretatione, chapter 9:

Imagine P refers to the statement "There will be a sea battle tomorrow."

The principle of bivalence here asserts: Either it is true that there will be a sea battle tomorrow, or it is not true that there will be a sea battle tomorrow.

Aristotle hesitated to embrace bivalence for such future contingents; Chrysippus, the Stoic logician, did embrace bivalence for this and all other propositions. The controversy continues to be of central importance in both metaphysics and the philosophy of logic.

One of the early motivations for the study of many-valued logics has been precisely this issue. In the early 20th century, the Polish formal logician Jan £ukasiewicz proposed three truth-values: the true, the false and the as-yet-undetermined. This approach was later developed by Arend Heyting and L. E. J. Brouwer.

Issues such as this have also been addressed in various temporal logics, where one can assert that "Eventually, either there will be a sea battle tomorrow, or there won't be." (Which is true if "tomorrow" eventually occurs.)

Vagueness

Such puzzles as the Sorites paradox and the related continuum fallacy have raised doubt as to the applicability of classical logic and the principle of bivalence to concepts that may be vague in their application. Fuzzy logic and some other multi-valued logics have been proposed as alternatives that handle vague concepts better. Truth (and falsity) in fuzzy logic, for example, comes in varying degrees. Consider the following statement in the circumstance of sorting apples on a moving belt:

This apple is red.

Upon observation, the apple is an undetermined colour between yellow and red, or it is motled both colours. Thus the colour falls into neither category " red " nor " yellow ", but these are the only categories available to us as we sort the apples. We might say it is "50% red". This could be rephrased: it is 50% true that the apple is red. Therefore, P is 50% true, and 50% false. Now consider:

This apple is red and it is not-red.

In other words, P and not-P. This violates the law of noncontradiction and, by extension, bivalence. However, this is only a partial rejection of these laws because P is only partially true. If P were 100% true, not-P would be 100% false, and there is no contradiction because P and not-P no longer holds. However, the law of the excluded middle is retained, because P and not-P implies P or not-P, since "or" is inclusive. The only two cases where P and not-P is false (when P is 100% true or false) are the same cases considered by two-valued logic, and the same rules apply.

Truth Value

In logic and mathematics, a truth value, sometimes called a logical value, is a value indicating the relation of a proposition to truth.

In classical logic, with its intended semantics, the truth values are true and false; that is, classical logic is a two-valued logic. Intuitionistic logic lacks a complete set of truth values because its semantics, the Brouwer–Heyting–Kolmogorov interpretation, is specified in terms of provability conditions, and not directly in terms of the truth of formulae. Multi-valued logics (such as fuzzy logic and relevance logic) allow for more than two truth values, possibly containing some internal structure.

Even non-truth-valuational logics can associate values with logical formulae, as is done in algebraic semantics. For example, the algebraic semantics of intuitionistic logic is given in terms of Heyting algebras.

Topos theory uses truth values in a special sense: the truth values of a topos are the global elements of the subobject classifier. Having truth values in this sense does not make a logic truth valuational.

Fuzzy Set

Fuzzy sets are sets whose elements have degrees of membership. Fuzzy sets were introduced simultaneously by Lotfi A. Zadeh and Dieter Klaua in 1965 as an extension of the classical notion of set. In classical set theory, the membership of elements in a set is assessed in binary terms according to a bivalent condition — an element either belongs or does not belong to the set. By contrast, fuzzy set theory permits the gradual assessment of the membership of elements in a set; this is described with the aid of a membership function valued in the real unit interval [0, 1].

Fuzzy sets generalise classical sets, since the indicator functions of classical sets are special cases of the membership functions of fuzzy sets, if the latter only take values 0 or 1. In fuzzy set theory, classical bivalent sets are usually called crisp sets. The fuzzy set theory can be used in a wide range of domains in which information is incomplete or imprecise, such as bioinformatics.

Fuzzy sets can be applied, for example, to the field of genealogical research. When an individual is searching in vital records such as birth records for possible ancestors, the researcher must contend with a number of issues that could be encapsulated in a membership function. Looking for an ancestor named John Henry Pittman, who you think was born in (probably eastern) Tennessee circa 1853 (based on statements of his age in later censuses, and a marriage record in Knoxville), what is the likelihood that a particular birth record for "John Pittman" is your John Pittman? What about a record in a different part of Tennessee for "J.H. Pittman" in 1851? (It has been suggested by Thayer Watkins that Zadeh's ethnicity is an example of a fuzzy set)

Definition

A fuzzy set is a pair (A,m) where A is a set and $m; A \to [0,1]$.

For each $x \in A$, m(x) is called the grade of membership of x in (A,m). For a finite setA = $\{x_1,...,x_n\}$, the fuzzy set (A,m) is often denoted by $\{m(x_1)/\ x_1,...,m(x_n)/\ x_n\}$.

Let $x \in A$. Then x is called not included in the fuzzy set (A,m) if m(x) = 0, x is called fully included if m(x) = 1, and x is called a fuzzy member if 0 < m(x) < 1. The set is $\{x \in A \mid m(x) > 0\}$ called the support of (A,m) and the set is $\{x \in A \mid m(x) = 1\}$ called its kernel.

Sometimes, more general variants of the notion of fuzzy set are used, with membership functions taking values in a (fixed or variable) algebra or structure L of a given kind; usually it is required that Lbe at least a poset or lattice. These are usually called L-fuzzy sets, to distinguish them from those valued over the unit interval. The usual membership functions with values in [0, 1] are then called [0, 1]-valued membership functions. These kinds of generalisations were first considered in 1967 by Joseph Goguen, who was a student of Zadeh.

Fuzzy Logic

As an extension of the case of multi-valued logic, valuations $(\mu : V_0 \to W)$ of propositional variables (V_o) into a set of membership degrees (W) can be thought of as membership functions mapping predicates into fuzzy sets (or more formally, into an ordered set of fuzzy pairs, called a fuzzy relation). With these valuations, many-valued logic can be extended to allow for fuzzy premises from which graded conclusions may be drawn.

This extension is sometimes called "fuzzy logic in the narrow sense" as opposed to "fuzzy logic in the wider sense," which originated in the engineering fields of automated control and knowledge engineering, and which encompasses many topics involving fuzzy sets and "approximated reasoning."

Industrial applications of fuzzy sets in the context of "fuzzy logic in the wider sense" can be found at fuzzy logic.

Fuzzy Number

A fuzzy number is a convex, normalized fuzzy set $\tilde{A} \subseteq \mathbf{R}$ whose membership function is at least segmentally continuous and has the functional value $\mu_A(x) = 1$ at precisely one element.

This can be likened to the funfair game "guess your weight," where someone guesses the contestant's weight, with closer guesses being more correct, and where the guesser "wins" if he or she guesses near enough to the contestant's weight, with the actual weight being completely correct (mapping to 1 by the membership function).

Fuzzy Interval

A fuzzy interval is an uncertain set $\tilde{A} \subseteq \mathbf{R}$ with a mean interval whose elements possess the membership function value $\mu_A(x) = 1$. As in fuzzy numbers, the membership function must be convex, normalized, at least segmentally continuous.

Fuzzy Relation Equation

The fuzzy relation equation is an equation of the form $A \cdot R = B$, where A and B are fuzzy sets, R is a fuzzy relation, and $A \cdot R$ stands for the composition of A with R.

Chapter 3

Propositional Fuzzy Logics

Monoidal t-norm Logic

Monoidal t-norm based logic (or shortly MTL), the logic of left-continuous t-norms, is one of t-norm fuzzy logics. It belongs to the broader class of substructural logics, or logics of residuated lattices; it extends the logic of commutative bounded integral residuated lattices (known as Höhle's monoidal logic, Ono's FL_{ew}, or intuitionistic logic without contraction) by the axiom of prelinearity.

Motivation

T-norms are binary functions on the real unit interval [0, 1] which are often used to represent a conjunction connective in fuzzy logic. Every left-continuous t-norm * has a unique residuum, that is, a function $\Rightarrow$ such that for all x, y, and z,

$$x * y \leq z \text{ if and only if } x \leq (y \Rightarrow z)$$

The residuum of a left-continuous t-norm can explicitly be defined as

$$(x \Rightarrow y) = \sup\{z \mid z * x \leq y\}.$$

This ensures that the residuum is the largest function such that for all x and y,

$$x * (x \Rightarrow y) \leq y.$$

The latter can be interpreted as a fuzzy version of the modus ponens rule of inference. The residuum of a left-continuous t-norm thus can be characterized as the weakest function that makes the fuzzy modus ponens valid, which makes it a suitable truth function for implication in fuzzy logic. Left-continuity of the t-norm is the necessary and sufficient condition for this relationship between a t-norm conjunction and its residual implication to hold.

Truth functions of further propositional connectives can be defined by means of the t-norm and its residuum, for instance the residual negation $\neg x = (x \Rightarrow 0)$. In this way, the left-continuous t-norm, its residuum, and the truth functions of additional propositional connectives determine the truth values of complex propositional formulae in [0, 1]. Formulae that always evaluate to 1 are then called tautologies with respect to the given left-continuous t-norm * , or * -tautologies.

The set of all * -tautologies is called the logic of the t-norm *, since these formulae represent the laws of fuzzy logic (determined by the t-norm) which hold (to degree 1) regardless of the truth degrees of atomic formulae. Some formulae are tautologies with respect to all left-continuous t-norms: they represent general laws of propositional fuzzy logic which are independent of the choice of a particular left-continuous t-norm. These formulae form the logic MTL, which can thus be characterized as the logic of left-continuous t-norms.

Syntax

Language

The language of the propositional logic MTL consists of countably many propositional variables and the following primitive logical connectives:

- Implication $\rightarrow$ (binary)
- Strong conjunction $\otimes$ (binary). The sign & is a more traditional notation $\otimes$ for strong conjunction in the literature on fuzzy logic, while the notation follows the tradition of substructural logics.
- Weak conjunction $\wedge$ (binary), also called lattice conjunction (as it is always realized by the lattice operation of meet in algebraic semantics). Unlike BL and stronger fuzzy logics, weak conjunction is not definable in MTL and has to be included among primitive connectives.
- Bottom $\perp$ (nullary — a propositional constant); 0 or are common alternative signs and zero a common alternative name for the propositional constant (as the constants bottom and zero of substructural logics coincide in MTL).

The following are the most common defined logical connectives:

- Negation (unary), defined as

- $\neg A \equiv A \to \bot$
- Equivalence (binary), defined as

  $A \leftrightarrow B \equiv (A \to B) \wedge (B \to A)$

In MTL, the definition is equivalent to $(A \to B) \otimes (B \to A)$.

- (Weak) disjunction (binary), also called lattice disjunction (as it is always realized by the lattice operation of join in algebraic semantics), defined as

  $A \vee B \equiv ((A \to B) \to B) \wedge ((B \to A) \to A)$

- Top (nullary), also called one and denoted by 1 or (as the constants top and zero of substructural logics coincide in MTL), defined as

  $T \equiv \bot \to \bot$

  Well-formed formulae of MTL are defined as usual in propositional logics. In order to save parentheses, it is common to use the following order of precedence:

- Unary connectives (bind most closely)
- Binary connectives other than implication and equivalence
- Implication and equivalence (bind most loosely)

Axioms

A Hilbert-style deduction system for MTL has been introduced by Esteva and Godo (2001). Its single derivation rule is modus ponens:

from A and $A \to B$ derive B.

The following are its axiom schemata:

$(MTL1)$: $(A \to B) \to ((B \to C) \to (a \to C))$

$(MTL2)$: $A \otimes B \to A$

$(MTL3)$: $A \otimes B \to B \otimes A$

$(MTL4a)$: $A \wedge B \to A$

$(MTL4b)$: $A \wedge B \to B \wedge A$

$(MTL4c)$: $A \otimes (A \to B) \to A \wedge B$

$(MTL5a)$: $(A \to (B \to C)) \to (A \otimes B \to C)$

$(MTL5b)$: $(A \otimes B \to C) \to (A \to (B \to C))$

$(MTL6)$: $((A \to B) \to C) \to (((B \to A) \to C) \to C)$

$(MTL7)$: $\bot \to A$

The traditional numbering of axioms, given in the left column, is derived from the numbering of axioms of Hájek's basic fuzzy logic BL. The axioms (MTL4a)–(MTL4c) replace the axiom of divisibility (BL4) of BL. The axioms (MTL5a) and (MTL5b) express the law of residuation and the axiom (MTL6) corresponds to the condition of prelinearity. The axioms (MTL2) and (MTL3) of the original axiomatic system were shown to be redundant (Chvalovský, 2008) and . All the other axioms were shown to be independent (Chvalovský, 2008).

Semantics

Like in other propositional t-norm fuzzy logics, algebraic semantics is predominantly used for MTL, with three main classes of algebras with respect to which the logic is complete:

- General semantics, formed of all MTL-algebras — that is, all algebras for which the logic is sound
- Linear semantics, formed of all linear MTL-algebras — that is, all MTL-algebras whose lattice order is linear
- Standard semantics, formed of all standard MTL-algebras — that is, all MTL-algebras whose lattice reduct is the real unit interval [0, 1] with the usual order; they are uniquely determined by the function that interprets strong conjunction, which can be any left-continuous t-norm

General Semantics

MTL-algebras

Algebras for which the logic MTL is sound are called MTL-algebras. They can be characterized a sprelinear commutative bounded integral residuated lattices. In more detail, an algebraic structure $(L,\wedge,\vee,*,\Rightarrow,0,1)$ is an MTL-algebra if

- $(L,\wedge,\vee,0,1)$ is a bounded lattice with the top element 0 and bottom element 1
- $(L,*,1)$ is a commutative monoid
- $*$ and $\Rightarrow$ form an adjoint pair, that is, $z*x\le y$ if and only if $z\le x\Rightarrow y$, where $\le$ is the lattice order $(L,\wedge,\vee)$ of for all x, y, and z in L, (the residuation condition)
- $(x\Rightarrow y)\vee(y\Rightarrow x)=1$ holds for all x and y in L (the prelinearity condition).

Important examples of MTL algebras are standard MTL-algebras on the real unit interval [0, 1]. Further examples include all Boolean algebras, all linear Heyting algebras (both with $* = \wedge$), all MV-algebras, all BL-algebras, etc. Since the residuation condition can equivalently be expressed by identities, MTL-algebras form a variety.

Interpretation of the logic MTL in MTL-algebras

The connectives of MTL are interpreted in MTL-algebras as follows:

- Strong conjunction by the monoidal operation $*$
- Implication by the operation $\Rightarrow$ (which is called the residuum of $*$)
- Weak conjunction and weak disjunction by the lattice operations $\wedge$ and $\vee$ respectively (usually denoted by the same symbols as the connectives, if no confusion can arise)
- The truth constants zero (top) and one (bottom) by the constants 0 and 1
- The equivalence connective is interpreted by the operation $\Leftrightarrow$ defined as $x \Leftrightarrow y \equiv (x \Rightarrow y) \wedge (y \Rightarrow x)$.

Due to the prelinearity condition, this definition is equivalent to one that uses instead of thus $x \Leftrightarrow y \equiv (x \Rightarrow y) * (y \Rightarrow x)$

- Negation is interpreted by the definable operation.

With this interpretation of connectives, any evaluation e_v of propositional variables in L uniquely extends to an evaluation e of all well-formed formulae of MTL, by the following inductive definition (which generalises Tarski's truth conditions), for any formulae A, B, and any propositional variable p:

$$
\begin{aligned}
e(p) &= e_v(p) \\
e(\perp) &= 0 \\
e(T) &= 1 \\
e(A \otimes B) &= e(A) * e(B) \\
e(A \rightarrow B) &= e(A) \Rightarrow e(B) \\
e(A \wedge B) &= e(A) \wedge e(B) \\
e(A \vee B) &= e(A) \vee e(B) \\
e(A \leftrightarrow B) &= e(A) \Leftrightarrow e(B) \\
e(\neg A) &= e(A) \Rightarrow 0
\end{aligned}
$$

Informally, the truth value 1 represents full truth and the truth value 0 represents full falsity; intermediate truth values represent intermediate degrees of truth. Thus a formula is considered fully true under an evaluation e if e(A) = 1. A formula A is said to be valid in an MTL-algebra L if it is fully true under all evaluations in L, that is, if e(A) = 1 for all evaluations e in L. Some formulae (for instance,p $\rightarrow$ p) are valid in any MTL-algebra; these are called tautologies of MTL.

The notion of global entailment (or: global consequence) is defined for MTL as follows: a set of formulae Γ entails a formula A (or: A is a global consequence of Γ), in symbols $\Gamma \models A$, if for any evaluation e in any MTL-algebra, whenever e(B) = 1 for all formulae B in Γ, then also e(A) = 1. Informally, the global consequence relation represents the transmission of full truth in any MTL-algebra of truth values.

General Soundness and Completeness Theorems

The logic MTL is sound and complete with respect to the class of all MTL-algebras (Esteva & Godo, 2001):

A formula is provable in MTL if and only if it is valid in all MTL-algebras.

The notion of MTL-algebra is in fact so defined that MTL-algebras form the class of all algebras for which the logic MTL is sound. Furthermore, the strong completeness theorem holds:

A formula A is a global consequence in MTL of a set of formulae Ã if and only if A is derivable from Γ in MTL.

Linear Semantics

Like algebras for other fuzzy logics, MTL-algebras enjoy the following linear subdirect decomposition property:

Every MTL-algebra is a subdirect product of linearly ordered MTL-algebras.

(A subdirect product is a subalgebra of the direct product such that all projection maps are surjective. An MTL-algebra is linearly ordered if its lattice order is linear.)

In consequence of the linear subdirect decomposition property of all MTL-algebras, the completeness theorem with respect to linear MTL-algebras (Esteva & Godo, 2001) holds:

- A formula is provable in MTL if and only if it is valid in all linear MTL-algebras.

- A formula A is derivable in MTL from a set of formulae Γ if and only if A is a global consequence in all linear MTL-algebras of Γ.

Standard Semantics

Standard are called those MTL-algebras whose lattice reduct is the real unit interval [0, 1]. They are uniquely determined by the real-valued function that interprets strong conjunction, which can be any left-continuous t-norm $*$. The standard MTL-algebra determined by a left-continuous t-norm $*$ is usually denoted by $[0,1]_{*\cdot In}[0,1]_{*}$, In implication is represented by the residuum of $*$ weak conjunction and disjunction respectively by the minimum and maximum, and the truth constants zero and one respectively by the real numbers 0 and 1.

The logic MTL is complete with respect to standard MTL-algebras; this fact is expressed by the standard completeness theorem:

A formula is provable in MTL if and only if it is valid in all standard MTL-algebras.

Since MTL is complete with respect to standard MTL-algebras, which are determined by left-continuous t-norms, MTL is often referred to as the logic of left-continuous t-norms (similarly as BL is the logic of continuous t-norms).

BL (Logic)

Basic fuzzy Logic (or shortly BL), the logic of continuous t-norms, is one of t-norm fuzzy logics. It belongs to the broader class of substructural logics, or logics of residuated lattices; it extends the logic of all left-continuous t-norms MTL.

Lukasiewicz Logic

In mathematics, £ukasiewicz logic is a non-classical, many valued logic. It was originally defined in the early 20th-century by Jan £ukasiewicz as a three-valued logic; it was later generalised to n-valued (for all finite n) as well as infinitely-many-valued variants, both propositional and first-order. It belongs to the classes of t-norm fuzzy logics and substructural logics.

Language

The propositional connectives of £ukasiewicz logic are implication $\rightarrow$, negation $\neg$, equivalence ,weak conjunction $\leftrightarrow$, strong conjunction

$\wedge$, weak disjunction $\vee$, strong disjunction $\otimes$, and propositional constants $\overline{0}$ and $\overline{1}$. The presence of weak and strong conjunction and disjunction is a common feature of substructural logics without the rule of contraction, to which £ukasiewicz logic belongs.

Axioms

The original system of axioms for propositional infinite-valued £ukasiewicz logic used implication and negation as the primitive connectives:

$$A \rightarrow (B \rightarrow A)$$
$$(A \rightarrow B) \rightarrow ((B \rightarrow C) \rightarrow (A \rightarrow C))$$
$$((A \rightarrow B) \rightarrow B) \rightarrow ((B \rightarrow A) \rightarrow A)$$
$$(\neg B \rightarrow \neg A) \rightarrow (A \rightarrow B).$$

Propositional infinite-valued £ukasiewicz logic can also be axiomatised by adding the following axioms to the axiomatic system of monoidal t-norm logic:

- Divisibility: $(A \wedge B) \rightarrow (A \otimes (A \rightarrow B))$
- Double negation: $\neg\neg A \rightarrow A.$

That is, infinite-valued £ukasiewicz logic arises by adding the axiom of double negation to basic t-norm logic BL, or by adding the axiom of divisibility to the logic IMTL.

Real-valued Semantics

Infinite-valued £ukasiewicz logic is a real-valued logic in which sentences from sentential calculus may be assigned a truth value of not only zero or one but also any real number in between (e.g. 0.25). Valuations have a recursive definition where:

- $\omega(\theta \circ \phi) = F_{\circ}(\omega(\theta), \omega(\phi))$ for a binary connective
- $\omega(\neg\theta) = F_{\neg}(\omega(\theta)),$
- $\omega(\overline{0}) = 0$ *and* $\omega(\overline{1}) = 1,$ and

and where the definitions of the operations hold as follows:

- Implication: $F_{\rightarrow}(x, y) = \min\{1, 1 - x + y\}$

- Equivalence: $F_{\leftrightarrow}(x,y)=1-|x-y|$
- Negation: $F_{\neg}(x)=1-x$
- Weak Conjunction: $F_{\wedge}(x,y)=\min\{x,y\}$
- Weak Disjunction: $F_{\vee}(x,y)=\max\{x,y\}$
- Strong Conjunction: $F_{\otimes}(x,y)=\max\{0,x+y-1\}$
- Strong Disjunction: $F_{\otimes}(x,y)=\min\{1,x+y\}$.

The truth function $F_{\otimes}$ of strong conjunction is the £ukasiewicz t-norm and the truth function $F_{\otimes}$ of strong disjunction is its dual t-conorm. The truth function $F_{\rightarrow}$ is the residuum of the £ukasiewicz t-norm. All truth functions of the basic connectives are continuous.

By definition, a formula is a tautology of infinite-valued £ukasiewicz logic if it evaluates to 1 under any valuation of propositional variables by real numbers in the interval [0, 1].

General Algebraic Semantics

The standard real-valued semantics determined by the £ukasiewicz t-norm is not the only possible semantics of £ukasiewicz logic. General algebraic semantics of propositional infinite-valued £ukasiewicz logic is formed by the class of all MV-algebras. The standard real-valued semantics is a special MV-algebra, called the standard MV-algebra.

Like other t-norm fuzzy logics, propositional infinite-valued £ukasiewicz logic enjoys completeness with respect to the class of all algebras for which the logic is sound (that is, MV-algebras) as well as with respect to only linear ones. This is expressed by the general, linear, and standard completeness theorems:

The following conditions are equivalent:

- A is provable in propositional infinite-valued £ukasiewicz logic
- A is valid in all MV-algebras (general completeness)
- A is valid in all linearly ordered MV-algebras (linear completeness)
- A is valid in the standard MV-algebra (standard completeness).

Kurt Godel

Kurt Friedrich Gödel(listen); April 28, 1906 – January 14, 1978) was an Austrian logician, mathematician and philosopher. Later in his life he emigrated to the United States to escape the effects of World War II. One of the most significant logicians of all time, Gödel made an immense impact upon scientific and philosophical thinking in the 20th century, a time when many, such as Bertrand Russell, A. N. Whitehead and David Hilbert, were pioneering the use of logic and set theory to understand the foundations of mathematics.

Gödel is best known for his two incompleteness theorems, published in 1931 when he was 25 years old, one year after finishing his doctorate at the University of Vienna. The more famous incompleteness theorem states that for any self-consistent recursive axiomatic system powerful enough to describe the arithmetic of the natural numbers (for example Peano arithmetic), there are true propositions about the naturals that cannot be proved from the axioms. To prove this theorem, Gödel developed a technique now known as Gödel numbering, which codes formal expressions as natural numbers.

He also showed that neither the axiom of choicenor the continuum hypothesis can be disproved from the accepted axioms of set theory, assuming these axioms are consistent. The former result opened the door for "working mathematicians" to assume the axiom of choice in their proofs. There are many important results whose only known proofs use the axiom of choice, which is equivalent to Zorn's lemma. He also made important contributions to proof theory by clarifying the connections between classical logic, intuitionistic logic, and modal logic.

Life—Childhood

Gödel was born April 28, 1906, in Brno, Austria-Hungary into the ethnic German family of Rudolf Gödel, the manager of a textile factory, and Marianne Gödel (born Handschuh). At the time of his birth the town had a slight German-speaking majority, and this was the language of his parents. The ancestors of Kurt Gödel were often active in the cultural life of the Brno city. For example, his grandfather Joseph Gödel was a famous singer of that time and for some years a member of the "Brünner Männergesangverein".

Although he spoke very little Czech himself, Gödel automatically became a Czechoslovak citizen at age 12 when the Austro-Hungarian empire broke up at the end of World War I. According to his classmate Klepetaø, "Gödel considered himself always Austrian and an exile in Czechoslovakia" ("ein Österreicher im Exil in der Tschechoslowakei") during this time. He chose to become an Austrian citizen at age 23. When Nazi Germany annexed Austria, Gödel automatically became a German citizen at age 32. After World War II, at the age of 42, he became an American citizen.

In his family, young Kurt was known as Herr Warum ("Mr. Why") because of his insatiable curiosity. According to his brother Rudolf, at the age of six or seven Kurt suffered from rheumatic fever; he completely recovered, but for the rest of his life he remained convinced that his heart had suffered permanent damage.

Gödel attended the Evangelische Volksschule, a Lutheran school in Brno from 1912 to 1916, and was enrolled in the Deutsches Staats-Realgymnasium from 1916 to 1924, excelling with honours in all his subjects, particularly in mathematics, languages and religion. Although Kurt had first excelled in languages, he later became more interested in history and mathematics. His interest in mathematics increased when in 1920 his older brother Rudolf (born 1902) left for Vienna to go to medical school at the University of Vienna. During his teens, Kurt studied Gabelsberger shorthand, Goethe's Theory of Colours and criticisms of Isaac Newton, and the writings of Immanuel Kant.

Studying in Vienna

At the age of 18, Gödel joined his brother in Vienna and entered the University of Vienna. By that time, he had already mastered university-level mathematics. Although initially intending to study theoretical physics, he also attended courses on mathematics and philosophy. During this time, he adopted ideas of mathematical realism. He read Kant's Metaphysische Anfangsgründe der Naturwissenschaft, and participated in the Vienna Circle with Moritz Schlick, Hans Hahn, and Rudolf Carnap. Gödel then studied number theory, but when he took part in a seminar run by Moritz Schlick which studied Bertrand Russell's book Introduction to Mathematical Philosophy, he became interested in mathematical logic. According to Gödel mathematical logic was "a science prior to all others, which contains the ideas and principles underlying all sciences."

Attending a lecture by David Hilbert in Bologna on completeness and consistency of mathematical systems may have set Gödel's life course. In 1928, Hilbert and Wilhelm Ackermann publishedGrundzüge der theoretischen Logik (Principles of Mathematical Logic), an introduction to first-order logic in which the problem of completeness was posed: Are the axioms of a formal system sufficient to derive every statement that is true in all models of the system?

This was the topic chosen by Gödel for his doctorate work. In 1929, at the age of 23, he completed his doctoral dissertation under Hans Hahn's supervision. In it, he established the completeness of the first-order predicate calculus (Gödel's completeness theorem). He was awarded his doctorate in 1930. His thesis, along with some additional work, was published by the Vienna Academy of Science.

The Incompleteness Theorem

In 1931 and while still in Vienna, Gödel published his incompleteness theorems in Über formal unentscheidbare Sätze der "Principia Mathematica" und verwandter Systeme (called in English "On Formally Undecidable Propositions of "Principia Mathematica" and Related Systems"). In that article, he proved for any computable axiomatic system that is powerful enough to describe the arithmetic of the natural numbers (e.g. the Peano axioms or Zermelo–Fraenkel set theory with the axiom of choice), that:

1. If the system is consistent, it cannot be complete.
2. The consistency of the axioms cannot be proven within the system.

These theorems ended a half-century of attempts, beginning with the work of Frege and culminating in Principia Mathematica and Hilbert's formalism, to find a set of axioms sufficient for all mathematics. The incompleteness theorems also imply that not all mathematical questions are computable.

In hindsight, the basic idea at the heart of the incompleteness theorem is rather simple. Gödel essentially constructed a formula that claims that it is unprovable in a given formal system. If it were provable, it would be false, which contradicts the idea that in a consistent system, provable statements are always true. Thus there will always be at least one true but unprovable statement. That is, for any computably enumerable set of axioms for arithmetic (that is, a set that can in principle be printed out by an idealized computer with unlimited resources), there is a formula that obtains in arithmetic, but which is not provable in that system. To make this precise, however, Gödel needed to produce a method to encode statements, proofs, and the concept of provability as natural numbers. He did this using a process known as Gödel numbering.

In his two-page paper Zum intuitionistischen Aussagenkalkül (1932) Gödel refuted the finite-valuedness of intuitionistic logic. In the proof he implicitly used what has later become known as Gödel–Dummett intermediate logic (or Gödel fuzzy logic).

The Mid 1930s: Further Work and Visits to the US

Gödel earned his habilitation at Vienna in 1932, and in 1933 he became a Privatdozent (unpaid lecturer) there. In 1933 Adolf Hitler came to power in Germany and over the following years the Nazis rose in influence in Austria, and among Vienna's mathematicians. In June 1936, Moritz Schlick, whose seminar had aroused Gödel's interest in logic, was assassinated by a pro-Nazi student. This triggered "a severe nervous crisis" in Gödel. He developed paranoid symptoms, including a fear of being poisoned, and spent several months in a sanitarium for nervous diseases.

In 1933, Gödel first travelled to the U.S., where he met Albert Einstein, who became a good friend. He delivered an address to the annual meeting of the American Mathematical Society. During this year, Gödel also developed the ideas of computability and recursive functions to the point where he delivered a lecture on general recursive functions and the concept of truth. This work was developed in number theory, using Gödel numbering.

In 1934 Gödel gave a series of lectures at the Institute for Advanced Study (IAS) in Princeton, New Jersey, entitled On undecidable propositions of formal mathematical systems. Stephen Kleene, who had just completed his PhD at Princeton, took notes of these lectures which have been subsequently published.

Gödel would visit the IAS again in the autumn of 1935. The travelling and the hard work had exhausted him, and the next year he took a break to recover from a depression. He returned to teaching in 1937. During this time, he worked on the proof of consistency of the axiom of choice and of the continuum hypothesis; he would go on to show that these hypotheses cannot be disproved from the common system of axioms of set theory.

He married Adele Nimbursky (née Porkert, 1899–1981), whom he had known for over 10 years, on September 20, 1938. Their relationship had been opposed by his parents on the grounds that she was a divorced dancer, six years older than he.

Subsequently, he left for another visit to the USA, spending the autumn of 1938 at the IAS and the spring of 1939 at the University of Notre Dame.

Gödel and his wife Adele spent the summer of 1942 in Blue Hill, Maine, in the Blue Hill Inn at the top of the bay. Gödel was taking a vacation from the IAS.

Gödel was not merely vacationing, and had a very productive summer of work. Using Heft 15 [volume 15] of Gödel's still-unpublished Arbeitshefte [working notebooks], John W. Dawson, Jr. conjectures that Gödel discovered a proof for the independence of the axiom of choice from finite type theory, a weakened form of set theory, while in Blue Hill in 1942. Gödel's close friend Hao Wang supports this conjecture, noting that Gödel's Blue Hill notebooks contain his most extensive treatment of the problem.

Relocation to Princeton, Einstein and US Citizenship

After the Anschluss in 1938, Austria had become a part of Nazi Germany. Germany abolished the title of Privatdozent, so Gödel had to apply for a different position under the new order. His former association with Jewish members of the Vienna Circle, especially with Hahn, weighed against him. The University of Vienna turned his application down. His predicament intensified when the German army found him fit for conscription. World War II started in September 1939. Before the year was up, Gödel and his wife left Vienna for Princeton. To avoid the difficulty of an Atlantic crossing, the Gödels took the trans-Siberian railway to the Pacific, sailed from Japan to San Francisco (which they reached on March 4, 1940), then crossed the U.S. by train to Princeton, where Gödel would accept a position at the Institute for Advanced Study (IAS).

Gödel very quickly resumed his mathematical work. In 1940, he published his work Consistency of the axiom of choice and of the generalised continuum-hypothesis with the axioms of set theory which is a classic of modern mathematics. In that work he introduced the constructible universe, a model of set theory in which the only sets that exist are those that can be constructed from simpler sets. Gödel showed that both the axiom of choice (AC) and the generalised continuum hypothesis (GCH) are true in the constructible universe, and therefore must be consistent with the Zermelo–Fraenkel axioms for set theory (ZF). Paul Cohen later constructed a model of ZF in which AC and GCH are false; together these proofs mean that AC and GCH are independent of the ZF axioms for set theory.

Albert Einstein was also living at Princeton during this time. Gödel and Einstein subsequently developed a strong friendship, and were known to take long walks together to and from the Institute for Advanced Study. The nature of their conversations was a mystery to the other Institute members. Economist Oskar Morgenstern recounts that toward the end of his life Einstein confided that his "own work no longer meant much, that he came to the Institute merely...to have the privilege of walking home with Gödel".

On December 5, 1947, Einstein and Morgenstern accompanied Gödel to his U.S. citizenship exam, where they acted as witnesses. Gödel had confided in them that he had discovered an inconsistency in the U.S. Constitution, one that would allow the U.S. to become a dictatorship. Einstein and Morgenstern were concerned that their friend's unpredictable behaviour might jeopardize his chances. Fortunately, the judge turned out to be Phillip Forman. Forman knew Einstein and had administered the oath at Einstein's own citizenship hearing. Everything went smoothly until Forman happened to ask Gödel if he thought a dictatorship like the Nazi regime could happen in the U.S. Gödel then started to explain his discovery to Forman. Forman understood what was going on, cut Gödel off, and moved the hearing on to other questions and a routine conclusion.

Later Years and Death

Gödel became a permanent member of the Institute of Advanced Study at Princeton in 1946. Around this time he stopped publishing, though he continued to work. He became a full professor at the Institute in 1953 and an emeritus professor in 1976.

In 1951, Gödel demonstrated the existence of paradoxical solutions to Albert Einstein's field equations in general relativity. He gave this elaboration to Einstein as a present for his 70th birthday. These "rotating universes" would allow time travel and caused Einstein to have doubts about his own theory. His solutions are known as the Gödel metric.

During his many years at the Institute, Gödel's interests turned to philosophy and physics. He studied and admired the works of

Gottfried Leibniz, but came to believe that a hostile conspiracy had caused some of Leibniz's works to be suppressed. To a lesser extent he studied Immanuel Kant and Edmund Husserl. In the early 1970s, Gödel circulated among his friends an elaboration of Leibniz's version of Anselm of Canterbury's ontological proof of God's existence. This is now known as Gödel's ontological proof. Gödel was awarded (with Julian Schwinger) the first Albert Einstein Award in 1951, and was also awarded the National Medal of Science, in 1974.

In later life, Gödel suffered periods of mental instability and illness. He had an obsessive fear of being poisoned; he would eat only food that his wife, Adele, prepared for him. Late in 1977, Adele was hospitalized for six months and could no longer prepare Gödel's food. In her absence, he refused to eat, eventually starving to death. He weighed 65 pounds (approximately 30 kg) when he died. His death certificate reported that he died of "malnutrition and inanition caused by personality disturbance" in Princeton Hospital on January 14, 1978.

Religious Views

Gödel was a convinced theist. He rejected the notion of others like his friend Albert Einstein that God was impersonal.

He believed firmly in an afterlife, stating: "Of course this supposes that there are many relationships which today's science and received wisdom haven't any inkling of. But I am convinced of this [the afterlife], independently of any theology." It is "possible today to perceive, by pure reasoning" that it "is entirely consistent with known facts." "If the world [Welt] is rationally constructed and has meaning, then there must be such a thing [as an afterlife]."

In an unmailed answer to a questionnaire, Gödel described his religion as "baptized Lutheran (but not member of any religious congregation). My belief is theistic, not pantheistic, following Leibniz rather than Spinoza."

Legacy

The Kurt Gödel Society, founded in 1987, was named in his honour. It is an international organization for the promotion of research in the areas of logic, philosophy, and the history of mathematics. The University of Vienna hosts the Kurt Gödel Research Centre for Mathematical Logic. The Association of Symbolic Logic has invited an annual Kurt Gödel lecture each year since 1990.

Five volumes of Gödel's collected works have been published. The first two include Gödel's publications; the third includes unpublished manuscripts from Gödel's Nachlass, and the final two include correspondence.

A biography of Gödel was published by John Dawson in 2005. Gödel was also one of four mathematicians examined in the 2008 BBC documentary entitled "Dangerous Knowledge".

Douglas Hofstadter wrote a popular book in 1979 called Gödel, Escher, Bach: An Eternal Golden Braid to celebrate the work and ideas of Gödel, along with those of artist M. C. Escher and composer Johann Sebastian Bach. The book partly explores the ramifications of the fact that Gödel's incompleteness theorem can be applied to any Turing-complete computational system, which may include the human brain.

Artificial Intelligence

Artificial intelligence (AI) is the intelligence of machines and the branch of computer science that aims to create it. AI textbooks define the field as "the study and design of intelligent agents" where an intelligent agent is a system that perceives its environment and takes actions that maximize its chances of success. John McCarthy, who coined the term in 1956, defines it as "the science and engineering of making intelligent machines."

The field was founded on the claim that a central property of humans, intelligence—the sapience of Homo sapiens—can be so precisely described that it can be simulated by a machine. This raises philosophical issues about the nature of the mind and the ethics of creating artificial beings, issues which have been addressed by myth, fiction and philosophy since antiquity. Artificial intelligence has been the subject of optimism, but has also suffered setbacks and, today, has become an essential part of the technology industry, providing the heavy lifting for many of the most difficult problems in computer science.

AI research is highly technical and specialized, deeply divided into subfields that often fail in the task of communicating with each other. Subfields have grown up around particular institutions, the work of individual researchers, the solution of specific problems, longstanding differences of opinion about how AI should be done and the application of widely differing tools. The central problems of AI include such traits as reasoning, knowledge, planning, learning, communication, perception and the ability to move and manipulate objects. General intelligence (or "strong AI") is still among the field's long term goals.

History

Thinking machines and artificial beings appear in Greek myths, such as Talos of Crete, the bronze robot of Hephaestus, and Pygmalion's Galatea. Human likenesses believed to have intelligence were built in every major civilization: animated cult images were worshipped in Egypt and Greeceand humanoid automatons were built by Yan Shi, Hero of Alexandria and Al-Jazari. It was also widely believed that artificial beings had been created by Jâbir ibn Hayyân, Judah Loew andParacelsus. By the 19th and 20th centuries, artificial beings had become a common feature in fiction, as in Mary Shelley's Frankenstein or Karel Èapek's R.U.R. (Rossum's Universal Robots). Pamela McCorduck argues that all of these are examples of an ancient urge, as she describes it, "to forge the gods". Stories of these creatures and their fates discuss many of the same hopes, fears and ethical concerns that are presented by artificial intelligence.

Mechanical or "formal" reasoning has been developed by philosophers and mathematicians since antiquity. The study of logic led directly to the invention of the programmable digital electronic computer, based on the work of mathematician Alan Turing and others. Turing's theory of computation suggested that a machine, by shuffling symbols as simple as "0" and "1", could simulate any conceivable act of mathematical deduction. This, along with concurrent discoveries in neurology, information theory and cybernetics, inspired a small group of researchers to begin to seriously consider the possibility of building an electronic brain.

The field of AI research was founded at a conference on the campus of Dartmouth College in the summer of 1956. The attendees, including John McCarthy, Marvin Minsky, Allen Newell and Herbert Simon, became the leaders of AI research for many decades. They and their students wrote programs that were, to most people, simply astonishing: Computers were solving word problems in algebra, proving logical theorems and speaking English. By the middle of the 1960s, research in the U.S. was heavily funded by the Department of Defence and laboratories had been established around the world. AI's founders were profoundly optimistic about the future of the new field: Herbert

Simon predicted that "machines will be capable, within twenty years, of doing any work a man can do" and Marvin Minsky agreed, writing that "within a generation ... the problem of creating 'artificial intelligence' will substantially be solved".

They had failed to recognize the difficulty of some of the problems they faced. In 1974, in response to the criticism of Sir James Lighthill and ongoing pressure from the US Congress to fund more productive projects, both the U.S. and British governments cut off all undirected exploratory research in AI. The next few years, when funding for projects was hard to find, would later be called the "AI winter".

In the early 1980s, AI research was revived by the commercial success of expert systems, a form of AI program that simulated the knowledge and analytical skills of one or more human experts. By 1985 the market for AI had reached over a billion dollars. At the same time, Japan's fifth generation computer project inspired the U.S and British governments to restore funding for academic research in the field. However, beginning with the collapse of the Lisp Machine market in 1987, AI once again fell into disrepute, and a second, longer lasting AI winter began.

In the 1990s and early 21st century, AI achieved its greatest successes, albeit somewhat behind the scenes. Artificial intelligence is used for logistics, data mining, medical diagnosis and many other areas throughout the technology industry. The success was due to several factors: the increasing computational power of computers, a greater emphasis on solving specific subproblems, the creation of new ties between AI and other fields working on similar problems, and a new commitment by researchers to solid mathematical methods and rigorous scientific standards.

On 11 May 1997, Deep Blue became the first computer chess-playing system to beat a reigning world chess champion, Garry Kasparov. In 2005, a Stanford robot won the DARPA Grand Challenge by driving autonomously for 131 miles along an unrehearsed desert trail. Two years later, a team from CMU won the DARPA Urban Challenge by autonomously navigating 55 miles in an Urban environment while adhering to traffic hazards and all traffic laws. In February 2011, in a Jeopardy! quiz show exhibition match, IBM's question answering system, Watson, defeated the two greatest Jeopardy! champions, Brad Rutter and Ken Jennings, by a significant margin.

The leading-edge definition of artificial intelligence research is changing over time. One pragmatic definition is: "AI research is that which computing scientists do not know how to do cost-effectively today." For example, in 1956 optical character recognition (OCR) was considered AI, but today, sophisticated OCR software with a context-sensitive spell checker and grammar checker software comes for free with most image scanners. No one would any longer consider already-solved computing science problems like OCR "artificial intelligence" today.

Low-cost entertaining chess-playing software is commonly available for tablet computers. DARPA no longer provides significant funding for chess-playing computing system development. The Kinect which provides a 3D body–motion interface for the Xbox 360 uses algorithms that emerged from lengthy AI research, but few consumers realize the technology source.

AI applications are no longer the exclusive domain of Department of defence R&D, but are now common place consumer items and inexpensive intelligent toys.

In common usage, the term "AI" no longer seems to apply to off-the-shelf solved computing-science problems, which may have originally emerged out of years of AI research.

Problems

"Can a machine act intelligently?" is still an open problem. Taking "A machine can act intelligently" as a working hypothesis, many researchers have attempted to build such a machine.

The general problem of simulating (or creating) intelligence has been broken down into a number of specific sub-problems. These consist of particular traits or capabilities that researchers would like an intelligent system to display. The traits described below have received the most attention.

Deduction, reasoning, problem solving

Early AI researchers developed algorithms that imitated the step-by-step reasoning that humans use when they solve puzzles or make logical deductions. By the late 1980s and '90s, AI research had also developed highly successful methods for dealing with uncertain or incomplete information, employing concepts from probability and economics.

For difficult problems, most of these algorithms can require enormous computational resources — most experience a "combinatorial explosion": the amount of memory or computer time required becomes astronomical when the problem goes beyond a certain size. The search for more efficient problem-solving algorithms is a high priority for AI research.

Human beings solve most of their problems using fast, intuitive judgments rather than the conscious, step-by-step deduction that early AI research was able to model. AI has made some progress at imitating this kind of "sub-symbolic" problem solving: embodied agent approaches emphasize the importance of sensorimotor skills to higher reasoning; neural net research attempts to simulate the structures inside human and animal brains that give rise to this skill.

Knowledge Representation

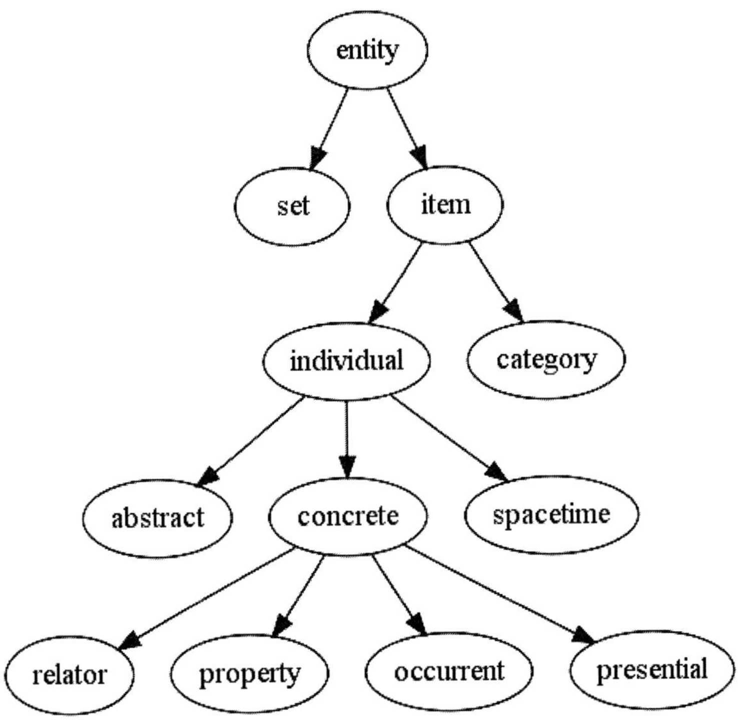

Figure: An ontology represents knowledge as a set of concepts within a domain and the relationships between those concepts.

Knowledge representation and knowledge engineering are central to AI research. Many of the problems machines are expected to solve will require extensive knowledge about the world. Among the things that AI needs to represent are: objects, properties, categories and relations between objects; situations, events, states and time; causes and effects; knowledge about knowledge (what we know about what other people know); and many other, less well researched domains. A representation of "what exists" is an ontology (borrowing a word from traditional philosophy), of which the most general are called upper on tologies.

Among the most difficult problems in knowledge representation are:

Default reasoning and the qualification problem

Many of the things people know take the form of "working assumptions." For example, if a bird comes up in conversation, people typically picture an animal that is fist sized, sings, and flies. None of these things are true about all birds. John McCarthy identified this problem in 1969 as the qualification problem: for any commonsense rule that AI researchers care to represent, there tend to be a huge number of exceptions. Almost nothing is simply true or false in the way that abstract logic requires. AI research has explored a number of solutions to this problem.

The Breadth of Commonsense Knowledge

The number of atomic facts that the average person knows is astronomical. Research projects that attempt to build a complete knowledge base of commonsense knowledge (e.g., Cyc) require enormous amounts of laborious ontological engineering — they must be built, by hand, one complicated concept at a time. A major goal is to have the computer understand enough concepts to be able to learn by reading from sources like the internet, and thus be able to add to its own ontology.

The Subsymbolic Form of Some Commonsense Knowledge

Much of what people know is not represented as "facts" or "statements" that they could express verbally. For example, a chess master will avoid a particular chess position because it "feels too exposed" or an art critic can take one look at a statue and instantly realize that it is a fake. These are intuitions or tendencies that are represented in the brain non-consciously and sub-symbolically. Knowledge like this informs, supports and provides a context for symbolic, conscious knowledge. As with the related problem of sub-symbolic reasoning, it is hoped that situated AI or computational intelligence will provide ways to represent this kind of knowledge.

Planning

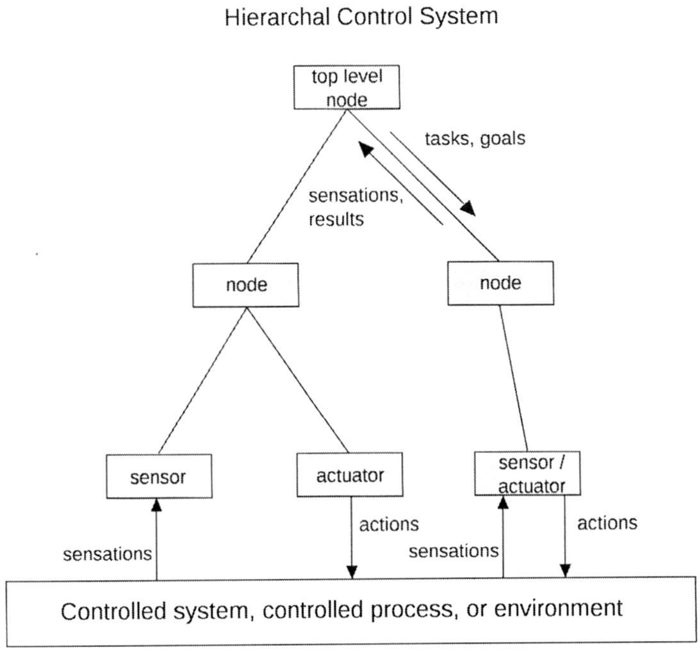

Figure: A hierarchical control system is a form of control system in which a set of devices and governing software is arranged in a hierarchy.

Intelligent agents must be able to set goals and achieve them. They need a way to visualize the future (they must have a representation of the state of the world and be able to make predictions about how their actions will change it) and be able to make choices that maximize the utility (or "value") of the available choices.

In classical planning problems, the agent can assume that it is the only thing acting on the world and it can be certain what the consequences of its actions may be. However, if this is not true, it must periodically check if the world matches its predictions and it must change its plan as this becomes necessary, requiring the agent to reason under uncertainty.

Multi-agent planning uses the cooperation and competition of many agents to achieve a given goal. Emergent behaviour such as this is used by evolutionary algorithms and swarm intelligence.

Learning

Machine learning has been central to AI research from the beginning. In 1956, at the original Dartmouth AI summer conference, Ray Solomon off wrote a report on unsupervised probabilistic machine learning: "An Inductive Inference Machine". Unsupervised learning is the ability to find patterns in a stream of input. Supervised learning includes both classification and numerical regression. Classification is used to determine what category something belongs in, after seeing a number of examples of things from several categories. Regression is the attempt to produce a function that describes the relationship between inputs and outputs and predicts how the outputs should change as the inputs change. In reinforcement learning the agent is rewarded for good responses and punished for bad ones. These can be analysed in terms of decision theory, using concepts like utility. The mathematical analysis of machine learning algorithms and their performance is a branch of theoretical computer science known as computational learning theory.

Natural Language Processing

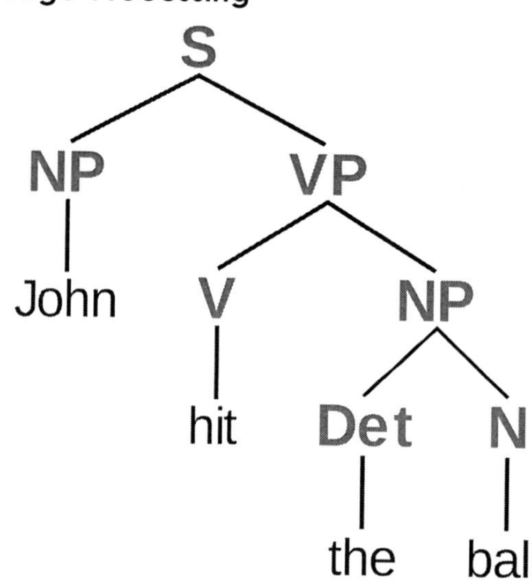

Figure: A parse tree represents the syntactic structure of a sentence according to some formal grammar.

Natural language processing gives machines the ability to read and understand the languages that humans speak. Many researchers hope that a sufficiently powerful natural language processing system would be able to acquire knowledge on its own, by reading the existing text available over the internet. Some straightforward applications of natural language processing include information retrieval (ortext mining) and machine translation.

Motion and Manipulation

The field of robotics is closely related to AI. Intelligence is required for robots to be able to handle such tasks as object manipulation and navigation, with sub-problems of localization (knowing where you are), mapping (learning what is around you) and motion planning (figuring out how to get there).

Perception

Machine perception is the ability to use input from sensors (such as cameras, microphones, sonar and others more exotic) to deduce aspects of the world. Computer vision is the ability to analyse visual input. A few selected subproblems are speech recognition, facial recognition and object recognition.

Social Intelligence

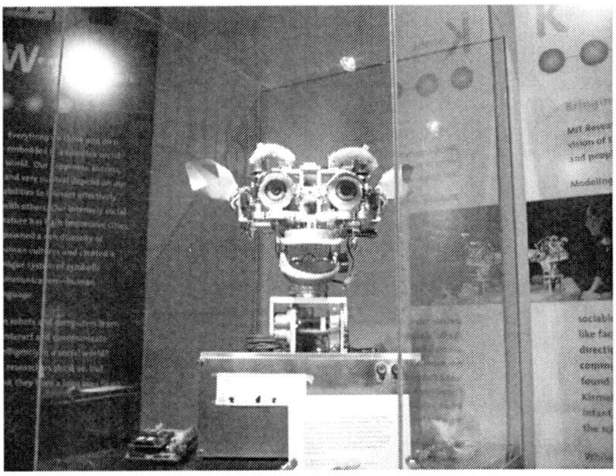

Figure: Kismet, a robot with rudimentary social skills

Emotion and social skills play two roles for an intelligent agent. First, it must be able to predict the actions of others, by understanding their motives and emotional states. (This involves elements of game theory, decision theory, as well as the ability to model human emotions and the perceptual skills to detect emotions.)

Also, for good human-computer interaction, an intelligent machine needs to display emotions. At the very least it must appear polite and sensitive to the humans it interacts with. At best, it should have normal emotions itself.

Creativity

A sub-field of AI addresses creativity both theoretically (from a philosophical and psychological perspective) and practically (via specific implementations of systems that generate outputs that can be considered creative, or systems that identify and assess creativity). A related area of computational research is Artificial intuition and Artificial imagination.

In the field of musical composition, the patented works» by René-Louis Baron allowed to make a robot that can create and play a multitude of melodies orchestrated so-called "coherent" in any musical style. All outdoor physical parameter associated with one or more specific musical parameters, can influence and develop each of these songs. The patented invention Medal-Composer raises problems of copyright.

General Intelligence

Most researchers hope that their work will eventually be incorporated into a machine with general intelligence (known as strong AI), combining all the skills above and exceeding human abilities at most or all of them. A few believe that anthropomorphic features like artificial consciousness or an artificial brain may be required for such a project.

Many of the problems above are considered AI-complete: to solve one problem, you must solve them all. For example, even a straightforward, specific task like machine translation requires that the machine follow the author's argument (reason), know what is being talked about (knowledge), and faithfully reproduce the author's intention (social intelligence). Machine translation, therefore, is believed to be AI-complete: it may require strong AI to be done as well as humans can do it.

Approaches

There is no established unifying theory or paradigm that guides AI research. Researchers disagree about many issues. A few of the most long standing questions that have remained unanswered are these: should artificial intelligence simulate natural intelligence by studying psychology or neurology? Or is human biology as irrelevant to AI research as bird biology is to aeronautical engineering? Can intelligent behaviour be described using simple, elegant principles (such as logic or optimisation)? Or does it necessarily require solving a large number of completely unrelated problems? Can intelligence be reproduced using high-level symbols, similar to words and ideas? Or does it require "sub-symbolic" processing? John Haugeland, who coined the term GOFAI (Good Old-Fashioned Artificial Intelligence), also proposed that AI should more properly be referred to as synthetic intelligence, a term which has since been adopted by some non-GOFAI researchers.

Cybernetics and Brain Simulation

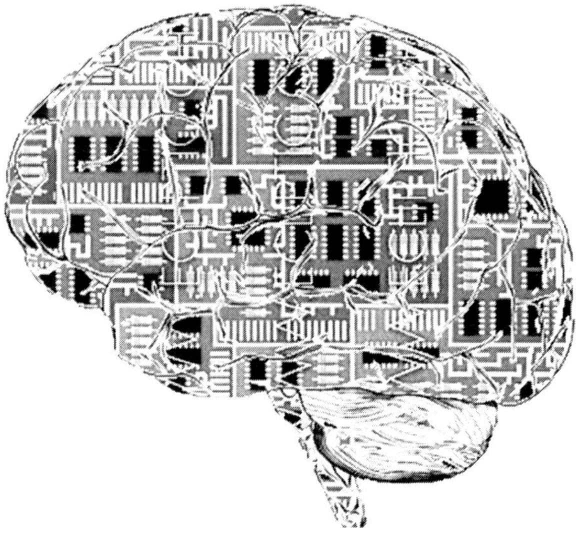

Figure: There is currently no consensus on how closely the brain should be simulated.

In the 1940s and 1950s, a number of researchers explored the connection between neurology, information theory, and cybernetics. Some of them built machines that used electronic networks to exhibit rudimentary intelligence, such as W. Grey Walter's turtles and the Johns Hopkins Beast. Many of these researchers gathered for meetings of the Teleological Society at Princeton University and the Ratio Club in England. By 1960, this approach was largely abandoned, although elements of it would be revived in the 1980s.

Symbolic

When access to digital computers became possible in the middle 1950s, AI research began to explore the possibility that human intelligence could be reduced to symbol manipulation. The research was centred in three institutions: CMU, Stanford and MIT, and each one developed its own style of research. John Haugeland named these approaches to AI "good old fashioned AI" or "GOFAI".

Cognitive Simulation

Economist Herbert Simon and Allen Newell studied human problem-solving skills and attempted to formalize them, and their work laid the foundations of the field of artificial intelligence, as well as cognitive science, operations research and management science. Their research team used the results of psychological experiments to develop programs that simulated the techniques that people used to solve problems. This tradition, centred at Carnegie Mellon University would eventually culminate in the development of the Soar architecture in the middle 80s.

Logic-based

Unlike Newell and Simon, John McCarthy felt that machines did not need to simulate human thought, but should instead try to find the essence of abstract reasoning and problem solving, regardless of whether people used the same algorithms. His laboratory at Stanford (SAIL) focused on using formal logic to solve a wide variety of problems, including knowledge representation, planning and learning. Logic was also focus of the work at the University of Edinburgh and elsewhere in Europe which led to the development of the programming language Prolog and the science of logic programming.

"Anti-logic" or "Scruffy"

Researchers at MIT (such as Marvin Minsky and Seymour Papert) found that solving difficult problems in vision and natural language processing required ad-hoc solutions – they argued that there was no simple and general principle (like logic) that would capture all the aspects of intelligent behaviour. Roger Schank described their "anti-logic" approaches as "scruffy" (as opposed to the "neat" paradigms at CMU and Stanford). Commonsense knowledge bases (such as Doug Lenat's Cyc) are an example of "scruffy" AI, since they must be built by hand, one complicated concept at a time.

Knowledge-based

When computers with large memories became available around 1970, researchers from all three traditions began to build knowledge into AI applications. This "knowledge revolution" led to the development and deployment of expert systems (introduced by Edward Feigenbaum), the first truly successful form of AI software. The knowledge revolution was also driven by the realization that enormous amounts of knowledge would be required by many simple AI applications.

Sub-symbolic

During the 1960s, symbolic approaches had achieved great success at simulating high-level thinking in small demonstration programs. Approaches based on cybernetics or neural networks were abandoned or pushed into the background. By the 1980s, however, progress in symbolic AI seemed to stall and many believed that symbolic systems would never be able to imitate all the processes of human cognition, especially perception, robotics, learning and pattern recognition. A number of researchers began to look into "sub-symbolic" approaches to specific AI problems.

Bottom-up, embodied, situated, behaviour-based or nouvelle AI Researchers from the related field of robotics, such as Rodney Brooks, rejected symbolic AI and focused on the basic engineering problems that would allow robots to move and survive. Their work revived the non-symbolic viewpoint of the early cybernetics researchers of the 50s and reintroduced the use of control theory in AI. This coincided with the development of the embodied mind thesis in the related field of cognitive science: the idea that aspects of the body (such as movement, perception and visualization) are required for higher intelligence.

Computational Intelligence

Interest in neural networks and "connectionism" was revived by David Rumelhart and others in the middle 1980s. These and other sub-symbolic approaches, such as fuzzy systems and evolutionary computation, are now studied collectively by the emerging discipline of computational intelligence.

Statistical

In the 1990s, AI researchers developed sophisticated mathematical tools to solve specific subproblems. These tools are truly scientific, in the sense that their results are both measurable and verifiable, and they have been responsible for many of AI's recent successes. The shared mathematical language has also permitted a high level of collaboration with more established fields (like mathematics, economics or operations research). Stuart Russell and Peter Norvig describe this movement as nothing less than a "revolution" and "the victory of the neats." Critiques argue that these techniques are too focussed on particular problems and have failed to address the long term goal of general intelligence.

Integrating the Approaches

Intelligent Agent Paradigm

An intelligent agent is a system that perceives its environment and takes actions which maximize its chances of success. The simplest intelligent agents are programs that solve specific problems. More complicated agents include human beings and organizations of human beings (such as firms). The paradigm gives researchers license to study isolated problems and find solutions that are both verifiable and useful, without agreeing on one single approach. An agent that solves a specific problem can use any approach that works — some agents are symbolic and logical, some are sub-symbolic neural networks and others may use new approaches. The paradigm also gives researchers a common language to communicate with other fields—such as decision theory and economics—that also use concepts of abstract agents. The intelligent agent paradigm became widely accepted during the 1990s.

Agent Architectures and Cognitive Architectures

Researchers have designed systems to build intelligent systems out of interacting intelligent agents in a multi-agent system. A system with both symbolic and sub-symbolic components is a hybrid intelligent system, and the study of such systems is artificial intelligence systems integration. A hierarchical control system provides a bridge between sub-symbolic AI at its lowest, reactive levels and traditional symbolic AI at its highest levels, where relaxed time constraints permit planning and world modelling. Rodney Brooks' subsumption architecture was an early proposal for such a hierarchical system.

Tools

In the course of 50 years of research, AI has developed a large number of tools to solve the most difficult problems in computer science. A few of the most general of these methods are discussed below.

Search and Optimisation

Many problems in AI can be solved in theory by intelligently searching through many possible solutions: Reasoning can be reduced to performing a search. For example, logical proof can be viewed as searching for a path that leads from premises to conclusions, where each step is the application of an inference rule. Planning algorithms search through trees of goals and subgoals, attempting to find a path to a target goal, a process called means-ends analysis. Robotics algorithms for moving limbs and grasping objects use local searches in configuration space. Many learning algorithms use search algorithms based on optimisation.

Simple exhaustive searches are rarely sufficient for most real world problems: the search space (the number of places to search) quickly grows to astronomical numbers. The result is a search that is too slow or never completes. The solution, for many problems, is to use "heuristics" or "rules of thumb" that eliminate choices that are unlikely to lead to the goal (called "pruning the search tree"). Heuristics supply the program with a "best guess" for the path on which the solution lies.

A very different kind of search came to prominence in the 1990s, based on the mathematical theory of optimisation. For many problems, it is possible to begin the search with some form of a guess and then refine the guess incrementally until no more refinements can be made. These algorithms can be visualized as blind hill climbing: we begin the search at a random point on the landscape, and then, by jumps or steps, we keep moving our guess uphill, until we reach the top. Other optimisation algorithms are simulated annealing, beam search and random optimisation.

Evolutionary computation uses a form of optimisation search. For example, they may begin with a population of organisms (the guesses) and then allow them to mutate and recombine, selecting only the fittest to survive each generation (refining the guesses). Forms of evolutionary computation include swarm intelligence algorithms (such as ant colony or particle swarm optimisation) and evolutionary algorithms (such as genetic algorithms and genetic programming).

Logic

Logic is used for knowledge representation and problem solving, but it can be applied to other problems as well. For example, the satplan algorithm uses logic for planning and inductive logic programming is a method for learning.

Several different forms of logic are used in AI research. Propositional or sentential logic is the logic of statements which can be true or false. First-order logic also allows the use of quantifiers and predicates, and can express facts about objects, their properties, and their relations with each other. Fuzzy logic, is a version of first-order logic which allows the truth of a statement to be represented as a value between 0 and 1, rather than simply True (1) or False (0). Fuzzy systems can be used for uncertain reasoning and have been widely used in modern industrial and consumer product control systems. Subjective logic models uncertainty in a different and more explicit manner than fuzzy-logic: a given binomial opinion satisfies belief + disbelief + uncertainty = 1 within a Beta distribution. By this method, ignorance can be distinguished from probabilistic statements that an agent makes with high confidence.

Default logics, non-monotonic logics and circumscription are forms of logic designed to help with default reasoning and the qualification problem. Several extensions of logic have been designed to handle specific domains of knowledge, such as: description logics; situation calculus, event calculus and fluent calculus (for representing events and time); causal calculus; belief calculus; and modal logics.

Probabilistic Methods for Uncertain Reasoning

Many problems in AI (in reasoning, planning, learning, perception and robotics) require the agent to operate with incomplete or uncertain information. AI researchers have devised a number of powerful tools to solve these problems using methods from probability theory and economics.

Bayesian networks are a very general tool that can be used for a large number of problems: reasoning (using the Bayesian inference algorithm), learning (using the expectation-maximization algorithm), planning (using decision networks) and perception (using dynamic Bayesian networks). Probabilistic algorithms can also be used for filtering, prediction, smoothing and finding explanations for streams of data, helping perception systems to analyse processes that occur over time (e.g., hidden Markov models or Kalman filters).

A key concept from the science of economics is "utility": a measure of how valuable something is to an intelligent agent. Precise mathematical tools have been developed that analyse how an agent can make choices and plan, using decision theory, decision analysis, information value theory. These tools include models such as Markov decision processes, dynamic decision networks, game theory and mechanism design.

Classifiers and Statistical Learning Methods

The simplest AI applications can be divided into two types: classifiers ("if shiny then diamond") and controllers ("if shiny then pick up"). Controllers do however also classify conditions before inferring actions, and therefore classification forms a central part of many AI systems. Classifiers are functions that use pattern matching to determine a closest match. They can be tuned according to examples, making them very attractive for use in AI. These examples are known as observations or patterns. In supervised learning, each pattern belongs to a certain predefined class. A class can be seen as a decision that has to be made. All the observations combined with their class labels are known as a data set. When a new observation is received, that observation is classified based on previous experience.

A classifier can be trained in various ways; there are many statistical and machine learning approaches. The most widely used classifiers are the neural network, kernel methods such as the support vector machine, k-nearest neighbour algorithm, Gaussian mixture model, naive Bayes classifier, and decision tree. The performance of these classifiers have been compared over a wide range of tasks. Classifier performance depends greatly on the characteristics of the data to be classified. There is no single classifier that works best on all given problems; this is also referred to as the "no free lunch" theorem. Determining a suitable classifier for a given problem is still more an art than science.

Neural Networks

The study of artificial neural networks began in the decade before the field AI research was founded, in the work of Walter Pitts and Warren McCullough. Other important early researchers were Frank Rosenblatt, who invented the perceptron and Paul Werbos who developed the back propagation algorithm.

The main categories of networks are acyclic or feedforward neural networks (where the signal passes in only one direction) and recurrent neural networks (which allow feedback). Among the most popular feedforward networks are perceptrons, multi-layer perceptrons and radial basis networks. Among recurrent networks, the most famous is the Hopfield net, a form of attractor network, which was first described by John Hopfield in 1982. Neural networks can be applied to the problem of intelligent control (for robotics) or learning, using such techniques as Hebbian learning and competitive learning.

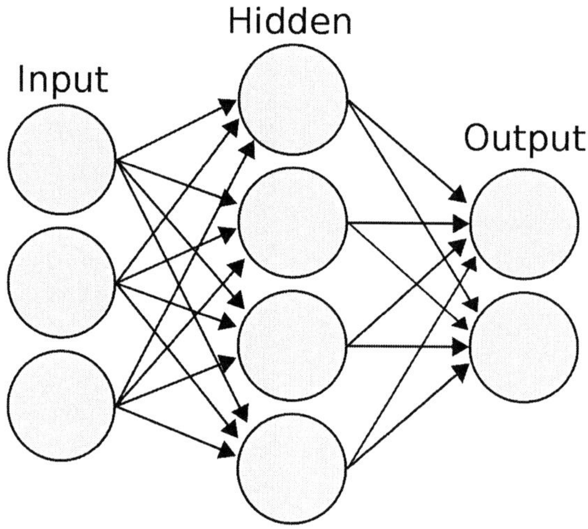

Figure: A neural network is an interconnected group of nodes, akin to the vast network of neurons in the human brain.

Hierarchical temporal memory is an approach that models some of the structural and algorithmic properties of the neocortex.

Control Theory

Control theory, the grandchild of cybernetics, has many important applications, especially in robotics.

Languages

AI researchers have developed several specialized languages for AI research, including Lisp and Prolog.

Evaluating Progress

In 1950, Alan Turing proposed a general procedure to test the intelligence of an agent now known as the Turing test. This procedure allows almost all the major problems of artificial intelligence to be tested. However, it is a very difficult challenge and at present all agents fail.

Artificial intelligence can also be evaluated on specific problems such as small problems in chemistry, hand-writing recognition and game-playing. Such tests have been termed subject matter expert Turing tests. Smaller problems provide more achievable goals and there are an ever-increasing number of positive results.

The broad classes of outcome for an AI test are: (1) Optimal: it is not possible to perform better. (2) Strong super-human: performs better than all humans. (3) Super-human: performs better than most humans. (4) Sub-human: performs worse than most humans. For example, performance at draughts is optimal, performance at chess is super-human and nearing strong super-human and performance at many everyday tasks (such as recognizing a face or crossing a room without bumping into something) is sub-human.

A quite different approach measures machine intelligence through tests which are developed from mathematical definitions of intelligence. Examples of these kinds of tests start in the late nineties devising intelligence tests using notions from Kolmogorov complexity and data compression. Two major advantages of mathematical definitions are their applicability to nonhuman intelligences and their absence of a requirement for human testers.

Applications

Artificial intelligence techniques are pervasive and are too numerous to list. Frequently, when a technique reaches mainstream use, it is no longer considered artificial intelligence; this phenomenon is described as the AI effect.

Competitions and Prizes

There are a number of competitions and prizes to promote research in artificial intelligence. The main areas promoted are: general machine intelligence, conversational behaviour, data-mining, driverless cars, robot soccer and games.

Platforms

A platform (or "computing platform") is defined as "some sort of hardware architecture or software framework (including application frameworks), that allows software to run." As Rodney Brooks pointed out many years ago, it is not just the artificial intelligence software that defines the AI features of the platform, but rather the actual platform itself that affects the AI that results, i.e., we need to be working out AI problems on real-world platforms rather than in isolation.

A wide variety of platforms has allowed different aspects of AI to develop, ranging from expert systems, albeit PC-based but still an entire real-world system, to various robot platforms such as the widely available Roomba with open interface.

Philosophy

Artificial intelligence, by claiming to be able to recreate the capabilities of the human mind, is both a challenge and an inspiration for philosophy. Are there limits to how intelligent machines can be? Is there an essential difference between human intelligence and artificial intelligence?

Turing's "polite convention": We need not decide if a machine can "think"; we need only decide if a machine can act as intelligently as a human being. This approach to the philosophical problems associated with artificial intelligence forms the basis of the Turing test.

The Dartmouth proposal: "Every aspect of learning or any other feature of intelligence can be so precisely described that a machine can be made to simulate it." This conjecture was printed in the proposal for the Dartmouth Conference of 1956, and represents the position of most working AI researchers.

Newell and Simon's physical symbol system hypothesis: "A physical symbol system has the necessary and sufficient means of general intelligent action." Newell and Simon argue that intelligences consist of formal operations on symbols. Hubert Dreyfus argued that, on the contrary, human expertise depends on unconscious instinct rather than conscious symbol manipulation and on having a "feel" for the situation rather than explicit symbolic knowledge.

Gödel's incompleteness theorem: A formal system (such as a computer program) cannot prove all true statements. Roger Penrose is among those who claim that Gödel's theorem limits what machines can do.

Searle's strong AI hypothesis: "The appropriately programmed computer with the right inputs and outputs would thereby have a mind in exactly the same sense human beings have minds." John Searle counters this assertion with his Chinese room argument, which asks us to look inside the computer and try to find where the "mind" might be.

The artificial brain argument: The brain can be simulated. Hans Moravec, Ray Kurzweil and others have argued that it is technologically feasible to copy the brain directly into hardware and software, and that such a simulation will be essentially identical to the original.

Predictions and Ethics

Artificial Intelligence is a common topic in both science fiction and projections about the future of technology and society. The existence of an artificial intelligence that rivals human intelligence raises difficult ethical issues, and the potential power of the technology inspires both hopes and fears.

In fiction, Artificial Intelligence has appeared fulfilling many roles, including a servant (R2D2 in Star Wars), a law enforcer (K.I.T.T. "Knight Rider"), a comrade (Lt. Commander Data in Star Trek: The Next Generation), a conqueror/overlord (The Matrix), a dictator (With Folded Hands), a benevolent provider/de facto ruler (The Culture), an assassin (Terminator), a sentient race (Battlestar Galactica/ Transformers), an extension to human abilities (Ghost in the Shell) and the saviour of the human race (R. Daneel Olivaw in the Asimov's Robot Series).

Mary Shelley's Frankenstein considers a key issue in the ethics of artificial intelligence: if a machine can be created that has intelligence, could it also feel? If it can feel, does it have the same rights as a human? The idea also appears in modern science fiction, including the films I Robot, Blade Runner and A.I.: Artificial Intelligence, in which humanoid machines have the ability to feel human emotions. This issue, now known as "robot rights", is currently being considered by, for example, California's Institute for the Future, although many critics believe that the discussion is premature. The subject is profoundly discussed in the 2010 documentary film Plug & Pray.

Martin Ford, author of The Lights in the Tunnel: Automation, Accelerating Technology and the Economy of the Future, and others argue that specialized artificial intelligence applications, robotics and other forms of automation will ultimately result in significant unemployment as machines begin to match and exceed the capability of workers to perform most routine and repetitive jobs. Ford predicts that many knowledge-based occupations—and in particular entry level jobs—will be increasingly susceptible to automation via expert systems, machine learning and other AI-enhanced applications. AI-based applications may also be used to amplify the capabilities of low-wage offshore workers, making it more feasible to outsource knowledge work.

Joseph Weizenbaum wrote that AI applications can not, by definition, successfully simulate genuine human empathy and that the use of AI technology in fields such as customer service or psychotherapy was deeply misguided. Weizenbaum was also bothered that AI researchers (and some philosophers) were willing to view the human mind as nothing more than a computer program (a position now known as computationalism). To Weizenbaum these points suggest that AI research devalues human life.

Many futurists believe that artificial intelligence will ultimately transcend the limits of progress. Ray Kurzweil has used Moore's law (which describes the relentless exponential improvement in digital technology) to calculate that desktop computers will have the same processing power as human brains by the year 2029. He also predicts that by 2045 artificial intelligence will reach a point where it is able to improve itself at a rate that far exceeds anything conceivable in the past, a scenario that science fiction writer Vernor Vinge named the "singularity".

Robot designer Hans Moravec, cyberneticist Kevin Warwick and inventor Ray Kurzweil have predicted that humans and machines will merge in the future into cyborgs that are more capable and powerful than either. This idea, called transhumanism, which has roots in Aldous Huxley and Robert Ettinger, has been illustrated in fiction as well, for example in the manga Ghost in the Shell and the science-fiction series Dune.

Edward Fredkin argues that "artificial intelligence is the next stage in evolution," an idea first proposed by Samuel Butler's "Darwin among the Machines" (1863), and expanded upon by George Dyson in his book of the same name in 1998.

Pamela McCorduck writes that all these scenarios are expressions of the ancient human desire to, as she calls it, "forge the gods".

Chapter 4

Logic and Dilemma

Dynamic Logic (Digital Electronics)

In integrated circuit design, dynamic logic (or sometimes clocked logic) is a design methodology in combinatorial logic circuits, particularly those implemented in MOS technology. It is distinguished from the so-called static logic by exploiting temporary storage of information in stray and gate capacitances. It was popular in the 1970s and has seen a recent resurgence in the design of high speed digital electronics, particularly computer CPUs. Dynamic logic circuits are usually faster than static counterparts, and require less surface area, but are more difficult to design, and have higher power dissipation. When referring to a particular logic family, the dynamic adjective usually suffices to distinguish the design methodology, e.g. dynamic CMOS or dynamic SOI design.

Dynamic logic is distinguished from so-called static logic in that dynamic logic uses a clock signal in its implementation of combinational logic circuits. The usual use of a clock signal is to synchronize transitions in sequential logic circuits. For most implementations of combinational logic, a clock signal is not even needed.

The static/dynamic terminology used to refer to combinatorial circuits should not be confused with how the same adjectives are used to distinguish memory devices, e.g. static RAM from dynamic RAM.

Terminology

In the context of logic design, the term dynamic logic is more commonly used as compared to clocked logic, as it makes clear the distinction between this type of design and static logic. To additionally confuse the matter, clocked logic is sometimes used as a synonym for sequential logic. This usage is nonstandard and should be avoided.

Static versus Dynamic Logic

The largest difference between static and dynamic logic is that in dynamic logic, a clock signal is used to evaluate combinational logic. However, to truly comprehend the importance of this distinction, the reader will need some background on static logic.

In most types of logic design, termed static logic, there is at all times some mechanism to drive the output either high or low. In many of the popular logic styles, such as TTL and traditional CMOS, this principle can be rephrased as a statement that there is always a low-impedance path between the output and either the supply voltage or the ground. As a sidenote, there is of course an exception in this definition in the case of high impedance outputs, such as a tri-state buffer; however, even in these cases, the circuit is intended to be used within a larger system where some mechanism will drive the output, and they do not qualify as distinct from static logic.

In contrast, in dynamic logic, there is not always a mechanism driving the output high or low. In the most common version of this concept, the output is driven high or low during distinct parts of the clock cycle.

Dynamic logic requires a minimum clock rate fast enough that the output state of each dynamic gate is used before it leaks out of the capacitance holding that state, during the part of the clock cycle that the output is not being actively driven.

Static logic has no minimum clock rate—the clock can be paused indefinitely. While it may seem that doing nothing for long periods of time is not particularly useful, it leads to two advantages:

- being able to pause a system at any time makes debugging and testing much easier, enabling techniques such as single stepping.
- being able to run a system at extremely low clock rates allows low-power electronics to run longer on a given battery.

In particular, although many popular CPUs use dynamic logic , only static cores — CPUs designed with fully static CMOS technology — are usable in space satellites due to their higher radiation hardness

Dynamic logic, when properly designed, can be over twice as fast as static logic. It uses only the faster N transistors, which improve transistor sizing optimisations. Static logic is slower because it has twice the capacitive loading, higher thresholds, and uses slow P transistors for logic. Dynamic logic can be harder to work with, but it may be the only choice when increased processing speed is needed. Most electronics running at over 2 GHz these days require the use of dynamic, although some manufacturers such as Intel have completely switched to static logic to save on power.

In general, dynamic logic greatly increases the number of transistors that are switching at any given time, which increases power consumption over static CMOS. There are several powersaving techniques that can be implemented in a dynamic logic based system. In addition, each rail can convey an arbitrary number of bits, and there are no power-wasting glitches. Power-saving clock gating and asynchronous techniques are much more natural in dynamic logic.

Dynamic Logic Example

As an example, consider first the static logic implementation of a NAND gate (here in CMOS):

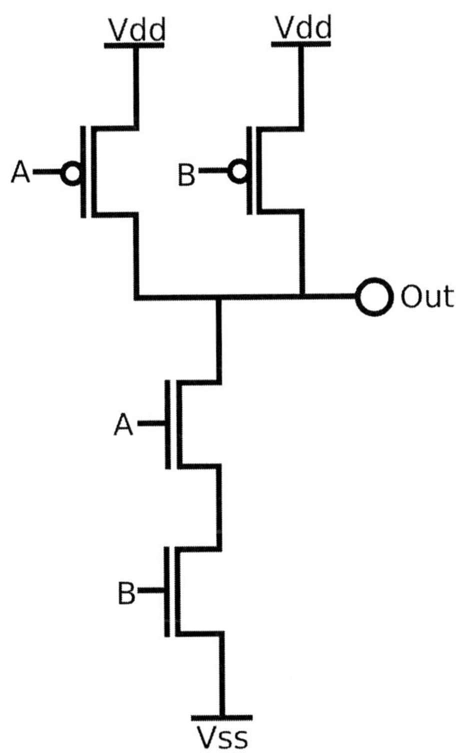

Figure: This circuit implements the logic function

$$Out = \overline{AB}$$

If A and B are both high, the output will be pulled low, whereas if one of A and B are low, the output will be pulled high. Most importantly, though, at all times, the output is pulled either low or high.

Consider now a dynamic logic implementation:

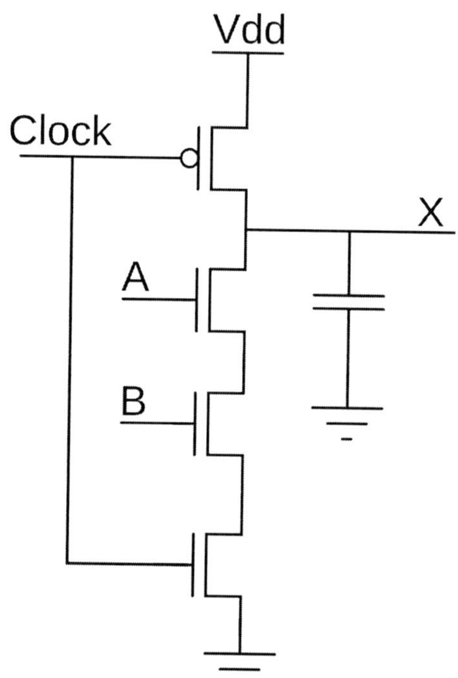

The dynamic logic circuit requires two phases. The first phase, when Clock is low, is called the setup phase or the precharge phase and the second phase, when Clock is high, is called the evaluation phase. In the setup phase, the output is driven high unconditionally (no matter the values of the inputs A and B). The capacitor, which represents the load capacitance of this gate, becomes charged. Because the transistor at the bottom is turned off, it is impossible for the output to be driven low during this phase.

During the evaluation phase, Clock is high. If A and B are also high, the output will be pulled low. Otherwise, the output stays high (due to the load capacitance).

Dynamic logic has a few potential problems that static logic does not. For example, if the clock speed is too slow, the output will decay too quickly to be of use. A popular implementation is domino logic.

Leonid Perlovsky

Dr. Leonid Perlovsky is a Visiting Scholar at Harvard University, Principal Research Physicist and Technical Advisor at the United States Air Force Research Laboratory, Hanscom Air Force Base. He is the Program Manager for United States Department of Defence (DOD) Semantic Web program and leads several research projects, including cognitivealgorithms, modelling of evolution of languages and cultures. From 1985 to 1999, he served as Chief Scientist at Nichols Research, a $0.5B hightech DOD contractor leading the corporate research in intelligent systems, neural networks, sensor fusion, and automatic target recognition.

He served as professor at Novosibirsk State University and New York University, and participated as a principal in commercial startups developing tools for text understanding, Biotechnology , and financial predictions. His company predicted the market crash following September 11, 2001 attacks a week before the event, detecting activities of Al-Qaeda traders, and later helped SEC tracking the perpetrators. He is invited as a keynote plenary speaker and tutorial lectures worldwide, and has published more than 320 papers and 10 book chapters and authored three books, including "Neural Networks and Intellect," Oxford University Press, 2000 (currently in the 3rd printing) and two books with Springer in 2007,. Dr. Perlovsky organizes conferences on Computational intelligence, Chairs IEEE Boston Computational Intelligence Chapter. He serves as Associate Editor for IEEE Transactions on Neural Networks, , Editor-at-Large for "New Mathematics and Natural Computation" and Editor-in-Chief for "Physics of Life Reviews." He received National and International awards including the IEEE Distinguished Member of Boston Section Award 2005; the US AFRL Charles Ryan Memorial Award for Basic Research, 2007; Gabor Award 2007, the top engineering award from the International Neural Network Society; and John McLucas Award 2007, the highest US Air Force Award for science.

His current research interests include modelling mechanisms of the mind: neural modelling fields, knowledge instinct, aesthetic emotions, emotions of beautiful and sublime, language, language evolution, emotionality of languages, language and cognition, evolution of languages and cultures, symbols as psychological processes, evolution of consciousness, languages, and cultures, mathematical intelligence and art, role of music in evolution of consciousness and cultures, science and religion, including scientific explanations for the role of sacred values in the workings of the mind, and why religious teleology is equivalent to scientific causality.

Knowledge Instinct

The term knowledge instinct is used by Leonid Perlovsky in his book Neural Networks and Intellect: Using Model-Based Concepts and other publications. In his works the knowledge instinct is recognized on a par with other 'basic instincts' such as instincts for food and procreation as a fundamental mechanism of human functioning.

The existence of knowledge instinct follows from the cognitive and neural evidence about the brain mechanisms of perception and cognition, as well as mathematical modelling of these mechanisms. The conclusion that humans and higher animals have a special instinct responsible for cognition is supported by several other researchers. Harry Harlow discovered that monkeys as well as humans have the drive for positive stimulation, regardless of satisfaction of drives such as hunger; David Berlyne discussed curiosity in this regard; Leon Festinger, introduced the notion of cognitive dissonance and described many experiments on the drive of humans to reduce dissonance; John Cacioppo discussed the need for cognition.

The fundamental nature of this mechanism is related to the fact that our knowledge always has to be modified to fit the current situations. One rarely sees exactly the same object: illumination, angles, surrounding objects are usually different; therefore, adaptation-learning is required. A mathematical formulation of the mind mechanisms (Perlovsky 2006) emphasizes the fundamental nature of our desire for knowledge.

Virtually all learning and adaptive algorithms (tens of thousands of publications) maximize correspondence between the algorithm internal structure (knowledge in a wide sense) and objects of recognition. Concept-models that our mind uses for understanding the world are in a constant need of adaptation. Knowledge is not just a static state; it is in a constant process of adaptation and learning. Without adaptation of concept-models humans and animals will not be able to understand the ever-changing surrounding world. They will not be able to orient ourselves or satisfy any of the bodily needs. Therefore, animals must have an inborn need, a drive, an instinct to improve knowledge, called the knowledge instinct. Mathematically it is described as a maximization of a similarity measure between the knowledge stored in mind concepts and the world as it is sensed by sensory organs.

Dynamic Logic (Neural)

In Perlovsky's works, the term Dynamic logic refers to a logic-process describing mathematically a fundamental mind mechanism of interactions between bottom-up signals and top-down signals as a process of adaptaton from vague to crisp concepts. Dynamic logic is a mathematical description of the Knowledge instinct. This mathematical formulation results in practically usable algorithms used within the framework of Neural modelling fields. It resulted in significant improvement in solving classical problems (such as detection, recognition, tracking, fusion) and new approaches to recently emerging problems (such as text search engines and cultural prediction models).

Physics of the Mind

Physics occupies itself with the search for basic laws, a few universal "first principles" describing a wealth of observed phenomena. Perlovsky aims to develop a physical theory of the mind and suggests the first principles that need to be included in such theory. Among "the first principles" of the mind are interactions between bottom-up signals and top-down signals, which is the essence of perception, cognition, and concept formation; mechanisms of instincts and emotions, and their interaction with cognition; the knowledge instinct driving cognition, higher mental abilities, and related aesthetic emotions. Dynamic logic mathematically describes these mechanisms.

Defuzzification

Defuzzification is the process of producing a quantifiable result in fuzzy logic, given fuzzy sets and corresponding membership degrees. It is typically needed in fuzzy control systems. These will have a number of rules that transform a number of variables into a fuzzy result, that is, the result is described in terms of membership in fuzzy sets. For example, rules designed to decide how much pressure to apply might result in "Decrease Pressure (15%), Maintain Pressure (34%), Increase Pressure (72%)". Defuzzification is interpreting the membership degrees of the fuzzy sets into a specific decision or real value.

The simplest but least useful defuzzification method is to choose the set with the highest membership, in this case, "Increase Pressure" since it has a 72% membership, and ignore the others, and convert this 72% to some number. The problem with this approach is that it loses information. The rules that called for decreasing or maintaining pressure might as well have not been there in this case.

A common and useful defuzzification technique is centre of gravity. First, the results of the rules must be added together in some way. The most typical fuzzy set membership function has the graph of a triangle. Now, if this triangle were to be cut in a straight horizontal line somewhere between the top and the bottom, and the top portion were to be removed, the remaining portion forms a trapezoid. The first step of defuzzification typically "chops off" parts of the graphs to form trapezoids (or other shapes if the initial shapes were not triangles). For example, if the output has "Decrease Pressure (15%)", then this triangle will be cut 15% the way up from the bottom. In the most common technique, all of these trapezoids are then superimposed one upon another, forming a single geometric shape. Then, the centroid of this shape, called the fuzzy centroid, is calculated. The x coordinate of the centroid is the defuzzified value.

Methods

There are many different methods of defuzzification available, including the following:

- AI (adaptive integration) DOI 10.1109/ICMNN.1994.593726
- BADD (basic defuzzification distributions)
- CDD (constraint decision defuzzification)
- COA (centre of area)
- COG (centre of gravity)
- ECOA (extended centre of area)
- EQM (extended quality method)
- FCD (fuzzy clustering defuzzification)
- FM (fuzzy mean)

- FOM (first of maximum)
- GLSD (generalised level set defuzzification)
- ICOG (indexed centre of gravity)
- IV (influence value) DOI 10.1109/FUZZY.1996.552647
- LOM (last of maximum)
- MeOM (mean of maxima)
- MOM (middle of maximum)
- QM (quality method)
- RCOM (random choice of maximum)
- SLIDE (semi-linear defuzzification)
- WFM (weighted fuzzy mean)

The maxima methods are good candidates for fuzzy reasoning systems. The distribution methods and the area methods exhibit the property of continuity that makes them suitable for fuzzy controllers.

False Dilemma

A false dilemma (also called false dichotomy, the either-or fallacy, fallacy of false choice, black-and-white thinking, or the fallacy of exhaustive hypotheses) is a type of logical fallacy that involves a situation in which only two alternatives are considered, when in fact there are additional options (sometimes shades of grey between the extremes). For example, "It wasn't medicine that cured Ms. X, so it must have been a miracle."

False dilemma can arise intentionally, when fallacy is used in an attempt to force a choice ("If you are not with us, you are against us"). But the fallacy can also arise simply by accidental omission of additional options rather than by deliberate deception (e.g., "I thought we were friends, but all my friends were at my apartment last night and you weren't there").

In the community of philosophers and scholars, many believe that "unless a distinction can be made rigorous and precise it isn't really a distinction." An exception is analytic philosopher John Searle, who called it an incorrect assumption which produces false dichotomies. Searle insists that "it is a condition of the adequacy of a precise theory of an indeterminate phenomenon that it should precisely characterize that phenomenon as indeterminate; and a distinction is no less a distinction for allowing for a family of related, marginal, diverging cases." Similarly, when two alternatives are presented, they are often, though not always, two extreme points on some spectrum of possibilities; this can lend credence to the larger argument by giving the impression that the options are mutually exclusive, even though they need not be. Furthermore, the options in false dichotomies are typically presented as being collectively exhaustive, in which case the fallacy can be overcome, or at least weakened, by considering other possibilities, or perhaps by considering a whole spectrum of possibilities, as in fuzzy logic.

Examples

Morton's Fork

Morton's Fork, a choice between two equally unpleasant options, is often a false dilemma. The phrase originates from an argument for taxing English nobles:

Either the nobles of this country appear wealthy, in which case they can be taxed for good; or they appear poor, in which case they are living frugally and must have immense savings, which can be taxed for good.

This is a false dilemma and a catch-22, because it fails to allow for the possibility that some members of the nobility may in fact lack liquid assets as well as the probability that those who appear poor also lack liquid assets.

False Choice

The presentation of a false choice often reflects a deliberate attempt to eliminate the middle ground on an issue. Eldridge Cleaver used such a quotation during his 1968 presidential campaign: "You're either part of the solution or part of the problem." Another example would be the former US president George W. Bush stating that the world had a choice to make; "Either you are with us, or you are with the terrorists." A common argument against noise pollution laws involves a false choice. It might be argued that in New York City noise should not be regulated, because if it were, the city would drastically change in a negative way. This argument involves assuming that, for example, a bar must be shut down for it to not cause disturbing levels of noise after midnight. This ignores the fact that the bar could simply lower its noise levels, and/or install more soundproof structural elements to keep the noise from excessively transmitting onto others' properties.

Black-and-White Thinking

In psychology, a related phenomenon to the false dilemma is black-and-white thinking. Many people routinely engage in black-and-white thinking, an example of which is feeling boundless optimism when things are going well and suddenly switching to total despair at the first setback. Another example is someone who labels other people as all good or all bad.

Falsum in Uno, Falsum in Omnibus

The Latin phrase falsum in uno, falsum in omnibus which, roughly translated, means "false in one thing, false in everything", is fallacious in so far as someone found to be wrong about one thing, is presumed to be wrong about some other thing entirely. Arising in Roman courts, this principle meant that if a witness was proved false in some parts of his testimony, any further statements were also regarded as false unless they were independently corroborated. Falsus is thus a fallacy of logic. The description that an initial false statement is a prelude to the making of more false statements is false, however, even one false premise will suffice to disprove an argument. This is a special case of the associatory fallacy.

It must be noted that falsum in uno, falsum in omnibus status as a logical fallacy is independent of whether it is wise or unwise to use as a legal rule, with witnesses testifying in courts being held for perjury if part of their statements are false.

Fuzzy Architectural Spatial Analysis

Fuzzy architectural spatial analysis (FASA) (also fuzzy inference system (FIS) based architectural space analysis or fuzzy spatial analysis) is a spatial analysis method of analysing the spatial formation and architectural space intensity within any architectural organization.

Fuzzy architectural spatial analysis is used in architecture, interior design, urban planning and similar spatial design fields.

Fuzzy architectural spatial analysis was developed from the architectural theory of space syntax and visibility graph analysis, by Burcin Cem Arabacioglu (2010), and is applied with the help of a fuzzy system with a Mamdami inference system based on fuzzy logic within any architectural space. Fuzzy architectural spatial analysis model analyses the space by considering the perceivable architectural element by their boundary and stress characteristics and intensity properties. The method is capable of taking all sensorial factors into account during analyses in conformably with the perception process of architectural space which is a multi-sensored act.

Fuzzy Associative Matrix

A fuzzy associative matrix expresses fuzzy logic rules in tabular form. These rules usually take two variables as input, mapping cleanly to a two-dimensional matrix, although theoretically a matrix of any number of dimensions is possible.

Let's suppose we want to write fuzzy logic rules for a video game monster. We decide to start with two variables: hit points (HP) and firepower (FP). We might start with this:

HP/FP	Very low HP	Low HP	Medium HP	High HP	Very high HP
Very weak FP	Retreat!	Retreat!	Defend	Defend	Attack
Weak FP	Retreat!	Defend	Defend	Attack	Attack
Medium FP	Retreat!	Defend	Attack	Attack	Full attack!
High FP	Retreat!	Defend	Attack	Attack	Full attack!
Very high FP	Defend	Attack	Attack	Full attack!	Full attack!

This translates to:

IF MonsterHP IS VeryLowHP AND MonsterFP IS VeryWeakFP THEN Retreat

IF MonsterHP IS LowHP AND MonsterFP IS VeryWeakFP THEN Retreat

IF MonsterHP IS MediumHP AND MonsterFP is VeryWeakFP THEN Defend

...and so on. Multiple rules can fire at once, and very often, they will. The distinction between "very low" and "low" is probably fuzzy at many points, and at such points, both rules will fire. If it is more "very low" than it is low, then the "very low" rule will generate a stronger response. The program will evaluate all the rules that fire and use an appropriate defuzzification method to generate its actual response.

An implementation of this system might use either the matrix or the explicit IF/THEN form. The matrix makes it easy to visualize the system, but it also makes it impossible to add a third variable just for one rule, so it is less flexible.

There is no inherent pattern in the matrix. It appears as if the rules were just made up, and indeed they were. This is both a strength and a weakness of fuzzy logic in general. It is often impractical or impossible to find an exact set of rules or formulae for dealing with a specific situation. For a sufficiently complex game, a mathematician would not be able to study the system and figure out a mathematically accurate set of rules. However, this weakness is intrinsic to the realities of the situation, not of fuzzy logic itself. The strength of the system is that even if one of the rules is wrong, even greatly wrong, other rules that are correct are likely to fire as well and they may compensate for the error.

This does not mean a fuzzy system should be sloppy. Depending on the system, it might get away with being sloppy, but it will underperform. While the rules are fairly arbitrary, they should be chosen carefully. If possible, an expert should decide on the rules, and the sets and rules should be tested vigorously and refined as needed. In this way, a fuzzy system is like an expert system. (Fuzzy logic is used in many true expert systems, as well.)

Fuzzy Classification

Fuzzy classification is the process of grouping elements into a fuzzy set (Zadeh 1965) whose membership function is defined by the truth value of a fuzzy propositional function. It has been discussed for example by (Zimmermann H.-J., 2000), (Meier, Schindler, & Werro, 2008) or (Del Amo, Montero, & Cutello, 1999).

A fuzzy class ~C = { i | ~Π(i) } is defined as a fuzzy set ~C of individuals i satisfying a fuzzy classification predicate ~Π which is a fuzzy propositional function. The domain of the fuzzy class operator ~{ .| .} is the set of variables V and the set of fuzzy propositional functions ~PF, and the range is the fuzzy powerset (the set of fuzzy subsets) of this universe, ~P(U):

~{ .| .}:V × ~PF □ ~P(U)

A fuzzy propositional function is, analogous to (Russel, 1919, S. 155), an expression containing one or more variables, such that, when values are assigned to these variables, the expression becomes a fuzzy proposition in the sense of (Zadeh 1975).

Accordingly, fuzzy classification is the process of grouping individuals having the same characteristics into a fuzzy set. A fuzzy classification corresponds to a membership function μ that indicates whether an individual is a member of a class, given its fuzzy classification predicate ~Π.

μ:~PF × U □ ~T

Here, ~T is the set of fuzzy truth values (the interval between zero an one). The fuzzy classification predicate ~Π corresponds to a fuzzy restriction "i is R" (Zadeh, Calculus of fuzzy restrictions, 1975) of U, where R is a fuzzy set defined by a truth function.

The degree of membership of an individual i in the fuzzy class ~C is defined by the truth value of the corresponding fuzzy predicate.

μ~C(i):= T(~Π(i))

Classification

Intuitively, a class is a set that is defined by a certain property, and all objects having that property are elements of that class.

The process of classification evaluates for a given set of objects whether they fulfill the classification property, and consequentially are a member of the corresponding class. However, this intuitive concept has some logical subtleties that need clarification.

A class logic (Glubrecht, Oberschelp, & Todt, 1983) is a logical system which supports set construction using logical predicates with the class operator { .| .}. A class

C = { i | Π(i) }

is defined as a set C of individuals i satisfying a classification predicate Π which is a propositional function. The domain of the class operator { .| .} is the set of variables V and the set of propositional functions PF, and the range is the powerset of this universe P(U) that is, the set of possible subsets:

{ .| .} 6□V×PF□ P(U)

Here is an explanation of the logical elements that constitute this definition:

- An individual is a real object of reference.
- A universe of discourse is the set of all possible individuals considered.

- A variable V:□ R is a function which maps into a predefined range R without any given function arguments: a zero-place function.
- A propositional function is "an expression containing one or more undetermined constituents, such that, when values are assigned to these constituents, the expression becomes a proposition" (Russel, 1919, S. 155).

In contrast, classification is the process of grouping individuals having the same characteristics into a set. A classification corresponds to a membership function μ that indicates whether an individual is a member of a class, given its classification predicate Π.

μ:PF × U □ T

The membership function maps from the set of propositional functions PF and the universe of discourse U into the set of truth values T. The membership μ of individual i in Class C is defined by the truth value ô of the classification predicate Π.

μC(i):=T(Π(i))

In classical logic the truth values are certain. Therefore a classification is crisp, since the truth values are either exactly true or exactly false.

Fuzzy Concept

A fuzzy concept is a concept of which the content, value, or boundaries of application can vary according to context or conditions, instead of being fixed once and for all.

Usually this means the concept is vague, lacking a fixed, precise meaning, without however being meaningless altogether. It does have a meaning, or rather multiple meanings (it has different semantic associations). But these can become clearer only through further elaboration and specification, including a closer definition of the context in which they are used. Fuzzy concepts (Markusen, 2003) "lack clarity and are difficult to test or operationalize". In logic, fuzzy concepts are often regarded as concepts which in their application are neither completely true or completely false, or which are partly true and partly false. A fuzzy variable (such as "the temperature", "hot" or "cold") is a value which could lie in a probable range defined by quantitative limits or parameters and can be usefully described with imprecise categories (such as "high", "medium" or "low").

Fuzzy concepts may generate uncertainty (they do not provide a clear orientation for action or decision-making) and reducing fuzziness may generate more certainty. However, this is not necessarily always so, insofar as a concept, although it is not fuzzy at all and very exact, could equally well fail to capture the meaning of something adequately. A concept can be very precise, but not - or insufficiently - applicable or relevant in the situation to which it refers. A fuzzy concept may indeed provide more security, because it provides a meaning for something when an exact concept is unavailable - which is better than not being able to denote it at all. A concept such as God, although not easily definable, for instance can provide security to the believer.

Fuzzy Concepts and Language

Ordinary language, which uses symbolic conventions and associations which are often not logical, inherently contains many fuzzy concepts - "knowing what you mean" in this case depends on knowing the context or being familiar with the way in which a term is normally used, or what it is associated with. This can be easily verified for instance by consulting a dictionary, a thesaurus or an encyclopedia which show the multiple meanings of words, or by observing the behaviours involved in ordinary relationships which rely on mutually understood meanings.

To communicate, receive or convey a message, an individual somehow has to bridge his own intended meaning and the meanings which are understood by others, i.e. the message has to be conveyed in a way that it will be socially understood, preferably in the intended manner. Thus, people might state: "you have to say it in a way that I understand".

This may be done instinctively, habitually or unconsciously, but it usually involves a choice of terms, assumptions or symbols whose meanings may often not be completely fixed, but which depend among other things on how the receiver of the message responds to it, or the context. In this sense, meaning is often "negotiated" (or, more cynically, manipulated). This gives rise to many fuzzy concepts.

But even using ordinary set theory and binary logic to reason something out, logicians have discovered that it is possible to generate statements which are logically speaking not completely true or imply a paradox, even although in other respects they conform to logical rules.

Origin of Fuzzy Concepts

The origin of fuzzy concepts is partly de to the fact that the human brain does not operate like a computer. While computers use strict binary logic gates, the brain does not; i.e., it is capable of making all kinds of neural associations according to all kinds of ordering principles (or fairly chaotically) in associative patterns which are not logical but nevertheless meaningful. Something can be meaningful although we cannot name it, or we might only be able to name it and nothing else. The human brain can also interpret the same phenomenon in several different but interacting frames of reference, at the same time, or in quick succession.

In part, fuzzy concepts arise also because learning or the growth of understanding involves a transition from a vague awareness, which cannot orient behaviour greatly, to clearer insight, which can orient behaviour.

Some logicians argue that fuzzy concepts are a necessary consequence of the reality that any kind of distinction we might like to draw has limits of application. As a certain level of generality, it works fine. But if we pursued its application in a very exact and rigorous manner, or overextend its application, it appears that the distinction simply does not apply in some areas or contexts, or that we cannot fully specify how it should be drawn. An analogy might be that zooming a telescope, camera, or microscope in and out reveals that a pattern which is sharply focused at a certain distance disappears at another distance.

In psychophysics it has been discovered that the perceptual distinctions we draw in the mind are often more sharply defined than they are in the real world. Thus, the brain actually tends to "sharpen up" our perceptions of differences in the external world. Between black and white, we are able to detect only a limited number of shades of gray, or colour gradations. If there are more gradations and transitions in reality than our conceptual distinctions can capture, then it could be argued that how those distinctions will actually apply must necessarily become vaguer at some point. If, for example, one wants to count and quantify distinct objects using numbers, one needs to be able to distinguish between those separate objects, but if this is difficult or impossible, then, although this may not invalidate a quantitative procedure as such, quantification is not really possible in practice; at best, we may be able to assume or infer indirectly a certain distribution of quantities. Finally, in interacting with the external world, the human mind may often encounter new, or partly new phenomena or relationships which cannot (yet) be sharply defined given the background knowledge available, and by known distinctions, associations or generalisations.

"Crisis management plans cannot be put 'on the fly' after the crisis occurs. At the outset, information is often vague, even contradictory. Events move so quickly that decision makers experience a sense of loss of control. Often denial sets in, and managers unintentionally cut off information flow about the situation" - L. Paul Bremer, "Corporate governance and crisis management", in: Directors & Boards, Winter 2002. It also can be argued that fuzzy concepts are generated by a certain sort of lifestyle or way of working which evades definite distinctions, makes them impossible or inoperable, or which is in some way chaotic. To obtain concepts which are not fuzzy, it must be possible to test out their application in some way. But in the absence of any relevant clear distinctions, or when everything is "in a state of flux" or in transition, it may not be possible to do so, so that the amount of fuzziness increases.

Use of Fuzzy Concepts

Fuzzy concepts often play a role in the creative process of forming new concepts to understand something. In the most primitive sense, this can be observed in infants who, through practical experience, learn to identify, distinguish and generalise the correct application of a concept, and relate it to other concepts.

However, fuzzy concepts may also occur in scientific, journalistic, programming and philosophical activity, when a thinker is in the process of clarifying and defining a newly emerging concept which is based on distinctions which, for one reason or another, cannot (yet) be more exactly specified or validated. Fuzzy concepts are often used to denote complex phenomena, or to describe something which is developing and changing, which might involve shedding some old meanings and acquiring new ones.

- In politics, it can be highly important and problematic how exactly a conceptual distinction is drawn, or indeed whether a distinction is drawn at all; distinctions used in administration may be deliberately sharpened, or kept fuzzy, due to some political motive or power relationship. A politician may be deliberately vague about some things, and very clear and explicit about others. The "fuzzy area" can also refer simply to a residual number of cases which cannot be allocated to a known and identifiable group, class or set.

- In translation work, fuzzy concepts are analysed for the purpose of good translation. A concept in one language may not have quite the same meaning or significance in another language, or it may not be feasible to translate it literally, or at all. Some languages have concepts which do not exist in another language, raising the problem of how one would most easily render their meaning.
- In information services fuzzy concepts are frequently encountered because a customer or client asks a question about something which could be interpreted in many different ways, or, a document is transmitted of a type or meaning which cannot be easily allocated to a known type or category, or to a known procedure. It might take considerable inquiry to "place" the information, or establish in what framework it should be understood.
- In the legal system, it is essential that rules are interpreted and applied in a standard way, so that the same cases and the same circumstances are treated equally. Otherwise one would be accused of arbitrariness, which would not serve the interests of justice. Consequently, lawmakers aim to devise definitions and categories which are sufficiently precise that they are not open to different interpretations. For this purpose, it is critically important to remove fuzziness, and differences of interpretation are typically resolved through a court ruling based on evidence.
- In statistical research, it is an aim to measure the magnitudes of phenomena. For this purpose, phenomena have to be grouped and categorized so that distinct and discrete counting units can be defined. It must be possible to allocate all observations to mutually exclusive categories so that they are properly quantifiable. Survey observations do not spontaneously transform themselves into countable data; they have to be identified, categorized and classified in such a way that they are not counted twice or more. Again, for this purpose it is a requirement that the concepts used are exactly defined, and not fuzzy.

- In theology an attempt is made to define more precisely the meaning of spiritual concepts, which refer to how human beings construct the meaning of human existence, and, often, the relationship people have with a supernatural world. Many spiritual concepts and beliefs are fuzzy, to the extent that, although abstract, they often have a highly personalized meaning, or involve personal interpretation of a type that is not easy to define in a cut-and-dried way.
- In meteorology, where changes and effects of complex interactions in the atmosphere are studied, the weather reports often use fuzzy expressions indicating a broad trend, likelihood or level. The main reason is that the forecast can rarely be totally exact for any given location.
- In phenomenology which studies the structure of subjective experience, an important insight is that how someone experiences something can be influenced both by the influence of the thing being experienced itself, but also by how the person responds to it. Thus, the actual experience the person has, is shaped by an "interactive object-subject relationship". To describe this experience, fuzzy categories are often necessary, since it is often impossible to predict or describe with great exactitude what the interaction will be, and how it is experienced.

It could be argued that many concepts used fairly universally in daily life (e.g. "love" or "God" or "health" or "social") are inherently or intrinsically fuzzy concepts, to the extent that their meaning can never be completely and exactly specified with logical operators or objective terms, and can have multiple interpretations, which are in part exclusively subjective. Yet despite this limitation, such concepts are not meaningless.

It may also be possible to specify one personal meaning for the concept, without however placing restrictions on a different use of the concept in other contexts (as when, for example, one says "this is what I mean by X" in contrast to other possible meanings). In ordinary speech, concepts may sometimes also be uttered purely randomly; for example a child may repeat the same idea in completely unrelated contexts, or an expletive term may be uttered arbitrarily. Fuzzy concepts can be used deliberately to create ambiguity and vagueness, as an evasive tactic, or to bridge what would otherwise be immediately recognized as a contradiction of terms. They might be used to indicate that there is definitely a connection between two things, without giving a complete specification of what the connection is, for some or other reason. This could be due to a failure or refusal to be more precise. But it could also could be a prologue to a more exact formulation of a concept, or a better understanding. It could also simply be a practical method to describe something of which a complete description would be an unmanageably large undertaking, or very time-consuming.

Analysis of Fuzzy Concepts

In mathematical logic, programming, philosophy and linguistics fuzzy concepts can however be analysed and defined more accurately or comprehensively, for instance:

- by specifying a range of conditions to which the concept applies.
- by classifying or categorizing all or most cases or uses to which the concept applies (taxonomy).
- by probing the assumptions on which a concept is based, or which are associated with its use (Critical thought).
- by identifying operational rules for the use of the concept, which cover all or most cases.
- by allocating different applications of the concept to different but related sets (e.g. using Boolean logic).
- by examining how probable it is that the concept applies, statistically or intuitively.
- by examining the distribution or distributional frequency of (possibly different) uses of the concept.
- by some other kind of measure or scale of the degree to which the concept applies.
- by specifying a series of logical operators (an inferential system or algorithm) which captures all or most cases to which the concept applies.
- by mapping or graphing the applications of the concept using some basic parameters.
- by applying a meta-language which includes fuzzy concepts in a more inclusive categorical system which is not fuzzy.
- by reducing or restating fuzzy concepts in terms which are simpler or similar, and which are not fuzzy or less fuzzy.

- by relating the fuzzy concept to other concepts which are not fuzzy or less fuzzy, or simply by replacing the fuzzy concept altogether with another, alternative concept which is not fuzzy yet "works exactly the same way".

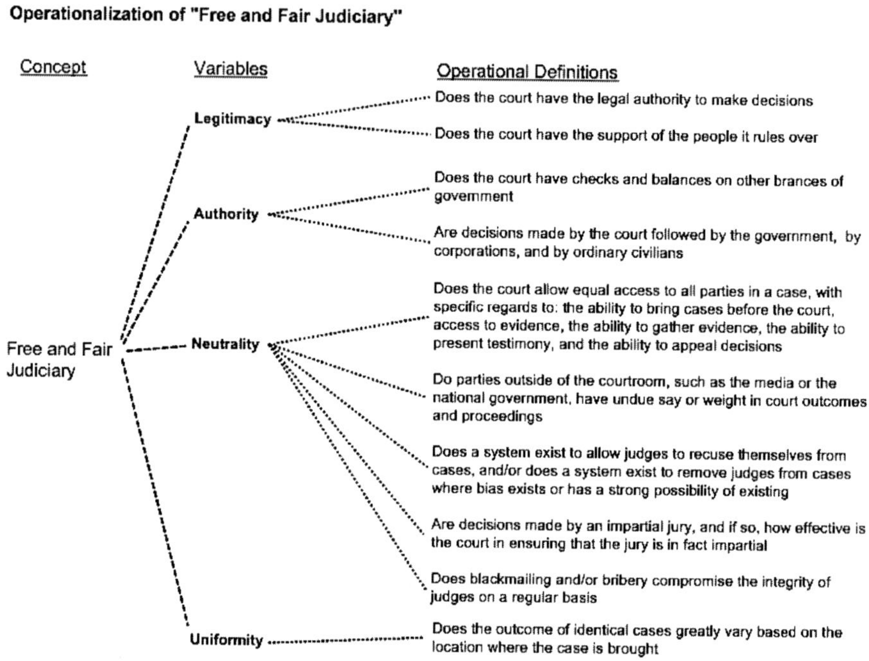

Figure: A operationalization diagram, one method of clarifing fuzzy concepts.

In this way, we can obtain a more exact understanding of the use of a fuzzy concept, and possibly decrease the amount of fuzziness. It may not be possible to specify all the possible meanings or applications of a concept completely and exhaustively, but if it is possible to capture the majority of them, statistically or otherwise, this may be useful enough for practical purposes.

The difficulty that can occur in judging the fuzziness of a concept can be illustrated with the question "Is this one of those?". If it is not possible to clearly answer this question, that could be because "this" (the object) is itself fuzzy and evades definition, or because "one of those" (the concept of the object) is fuzzy and inadequately defined.

Thus, the source of fuzziness may be in the nature of the reality being dealt with, the concepts used to interpret it, or the way in which the two are being related by a person.

Fuzzy Control Language

Fuzzy Control Language, or FCL, is a language for implementing fuzzy logic, especially fuzzy control. It was standardized by IEC 61131-7. It is a domain-specific programming language: it has no features unrelated to fuzzy logic, so it is impossible to even print "Hello, world!". Therefore, one does not write a program in FCL, but one may write part of it in FCL.

FCL allows the programmer to specify fuzzy sets, which are lists of points on a graph, as well as IF-THEN rules, for example:

RULE 0: IF (Temperature IS Cold) THEN (Output IS High)

FCL is not an entirely complete fuzzy language, for instance, it does not support "hedges", which are adverbs that modify the set. For instance, the programmer cannot write:

RULE 0: IF (Temperature IS VERY Cold) THEN (Output IS VERY High)

However, the programmer can simply define new sets for "very cold" and "very high". FCL also lacks support for higher-order fuzzy sets, subsets, and so on. None of these features are essential to fuzzy control, although they may be nice to have.

Fuzzy Control System

A fuzzy control system is a control system based on fuzzy logic—a mathematical system that analyses analogue input values in terms of logical variables that take on continuous values between 0 and 1, in contrast to classical or digital logic, which operates on discrete values of either 1 or 0 (true or false respectively).

Overview

Fuzzy logic is widely used in machine control. The term itself inspires a certain skepticism, sounding equivalent to "half-baked logic" or "bogus logic", but the "fuzzy" part does not refer to a lack of rigour in the method, rather to the fact that the logic involved can deal with fuzzy concepts—concepts that cannot be expressed as "true" or "false" but rather as "partially true".

Although genetic algorithms and neural networks can perform just as well as fuzzy logic in many cases, fuzzy logic has the advantage that the solution to the problem can be cast in terms that human operators can understand, so that their experience can be used in the design of the controller. This makes it easier to mechanize tasks that are already successfully performed by humans.

History and Applications

Fuzzy logic was first proposed by Lotfi A. Zadeh of the University of California at Berkeley in a 1965 paper. He elaborated on his ideas in a 1973 paper that introduced the concept of "linguistic variables", which in this article equates to a variable defined as a fuzzy set. Other research followed, with the first industrial application, a cement kiln built in Denmark, coming on line in 1975.

Fuzzy systems were largely ignored in the U.S. because they were associated with artificial intelligence, a field that periodically oversells itself, especially in the mid-1980s, resulting in a lack of credibility within the commercial domain.

The Japanese did not have this prejudice. Interest in fuzzy systems was sparked by Seiji Yasunobu and Soji Miyamoto of Hitachi, who in 1985 provided simulations that demonstrated the superiority of fuzzy control systems for the Sendai railway. Their ideas were adopted, and fuzzy systems were used to control accelerating, braking, and stopping when the line opened in 1987.

Another event in 1987 helped promote interest in fuzzy systems. During an international meeting of fuzzy researchers in Tokyo that year, Takeshi Yamakawa demonstrated the use of fuzzy control, through a set of simple dedicated fuzzy logic chips, in an "inverted pendulum" experiment. This is a classic control problem, in which a vehicle tries to keep a pole mounted on its top by a hinge upright by moving back and forth.

Observers were impressed with this demonstration, as well as later experiments by Yamakawa in which he mounted a wine glass containing water or even a live mouse to the top of the pendulum. The system maintained stability in both cases. Yamakawa eventually went on to organize his own fuzzy-systems research lab to help exploit his patents in the field.

Following such demonstrations, Japanese engineers developed a wide range of fuzzy systems for both industrial and consumer applications. In 1988 Japan established the Laboratory for International Fuzzy Engineering (LIFE), a cooperative arrangement between 48 companies to pursue fuzzy research.

Japanese consumer goods often incorporate fuzzy systems. Matsushita vacuum cleaners use microcontrollers running fuzzy algorithms to interrogate dust sensors and adjust suction power accordingly. Hitachi washing machines use fuzzy controllers to load-weight, fabric mix, and dirt sensors and automatically set the wash cycle for the best use of power, water, and detergent.

As a more specific example, Canon developed an autofocusing camera that uses a charge-coupled device (CCD) to measure the clarity of the image in six regions of its field of view and use the information provided to determine if the image is in focus. It also tracks the rate of change of lens movement during focusing, and controls its speed to prevent overshoot.

The camera's fuzzy control system uses 12 inputs: 6 to obtain the current clarity data provided by the CCD and 6 to measure the rate of change of lens movement. The output is the position of the lens. The fuzzy control system uses 13 rules and requires 1.1 kilobytes of memory.

As another example of a practical system, an industrial air conditioner designed by Mitsubishi uses 25 heating rules and 25 cooling rules. A temperature sensor provides input, with control outputs fed to an inverter, a compressor valve, and a fan motor. Compared to the previous design, the fuzzy controller heats and cools five times faster, reduces power consumption by 24%, increases temperature stability by a factor of two, and uses fewer sensors.

The enthusiasm of the Japanese for fuzzy logic is reflected in the wide range of other applications they have investigated or implemented: character and handwriting recognition; optical fuzzy systems; robots, including one for making Japanese flower arrangements; voice-controlled robot helicopters, this being no mean feat, as hovering is a "balancing act" rather similar to the inverted pendulum problem; control of flow of powders in film manufacture; elevator systems; and so on.

Work on fuzzy systems is also proceeding in the US and Europe, though not with the same enthusiasm shown in Japan. The US Environmental Protection Agency has investigated fuzzy control for energy-efficient motors, and NASA has studied fuzzy control for automated space docking: simulations show that a fuzzy control system can greatly reduce fuel consumption. Firms such as Boeing, General

Motors, Allen-Bradley, Chrysler, Eaton, and Whirlpool have worked on fuzzy logic for use in low-power refrigerators, improved automotive transmissions, and energy-efficient electric motors.

In 1995 Maytag introduced an "intelligent" dishwasher based on a fuzzy controller and a "one-stop sensing module" that combines a thermistor, for temperature measurement; a conductivity sensor, to measure detergent level from the ions present in the wash; a turbidity sensor that measures scattered and transmitted light to measure the soiling of the wash; and a magnetostrictive sensor to read spin rate. The system determines the optimum wash cycle for any load to obtain the best results with the least amount of energy, detergent, and water. It even adjusts for dried-on foods by tracking the last time the door was opened, and estimates the number of dishes by the number of times the door was opened.

Research and development is also continuing on fuzzy applications in software, as opposed to firmware, design, including fuzzy expert systems and integration of fuzzy logic with neural-network and so-called adaptive "genetic" software systems, with the ultimate goal of building "self-learning" fuzzy control systems.

Fuzzy Sets

The input variables in a fuzzy control system are in general mapped into by sets of membership functions similar to this, known as "fuzzy sets". The process of converting a crisp input value to a fuzzy value is called "fuzzification".

A control system may also have various types of switch, or "ON-OFF", inputs along with its analogue inputs, and such switch inputs of course will always have a truth value equal to either 1 or 0, but the scheme can deal with them as simplified fuzzy functions that happen to be either one value or another.

Given "mappings" of input variables into membership functions and truth values, the microcontroller then makes decisions for what action to take based on a set of "rules", each of the form:

IF Brake Temperature IS Warm AND Speed IS not Very Fast THEN brake pressure IS slightly decreased.

In this example, the two input variables are "brake temperature" and "speed" that have values defined as fuzzy sets. The output variable, "brake pressure", is also defined by a fuzzy set that can have values like “static”, “slightly increased”, “slightly decreased”, and so on. This rule by itself is very puzzling since it looks like it could be used without bothering with fuzzy logic, but remember that the decision is based on a set of rules:

- All the rules that apply are invoked, using the membership functions and truth values obtained from the inputs, to determine the result of the rule.
- This result in turn will be mapped into a membership function and truth value controlling the output variable.
- These results are combined to give a specific (“crisp”) answer, the actual brake pressure, a procedure known as “defuzzification”.

This combination of fuzzy operations and rule-based ”inference” describes a “fuzzy expert system”.

Traditional control systems are based on mathematical models in which the control system is described using one or more differential equations that define the system response to its inputs. Such systems are often implemented as “PID controllers” (proportional-integral-derivative controllers). They are the products of decades of development and theoretical analysis, and are highly effective.

If PID and other traditional control systems are so well-developed, why bother with fuzzy control? It has some advantages. In many cases, the mathematical model of the control process may not exist, or may be too “expensive” in terms of computer processing power and memory, and a system based on empirical rules may be more effective.

Furthermore, fuzzy logic is well suited to low-cost implementations based on cheap sensors, low-resolution analogue-to-digital converters, and 4-bit or 8-bit one-chip microcontroller chips. Such systems can be easily upgraded by adding new rules to improve performance or add new features. In many cases, fuzzy control can be used to improve existing traditional controller systems by adding an extra layer of intelligence to the current control method.

Fuzzy Control in Detail

Fuzzy controllers are very simple conceptually. They consist of an input stage, a processing stage, and an output stage. The input stage maps sensor or other inputs, such as switches, thumbwheels, and so on, to the appropriate membership functions and truth values.

The processing stage invokes each appropriate rule and generates a result for each, then combines the results of the rules. Finally, the output stage converts the combined result back into a specific control output value.

The most common shape of membership functions is triangular, although trapezoidal and bell curves are also used, but the shape is generally less important than the number of curves and their placement. From three to seven curves are generally appropriate to cover the required range of an input value, or the "universe of discourse" in fuzzy jargon.

As discussed earlier, the processing stage is based on a collection of logic rules in the form of IF-THEN statements, where the IF part is called the "antecedent" and the THEN part is called the "consequent". Typical fuzzy control systems have dozens of rules.

Consider a rule for a thermostat:

IF (temperature is "cold") THEN (heater is "high")

This rule uses the truth value of the "temperature" input, which is some truth value of "cold", to generate a result in the fuzzy set for the "heater" output, which is some value of "high". This result is used with the results of other rules to finally generate the crisp composite output. Obviously, the greater the truth value of "cold", the higher the truth value of "high", though this does not necessarily mean that the output itself will be set to "high", since this is only one rule among many. In some cases, the membership functions can be modified by "hedges" that are equivalent to adjectives. Common hedges include "about", "near", "close to", "approximately", "very", "slightly", "too", "extremely", and "somewhat". These operations may have precise definitions, though the definitions can vary considerably between different implementations. "Very", for one example, squares membership functions; since the membership values are always less than 1, this narrows the membership function. "Extremely" cubes the values to give greater narrowing, while "somewhat" broadens the function by taking the square root.

In practice, the fuzzy rule sets usually have several antecedents that are combined using fuzzy operators, such as AND, OR, and NOT, though again the definitions tend to vary: AND, in one popular definition, simply uses the minimum weight of all the antecedents, while OR uses the maximum value. There is also a NOT operator that subtracts a membership function from 1 to give the "complementary" function. There are several different ways to define the result of a rule, but one of the most common and simplest is the "max-min" inference method, in which the output membership function is given the truth value generated by the premise.

Rules can be solved in parallel in hardware, or sequentially in software. The results of all the rules that have fired are "defuzzified" to a crisp value by one of several methods. There are dozens in theory, each with various advantages and drawbacks.

The "centroid" method is very popular, in which the "centre of mass" of the result provides the crisp value. Another approach is the "height" method, which takes the value of the biggest contributor. The centroid method favours the rule with the output of greatest area, while the height method obviously favours the rule with the greatest output value.

Fuzzy Electronics

Fuzzy electronics is an electronic technology that uses fuzzy logic, instead of the two-state Boolean logic more commonly used in digital electronics. It has a wide range of applications, including control systems and artificial intelligence.

Fuzzy Mathematics

Fuzzy mathematics forms a branch of mathematics related to fuzzy set theory and fuzzy logic. It started in 1965 after the publication of Lotfi Asker Zadeh's seminal work Fuzzy sets. A fuzzy subsetA of a set X is a function A:X'!L, where L is the interval [0,1]. This function is also called a membership function. A membership function is a generalisation of a characteristic function or an indicator function of a subset defined for L = {0,1}. More generally, one can use a complete lattice L in a definition of a fuzzy subset A .

The evolution of the fuzzification of mathematical concepts can be broken down into three stages:

1. straightforward fuzzification during the sixties and seventies,
2. the explosion of the possible choices in the generalisation process during the eighties,
3. the standardization, axiomatisation and L-fuzzification in the nineties.

Usually, a fuzzification of mathematical concepts is based on a generalisation of these concepts from characteristic functions to membership functions. Let A and B be two fuzzy subsets of X. IntersectionA ∩ B and union A ∪ B are defined as follows: (A∩ B)(x) = min(A(x),B(x)), (A∪ B)(x) = max(A(x),B(x)) for all x – X. Instead of min and max one can use t-norm and t-conorm, respectively, for example,min(a,b) can be replaced by multiplication ab. A straightforward fuzzification is usually based on min and max operations because in this case more properties of traditional mathematics can be extended to the fuzzy case.

A very important generalisation principle used in fuzzification of algebraic operations is a closure property. Let * be a binary operation on X. The closure property for a fuzzy subset A of X is that for all x,y – X, A(x*y) e– min(A(x),B(x)). Let (G,*) be a group and A a fuzzy subset of G. Then A is a fuzzy subgroup of G if for all x,y in G, A(x*y) e" min(A(x),A(y)).

A similar generalisation principle is used, for example, for fuzzification of the transitivity property. Let Rbe a fuzzy relation in X, i.e. R is a fuzzy subset of X×X. Then R is transitive if for all x,y,z in X, R(x,z) e" min(R(x,y),R(y,z)).

Some Fields of Mathematics using Fuzzy Set Theory

Fuzzy subgroupoids and fuzzy subgroups were introduced in 1971 by A. Rosenfeld . Hundreds of papers on related topics have been published. Recent results and references can be found in, .

Fuzzy topology was introduced by C.L. Chang in 1968 and further was studied in many papers.

Main concepts of fuzzy geometry were introduced by A. Rosenfeld in 1974 and by J.J. Buckley and E. Eslami in 1997.

Basic types of fuzzy relations were introduced by Zadeh in 1971.

The properties of fuzzy graphs have been studied by A. Kaufman, A. Rosenfeld, and by R.T. Yeh and S.Y. Bang. Recent results can be found in a 2000 article.

Possibility theory, nonadditive measures, fuzzy measure theory and fuzzy integrals are studied in the cited articles and treatises.

Main results and references on formal fuzzy logic can be found in these citations.

Fuzzy Subalgebra

Fuzzy subalgebras theory is a chapter of fuzzy set theory. It is obtained from an interpretation in a multi-valued logic of axioms usually expressing the notion of subalgebra of a given algebraic structure. Indeed, consider a first order language for algebraic structures with a monadic predicate symbol S. Then a fuzzy subalgebra, is a fuzzy model of a theory containing, for any n-ary operation name h, the axiom

$$A1 \ \forall x_1,..., \ \forall x_n(S(x_1) \wedge ..... \wedge \ S(x_n) \rightarrow S(h(x_1,...,x_n))$$

and, for any constant c, the axiom

A2 S(c).

A1 expresses the closure of S with respect to the operation h, A2 expresses the fact that c is an element in S. As an example, assume that the valuation structure is defined in [0,1] and denote by $\odot$the operation in [0,1] used to interpret the conjunction. Then it is easy to see that a fuzzy subalgebra of an algebraic structure whose domain is D is defined by a fuzzy subset s : D '! [0,1] of D such that, for every $d_1,...,d_n$ in D, if h is the interpretation of the n-ary operation symbol h, then

i) $s(d_1)\odot...\odot s(d_n) \leq \ s(h(d_1,...,d_n))$

Moreover, if c is the interpretation of a constant c

ii) s(c) = 1.

A largely studied class of fuzzy subalgebras is the one in which the operation coincides with the minimum. In such a case it is immediate to prove the following proposition.

Proposition. A fuzzy subset s of an algebraic structure defines a fuzzy subalgebra if and only if for every λ in [0,1], the closed cut $\{x \ \ D : s(x) \geq \ \lambda\}$ of s is a subalgebra.

The fuzzy subgroups and the fuzzy submonoids are particularly interesting classes of fuzzy subalgebras. In such a case a fuzzy subsets of a monoid (M,•,u) is a fuzzy submonoid if and only if

1) s(u) =1

2) $s(x)s(y) \ \leq \leq \ s(x \cdot y)$

where u is the neutral element in A. Given a group G, a fuzzy subgroup of G is a fuzzy submonoid s of G such that

3) s(x) $\leq$ s(x).

It is possible to prove that the notion of fuzzy subgroup is strictly related with the notions of fuzzy equivalence. In fact, assume that S is a set, G a group of transformations in S and (G,s) a fuzzy subgroup of G. Then, by setting

e(x,y) = Sup{s(h) : h is an element in G such that h(x) = y}

we obtain a fuzzy equivalence. Conversely, let e be a fuzzy equivalence in S and, for every transformation h of S, set

s(h)= Inf{e(x,h(x)): xS}.

Then s defines a fuzzy subgroup of transformation in S. In a similar way we can relate the fuzzy submonoids with the fuzzy orders.

FuzzyCLIPS

FuzzyCLIPS is a fuzzy logic extension of the CLIPS (C Language Integrated Production System) expert system shell from NASA. It was developed by the Integrated Reasoning Group of the Institute for Information Technology of the National Research Council of Canada and has been widely distributed for a number of years. It enhances CLIPS by providing a fuzzy reasoning capability that is fully integrated with CLIPS facts and inference engine allowing one to represent and manipulate fuzzy facts and rules. FuzzyCLIPS can deal with exact, fuzzy (or inexact), and combined reasoning, allowing fuzzy and normal terms to be freely mixed in the rules and facts of an expert system. The system uses two basic inexact concepts, fuzziness and uncertainty. It has provided a useful environment for developing fuzzy applications but it does require significant effort to update and maintain as new versions of CLIPS are released.

Neuro-fuzzy

In the field of artificial intelligence, neuro-fuzzy refers to combinations of artificial neural networks and fuzzy logic. Neuro-fuzzy was proposed by J. S. R. Jang. Neuro-fuzzy hybridization results in a hybrid intelligent system that synergizes these two techniques by combining the human-like reasoning style of fuzzy systems with the learning and connectionist structure of neural networks. Neuro-fuzzy hybridization is widely termed as Fuzzy Neural Network (FNN) or Neuro-Fuzzy System (NFS) in the literature. Neuro-fuzzy system (the more popular term is used henceforth) incorporates the human-like reasoning style of fuzzy systems through the use of fuzzy sets and a linguistic model consisting of a set of IF-THEN fuzzy rules. The main strength of neuro-fuzzy systems is that they are universal approximators with the ability to solicit interpretable IF-THEN rules.

The strength of neuro-fuzzy systems involves two contradictory requirements in fuzzy modelling: interpretability versus accuracy. In practice, one of the two properties prevails. The neuro-fuzzy in fuzzy modelling research field is divided into two areas: linguistic fuzzy modelling that is focused on interpretability, mainly the Mamdani model; and precise fuzzy modelling that is focused on accuracy, mainly the Takagi-Sugeno-Kang (TSK) model.

Although generally assumed to be the realization of a fuzzy system through connectionist networks, this term is also used to describe some other configurations including:

- Deriving fuzzy rules from trained RBF networks.
- Fuzzy logic based tuning of neural network training parameters.
- Fuzzy logic criteria for increasing a network size.
- Realising fuzzy membership function through clustering algorithms in unsupervised learning in SOMs and neural networks.
- Representing fuzzification, fuzzy inference and defuzzification through multi-layers feed-forward connectionist networks.

It must be pointed out that interpretability of the Mamdani-type neuro-fuzzy systems can be lost. To improve the interpretability of neuro-fuzzy systems, certain measures must be taken, wherein important aspects of interpretability of neuro-fuzzy systems are also discussed.

Pseudo Outer-Product-based Fuzzy Neural Networks

Pseudo outer-product-based fuzzy neural networks ("POPFNN") are a family of neuro-fuzzy systems that are based on the linguistic fuzzy model.

Three members of POPFNN exist in the literature:

- POPFNN-AARS(S), which is based on the Approximate Analogical Reasoning Scheme
- POPFNN-CRI(S), which is based on commonly accepted fuzzy Compositional Rule of Inference

- POPFNN-TVR, which is based on Truth Value Restriction

The "POPFNN" architecture is a five-layer neural network where the layers from 1 to 5 are called: input linguistic layer, condition layer, rule layer, consequent layer, output linguistic layer. The fuzzification of the inputs and the defuzzification of the outputs are respectively performed by the input linguistic and output linguistic layers while the fuzzy inference is collectively performed by the rule, condition and consequence layers.

The learning process of POPFNN consists of three phases:

1. Fuzzy membership generation
2. Fuzzy rule identification
3. Supervised fine-tuning

Various fuzzy membership generation algorithms can be used: Learning Vector Quantization (LVQ), Fuzzy Kohonen Partitioning (FKP) or Discrete Incremental Clustering (DIC). Generally, the POP algorithm and its variant LazyPOP are used to identify the fuzzy rules.

Chapter 5

Neural Network

Biological Neural Network

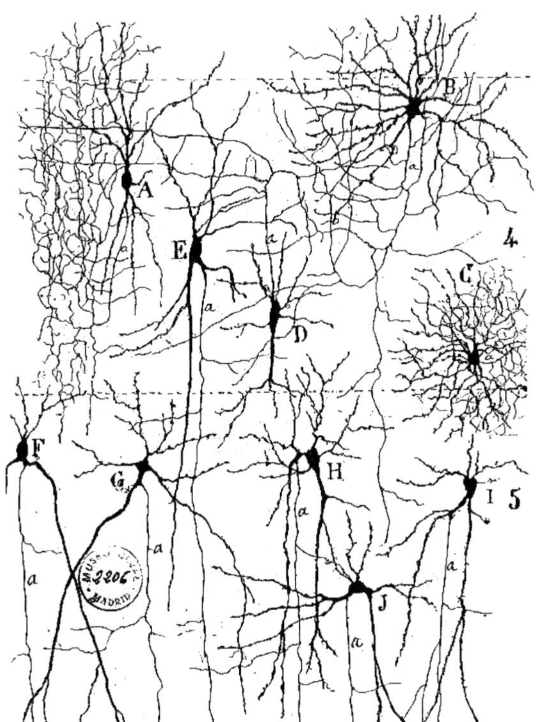

Figure: From "Texture of the Nervous System of Man and the Vertebrates" by Santiago Ramón y Cajal. The figure illustrates the diversity of neuronal morphologies in the auditory cortex.

In neuroscience, a biological neural network describes a population of physically interconnected neurons or a group of disparate neurons whose inputs or signalling targets define a recognizable circuit.

Communication between neurons often involves an electrochemical process. The interface through which they interact with surrounding neurons usually consists of several dendrites (input connections), which are connected via synapses to other neurons, and one axon (output connection). If the sum of the input signals surpasses a certain threshold, the neuron sends an action potential (AP) at the axon hillock and transmits this electrical signal along the axon.

In contrast, a neuronal circuit is a functional entity of interconnected neurons that influence each other (similar to a control loopin cybernetics).

Early Study

Early treatments of neural networks can be found in Herbert Spencer's Principles of Psychology, 3rd edition (1872), Theodor Meynert's Psychiatry (1884), William James' Principles of Psychology (1890), and Sigmund Freud's Project for a Scientific Psychology (composed 1895). The first rule of neuronal learning was described by Hebb in 1949, Hebbian learning. Thus, Hebbian pairing of pre-synaptic and post-synaptic activity can substantially alter the dynamic characteristics of the synaptic connection and therefore facilitate or inhibit signal transmission. The neuroscientists Warren Sturgis McCullochand Walter Pitts published the first works on the processing of neural networks called "What the frog's eye tells to the frog's brain." They showed theoretically that networks of artificial neurons could implement logical, arithmetic, and symbolic functions. Simplified models of biological neurons were set up, now usually called perceptrons or artificial neurons. These simple models accounted for neural summation, i.e., potentials at the post-synaptic membrane will summate in the cell body. Later models also provided for excitatory and inhibitory synaptic transmission.

Connections between Neurons

The connections between neurons are much more complex than those implemented in neural computing architectures. The basic kinds of connections between neurons are chemical synapses and electrical gap junctions. One principle by which neurons work is neural summation, i.e. potentials at the post synaptic membrane will sum up in the cell body. If the depolarization of the neuron at the axon goes above threshold an action potential will occur that travels down the axon to the terminal endings to transmit a signal to other neurons.

Excitatory and inhibitory synaptic transmission is realized mostly by inhibitory postsynaptic potentials and excitatory postsynaptic potentials.

On the electrophysiological level, there are various phenomena which alter the response characteristics of individual synapses (called synaptic plasticity) and individual neurons (intrinsic plasticity). These are often divided into short-term plasticity and long-term plasticity. Long-term synaptic plasticity is often contended to be the most likely memory substrate. Usually the term "plasticity" refers to changes in the brain that are caused by activity or experience.

Connections display temporal and spatial characteristics. Temporal characteristics refer to the continuously modified activity-dependent efficacy of synaptic transmission, called spike-dependent synaptic plasticity. It has been observed in several studies that the synaptic efficacy of this transmission can undergo short-term increase (called facilitation) or decrease (depression) according to the activity of the presynaptic neuron. The induction of long-term changes in synaptic efficacy, by long-term potentiation (LTP) or depression (LTD), depends strongly on the relative timing of the onset of the EPSP generated by the pre-synaptic AP, and the post-synaptic action potential. LTP is induced by a series of action potentials which cause a variety of biochemical responses. Eventually the reactions cause the insertion of new receptors into the cellular membrane of the dendrites, or serve to increase the efficacy of the receptors through phosphorylation.

Backpropagating APs are impossible because after an action potential travels down a given segment of the axon, the voltage gated sodium channels' (Na+ channels) m gate becomes closed, thus blocking any transient opening of the h gate from causing a change in the intracellular [Na+], and hence preventing the generation of an action potential back towards the cell body. In some cells, however, neural backpropagation does occur through the dendritic arbor and may have important effects on synaptic plasticity and computation.

A neuron in the brain requires a single impulse to a neuromuscular junction to fire for the contraction of the postsynaptic muscle cell. In the spinal cord, however, at least 75 afferent neurons are required to produce firing. This picture is further complicated by variation in time constant between neurons, as some cells can experience their EPSPs over a wider period of time than others.

While in synapses in the developing brain synaptic depression has been particularly widely observed it has been speculated that it changes to facilitation in adult brains.

Representations in Neural Networks

A receptive field is a small region within the entire visual field. Any given neuron only responds to a subset of stimuli within its receptive field. This property is called tuning. As for vision, in the earlier visual areas, neurons have simpler tuning. For example, a neuron in V1 may fire to any vertical stimulus in its receptive field. In the higher visual areas, neurons have complex tuning. For example, in the fusiform gyrus, a neuron may only fire when a certain face appears in its receptive field. It is also known that many parts of the brain generate patterns of electrical activity that correspond closely to the layout of the retinal image (this is known as retinotopy). It seems further that imagery that originates from the senses and internally generated imagery may have a shared ontology at higher levels of cortical processing. About many parts of the brain some characterization has been made as to what tasks are correlated with its activity.

In the brain, memories are very likely represented by patterns of activation amongst networks of neurons. However, how these representations are formed, retrieved and reach conscious awareness is not completely understood. Cognitive processes that characterize human intelligence are mainly ascribed to the emergent properties of complex dynamic characteristics in the complex systems that constitute neural networks. Therefore, the study and modelling of these networks have attracted broad interest under different paradigms and many different theories have been formulated to explain various aspects of their behaviour. One of these — and the subject of several theories — is considered a special property of a neural network: the ability to learn complex patterns.

Philosophical Issues

Today most researchers believe in mental representations of some kind (representationalism) or, more general, in particular mental states (cognitivism). For instance, perception can be viewed as information processing through transfer information from the world into the brain/mind where it is further processed and related to other information (cognitive processes). Few others envisage a direct path back into the external world in the form of action (radical behaviourism). Another issue, called the binding problem, relates to the question of how the activity of more or less distinct populations of neurons dealing with different aspects of perception are combined to form aunified perceptual experience and have qualia.

Neuronal networks are not full reconstructions of any cognitive system found in the human brain, and are therefore unlikely to form a complete representation of human perception. Some researchers argue that human perception must be studied as a whole; hence, the system cannot be taken apart and studied without destroying its original functionality. Furthermore, there is evidence that cognition is gained through a well-orchestrated barrage of sub-threshold synaptic activity throughout the network.

Study Methods

Different neuroimaging techniques have been developed to investigate the activity of neural networks. The use of "brain scanners" or functional neuroimaging to investigate the structure or function of the brain is common, either as simply a way of better assessing brain injury with high resolution pictures, or by examining the relative activations of different brain areas. Such technologies may include fMRI (functional magnetic resonance imaging), PET (positron emission tomography) and CAT (computed axial tomography). Functional neuroimaging uses specific brain imaging technologies to take scans from the brain, usually when a person is doing a particular task, in an attempt to understand how the activation of particular brain areas is related to the task. In functional neuroimaging, especially fMRI, which measures hemodynamic activity that is closely linked to neural activity, PET, and electroencephalography (EEG) is used.

Connectionist models serve as a test platform for different hypotheses of representation, information processing, and signal transmission. Lesioning studies in such models, e.g. artificial neural networks, where parts of the nodes are deliberately destroyed to see how the network performs, can also yield important insights in the working of several cell assemblies. Similarly, simulations of dysfunctional neurotransmitters in neurological conditions (e.g., dopamine in the basal ganglia of Parkinson'spatients) can yield insights into the underlying mechanisms for patterns of cognitive deficits observed in the particular patient group. Predictions from these models can be tested in patients and/or via pharmacological manipulations, and these studies can in turn be used to inform the models, making the process recursive.

Biocybernetics

Biocybernetics is the application of cybernetics to biological science, composed of biological disciplines that benefit from the application of cybernetics: neurology, multicellular systems and others. Biocybernetics plays a major role in systems biology, seeking to integrate different levels of information to understand how biological systems function.

Biocybernetics as an abstract science is a part of theoretical biology, and based upon the principles of systemics.

Terminology

Biocybernetics is a cojoined word from bio (Greek: âßï/life) and cybernetics (Greek: êõâåñíçôéêÞ/controlling-governing). It is sometimes written together or with a blank or written fully as biological cybernetics, whilst the same rules apply. Most write it together though, as Google statistics show. The same applies to neuro cybernetics which should also be looked up as neurological, when doing extensive research.

Early Fathers of Biocybernetics

Ross Ashby, 1956

Hans Drischel, 1972

Norbert Wiener, 1948.

Same or Familiar Fields

As those disciplines are dealing on theoretical/abstract foundations and are in accordance with the popularity of computers. Thus papers and research is in greater numbers going on under different names: e.g. molecular cybernetics -> molecular computational systems OR molecular systems theory OR molecular systemics OR molecular information/informational systems

Please heed this when you engage in an extensive search for information to assure access to a broad range of papers.

Categories

- biocybernetics - the study of an entire living organism

- neurocybernetics - cybernetics dealing with neurological models. (Psycho-Cybernetics was the title of a self-help book, and is not a scientific discipline)
- molecular cybernetics - cybernetics dealing with molecular systems (e.g. molecular biology cybernetics)
- cellular cybernetics - cybernetics dealing with cellular systems (e.g. information technology/cell phones,.. or biological cells)
- evolutionary cybernetics - study of the evolution of informational systems
- any distinct informational system within the realm of biology

Bio-inspired Computing

Bio-inspired computing, short for biologically-inspired computing, is a field of study that loosely knits together subfields related to the topics of connectionism, social behaviour and emergence. It is often closely related to the field of artificial intelligence, as many of its pursuits can be linked to machine learning. It relies heavily on the fields of biology, computer science and mathematics. Briefly put, it is the use of computers to model nature, and simultaneously the study of nature to improve the usage of computers. Biologically- inspired computing is a major subset of natural computation.

Areas of Research

Some areas of study encompassed under the canon of biologically-inspired computing, and their biological counterparts:

- genetic algorithms $\leftrightarrow$ evolution
- biodegradability prediction $\leftrightarrow$ biodegradation
- cellular automata $\leftrightarrow$ life
- emergent systems $\leftrightarrow$ ants, termites, bees, wasps
- neural networks $\leftrightarrow$ the brain
- artificial life $\leftrightarrow$ life
- artificial immune systems $\leftrightarrow$ immune system
- rendering (computer graphics) $\leftrightarrow$ patterning and rendering of animal skins, bird feathers, mollusk shells and bacterial colonies
- Lindenmayer systems $\leftrightarrow$ plant structures

- communication networks and protocols ↔ epidemiology and the spread of disease
- membrane computers ↔ intra-membrane molecular processes in the living cell
- excitable media ↔ forest fires, "the wave", heart conditions, axons, etc.
- sensor networks ↔ sensory organs

Bio-inspired Computing and AI

The way in which bio-inspired computing differs from traditional artificial intelligence (AI) is in how it takes a more evolutionary approach to learning, as opposed to the what could be described as 'creationist' methods used in traditional AI. In traditional AI, intelligence is often programmed from above: the programmer is the creator, and makes something and imbues it with its intelligence. Bio-inspired computing, on the other hand, takes a more bottom-up, decentralised approach; bio-inspired techniques often involve the method of specifying a set of simple rules, a set of simple organisms which adhere to those rules, and a method of iteratively applying those rules.

After several generations of rule application it is usually the case that some forms of complex behaviour arise. Complexity gets built upon complexity until the end result is something markedly complex, and quite often completely counterintuitive from what the original rules would be expected to produce. For this reason, in neural network models, it is necessary to accurately model an in vivo network, by live collection of "noise" coefficients that can be used to refine statistical inference and extrapolation as system complexity increases.

Natural evolution is a good analogy to this method–the rules of evolution (selection, recombination/reproduction, mutation and more recently transposition) are in principle simple rules, yet over thousands of years have produced remarkably complex organisms. A similar technique is used in genetic algorithms.

Artificial Neural Network

An artificial neural network (ANN), usually called neural network (NN), is a mathematical modelor computational model that is inspired by the structure and/or functional aspects of biological neural networks.

A neural network consists of an interconnected group of artificial neurons, and it processes information using a connectionist approach to computation. In most cases an ANN is an adaptive system that changes its structure based on external or internal information that flows through the network during the learning phase. Modern neural networks are non-linear statistical data modelling tools. They are usually used to model complex relationships between inputs and outputs or to find patterns in data.

Background

The original inspiration for the term Artificial Neural Network came from examination of central nervous systems and their neurons, axons, dendrites, and synapses, which constitute the processing elements of biological neural networks investigated by neuroscience. In an artificial neural network, simple artificial nodes, variously called "neurons", "neurodes", "processing elements" (PEs) or "units", are connected together to form a network of nodes mimicking the biological neural networks — hence the term "artificial neural network".

Because neuroscience is still full of unanswered questions, and since there are many levels of abstraction and therefore many ways to take inspiration from the brain, there is no single formal definition of what an artificial neural network is. Generally, it involves a network of simple processing elements that exhibit complex global behaviour determined by connections between processing elements and element parameters. While an artificial neural network does not have to be adaptive per se, its practical use comes with algorithms designed to alter the strength (weights) of the connections in the network to produce a desired signal flow.

These networks are also similar to the biological neural networks in the sense that functions are performed collectively and in parallel by the units, rather than there being a clear delineation of subtasks to which various units are assigned. Currently, the term Artificial Neural Network (ANN) tends to refer mostly to neural network models employed in statistics, cognitive psychology and artificial intelligence. Neural network models designed with emulation of the central nervous system (CNS) in mind are a subject of theoretical neuroscience and computational neuroscience.

In modern software implementations of artificial neural networks, the approach inspired by biology has been largely abandoned for a more practical approach based on statistics and signal processing. In some of these systems, neural networks or parts of neural networks (such as artificial neurons) are used as components in larger systems that combine both adaptive and non-adaptive elements.

While the more general approach of such adaptive systems is more suitable for real-world problem solving, it has far less to do with the traditional artificial intelligence connectionist models. What they do have in common, however, is the principle of non-linear, distributed, parallel and local processing and adaptation.

Models

Neural network models in artificial intelligence are usually referred to as artificial neural networks (ANNs); these are essentially simple mathematical models defining a function $f: X \rightarrow Y$ or a distribution over X or both X and Y, but sometimes models are also intimately associated with a particular learning algorithm or learning rule.

A common use of the phrase ANN model really means the definition of a class of such functions (where members of the class are obtained by varying parameters, connection weights, or specifics of the architecture such as the number of neurons or their connectivity).

Network Function

The word network in the term 'artificial neural network' refers to the inter–connections between the neurons in the different layers of each system.

An example system has three layers. The first layer has input neurons, which send data via synapses to the second layer of neurons, and then via more synapses to the third layer of output neurons. More complex systems will have more layers of neurons with some having increased layers of input neurons and output neurons. The synapses store parameters called "weights" that manipulate the data in the calculations.

An ANN is typically defined by three types of parameters:

1. The interconnection pattern between different layers of neurons
2. The learning process for updating the weights of the interconnections
3. The activation function that converts a neuron's weighted input to its output activation.

Mathematically, a neuron's network function $f(x)$ is defined as a composition of other functions $g_i(x)$, which can further be defined as a composition of other functions. This can be conveniently represented as a network structure, with arrows depicting the dependencies between variables. A widely used type of composition is the nonlinear weighted sum, where $f(x)=K\left(\sum_i \omega_i g_i(x)\right)$ K (commonly referred to as the activation function) is some predefined function, such as the hyperbolic tangent. It will be convenient for the following to refer to a collection of functions as simply a vector $g=(g_1,g_2,...,g_n)$..

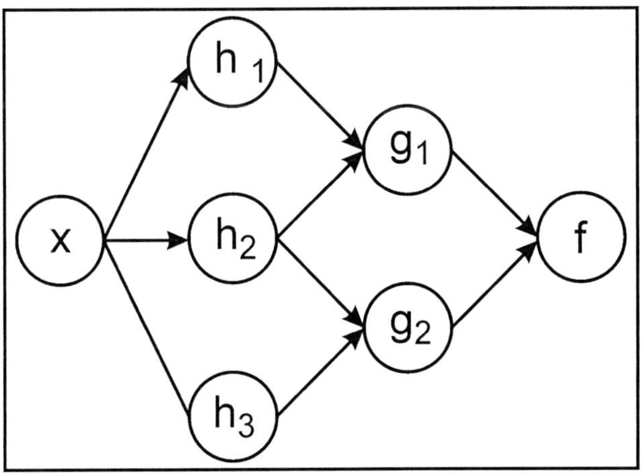

Figure: This figure depicts such a decomposition of f with dependencies between variables indicated by arrows. These can be interpreted in two ways.

The first view is the functional view: the input is transformed into a 3-dimensional vector , which is then transformed into a 2-dimensional vector , which is finally transformed into f. This view is most commonly encountered in the context of optimisation.

The second view is the probabilistic view: the random variable $F=f(G)$ depends upon the random variable $G=g(H)$, which depends upon $H=h(X)$, which depends upon the random variable X. This view is most commonly encountered in the context of graphical models.

The two views are largely equivalent. In either case, for this particular network architecture, the components of individual layers are independent of each other (e.g., the components of are independent of each other given their input). This naturally enables a degree of parallelism in the implementation.

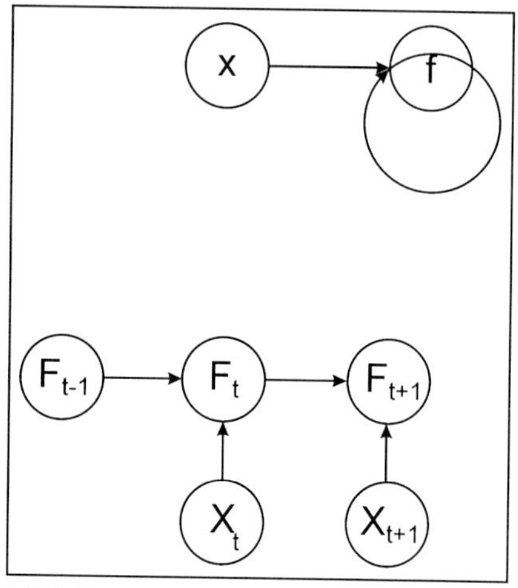

Figure: Recurrent ANN dependency graph

Networks such as the previous one are commonly called feedforward, because their graph is a directed acyclic graph. Networks with cycles are commonly called recurrent. Such networks are commonly depicted in the manner shown at the top of the figure, where is shown as being dependent upon itself. However, an implied temporal dependence is not shown.

Learning Algorithms

Training a neural network model essentially means selecting one model from the set of allowed models (or, in a Bayesian framework, determining a distribution over the set of allowed models) that minimizes the cost criterion. There are numerous algorithms available for training neural network models; most of them can be viewed as a straightforward application of optimisation theory and statistical estimation.

Most of the algorithms used in training artificial neural networks employ some form of gradient descent. This is done by simply taking the derivative of the cost function with respect to the network parameters and then changing those parameters in a gradient-related direction. Evolutionary methods, simulated annealing, expectation-maximization, non-parametric methods and particle swarm optimisation are some commonly used methods for training neural networks.

Employing Artificial Neural Networks

Perhaps the greatest advantage of ANNs is their ability to be used as an arbitrary function approximation mechanism that 'learns' from observed data. However, using them is not so straightforward and a relatively good understanding of the underlying theory is essential.

- Choice of model: This will depend on the data representation and the application. Overly complex models tend to lead to problems with learning.
- Learning algorithm: There are numerous trade-offs between learning algorithms. Almost any algorithm will work well with the correct hyperparameters for training on a particular fixed data set. However selecting and tuning an algorithm for training on unseen data requires a significant amount of experimentation.
- Robustness: If the model, cost function and learning algorithm are selected appropriately the resulting ANN can be extremely robust.

With the correct implementation, ANNs can be used naturally in online learning and large data set applications. Their simple implementation and the existence of mostly local dependencies exhibited in the structure allows for fast, parallel implementations in hardware.

Neural Network Software

Neural network software is used to simulate, research, develop and apply artificial neural networks, biological neural networks and in some cases a wider array of adaptive systems.

Types of Artificial Neural Networks

Artificial neural network types vary from those with only one or two layers of single direction logic, to complicated multi–input many directional feedback loop and layers. On the whole, these systems use algorithms in their programming to determine control and organization of their functions. Some may be as simple, one neuron layer with an input and an output, and others can mimic complex systems such as dANN, which can mimic chromosomal DNA through sizes at cellular level, into artificial organisms and simulate reproduction, mutation and population sizes.

Most systems use "weights" to change the parameters of the throughput and the varying connections to the neurons. Artificial neural networks can be autonomous and learn by input from outside "teachers" or even self-teaching from written in rules.

Theoretical Properties

Computational Power

The multilayer perceptron (MLP) is a universal function approximator, as proven by the Cybenko theorem. However, the proof is not constructive regarding the number of neurons required or the settings of the weights.

Work by Hava Siegelmann and Eduardo D. Sontag has provided a proof that a specific recurrent architecture with rational valued weights (as opposed to full precision real number-valued weights) has the full power of a Universal Turing Machine using a finite number of neurons and standard linear connections. They have further shown that the use of irrational values for weights results in a machine with super-Turing power.

Capacity

Artificial neural network models have a property called 'capacity', which roughly corresponds to their ability to model any given function. It is related to the amount of information that can be stored in the network and to the notion of complexity.

Convergence

Nothing can be said in general about convergence since it depends on a number of factors. Firstly, there may exist many local minima. This depends on the cost function and the model. Secondly, the optimisation method used might not be guaranteed to converge when far away from a local minimum. Thirdly, for a very large amount of data or parameters, some methods become impractical. In general, it has been found that theoretical guarantees regarding convergence are an unreliable guide to practical application.

Generalisation and Statistics

In applications where the goal is to create a system that generalises well in unseen examples, the problem of over-training has emerged. This arises in convoluted or over-specified systems when the capacity of the network significantly exceeds the needed free parameters.

There are two schools of thought for avoiding this problem: The first is to use cross-validation and similar techniques to check for the presence of overtraining and optimally select hyperparameters such as to minimize the generalisation error. The second is to use some form of regularization.

This is a concept that emerges naturally in a probabilistic (Bayesian) framework, where the regularization can be performed by selecting a larger prior probability over simpler models; but also in statistical learning theory, where the goal is to minimize over two quantities: the 'empirical risk' and the 'structural risk', which roughly corresponds to the error over the training set and the predicted error in unseen data due to overfitting.

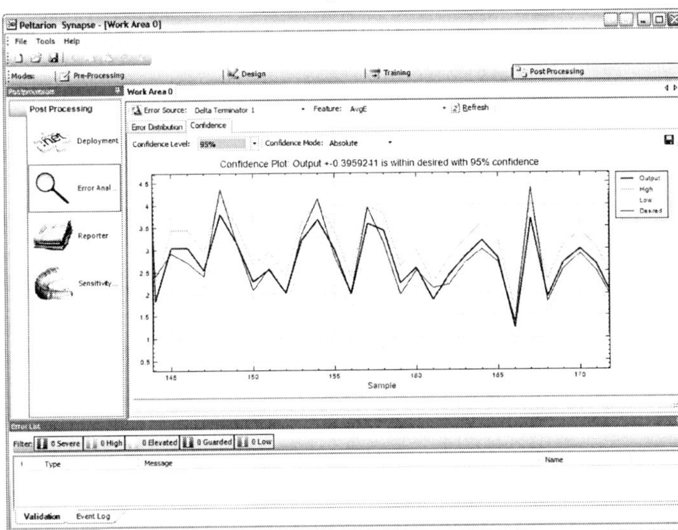

Figure: Confidence analysis of a neural network

Supervised neural networks that use an MSE cost function can use formal statistical methods to determine the confidence of the trained model. The MSE on a validation set can be used as an estimate for variance. This value can then be used to calculate the confidence interval of the output of the network, assuming a normal distribution. A confidence analysis made this way is statistically valid as long as the output probability distribution stays the same and the network is not modified.

By assigning a softmax activation function on the output layer of the neural network (or a softmax component in a component-based neural network) for categorical target variables, the outputs can be interpreted as posterior probabilities. This is very useful in classification as it gives a certainty measure on classifications.

The softmax activation function is:

$$y_i = \frac{e^{x_i}}{\sum_{j=1}^{c} e^{x_j}}$$

Dynamic Properties

Various techniques originally developed for studying disordered magnetic systems (i.e., the spin glass) have been successfully applied to simple neural network architectures, such as the Hopfield network. Influential work by E. Gardner and B. Derrida has revealed many interesting properties about perceptrons with real-valued synaptic weights, while later work by W. Krauth and M. Mezard has extended these principles to binary-valued synapses.

Criticism

A common criticism of artificial neural networks, particularly in robotics, is that they require a large diversity of training for real-world operation. Dean Pomerleau, in his research presented in the paper "Knowledge-based Training of Artificial Neural Networks for Autonomous Robot Driving," uses a neural network to train a robotic vehicle to drive on multiple types of roads (single lane, multi-lane, dirt, etc.). A large amount of his research is devoted to (1) extrapolating multiple training scenarios from a single training experience, and (2) preserving past training diversity so that the system does not become overtrained (if, for example, it is presented with a series of right turns – it should not learn to always turn right). These issues are common in neural networks that must decide from amongst a wide variety of responses.

A. K. Dewdney, a former Scientific American columnist, wrote in 1997, "Although neural nets do solve a few toy problems, their powers of computation are so limited that I am surprised anyone takes them seriously as a general problem-solving tool." (Dewdney, p. 82)

Arguments for Dewdney's position are that to implement large and effective software neural networks, much processing and storage resources need to be committed. While the brain has hardware tailored to the task of processing signals through a graph of neurons, simulating even a most simplified form on Von Neumann technology may compel a NN designer to fill many millions of database rows for its connections

- which can lead to excessive RAM and HD necessities. Furthermore, the designer of NN systems will often need to simulate the transmission of signals through many of these connections and their associated neurons - which must often be matched with incredible amounts of CPU processing power and time. While neural networks often yield effective programs, they too often do so at the cost of time and money efficiency.

Arguments against Dewdney's position are that neural nets have been successfully used to solve many complex and diverse tasks, ranging from autonomously flying aircraft to detecting credit card fraud. Technology writer Roger Bridgman commented on Dewdney's statements about neural nets:

Neural networks, for instance, are in the dock not only because they have been hyped to high heaven, (what hasn't?) but also because you could create a successful net without understanding how it worked: the bunch of numbers that captures its behaviour would in all probability be "an opaque, unreadable table...valueless as a scientific resource". In spite of his emphatic declaration that science is not technology, Dewdney seems here to pillory neural nets as bad science when most of those devising them are just trying to be good engineers. An unreadable table that a useful machine could read would still be well worth having.

Some other criticisms came from believers of hybrid models (combining neural networks and symbolic approaches). They advocate the intermix of these two approaches and believe that hybrid models can better capture the mechanisms of the human mind (Sun and Bookman 1994).

Gallery

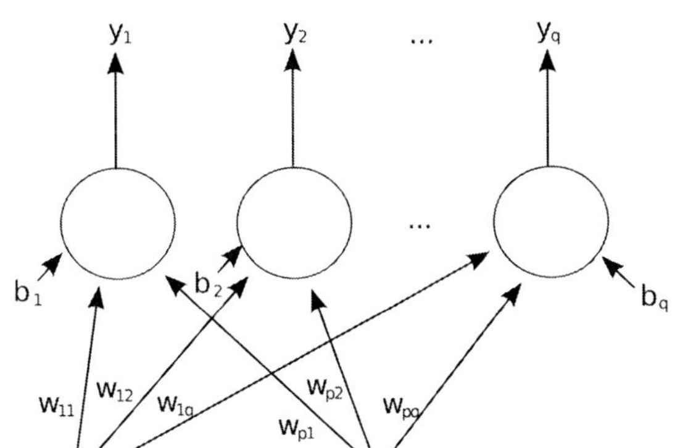

A single-layer feedforward artificial neural network. Arrows originating from $x2$ are omitted for clarity. There are p inputs to this network and q outputs. There is no activation function (or equivalently, the activation function is $g(x)=x$). In this system, the value of the qth output, yq would be calculated *as* $yq = \Sigma(x_i * w_{iq})$

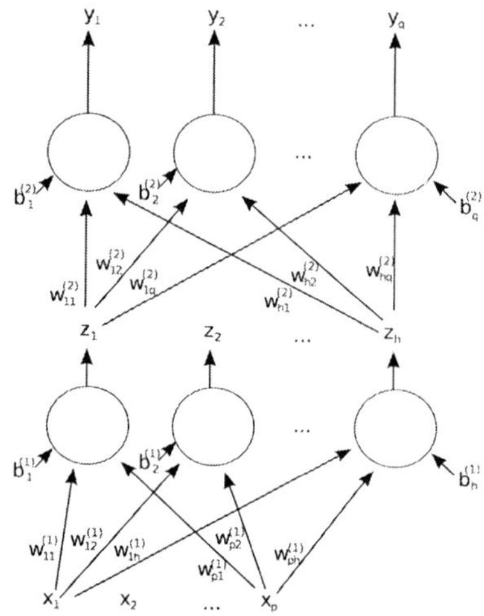

Connectionism

Connectionism is a set of approaches in the fields of artificial intelligence, cognitive psychology, cognitive science, neuroscience and philosophy of mind, that models mental or behavioural phenomena as the emergent processes of interconnected networks of simple units. There are many forms of connectionism, but the most common forms use neural network models.

Basic Principles

The central connectionist principle is that mental phenomena can be described by interconnected networks of simple and often uniform units. The form of the connections and the units can vary from model to model. For example, units in the network could represent neurons and the connections could represent synapses.

Spreading Activation

In most connectionist models, networks change over time. A closely related and very common aspect of connectionist models is activation. At any time, a unit in the network has an activation, which is a numerical value intended to represent some aspect of the unit. For example, if the units in the model are neurons, the activation could represent the probability that the neuron would generate an action potential spike. If the activation spreads to all the other units connected to it. Spreading activation is always a feature of neural network models, and it is very common in connectionist models used by cognitive psychologists.

Neural Networks

Neural networks are by far the most commonly used connectionist model today. Though there are a large variety of neural network models, they almost always follow two basic principles regarding the mind:

1. Any mental state can be described as an (N)-dimensional vector of numeric activation values over neural units in a network.
2. Memory is created by modifying the strength of the connections between neural units. The connection strengths, or "weights", are generally represented as an (N×N)-dimensional matrix.

Most of the variety among neural network models comes from:

- Interpretation of units: units can be interpreted as neurons or groups of neurons.
- Definition of activation: activation can be defined in a variety of ways. For example, in a Boltzmann machine, the activation is interpreted as the probability of generating an action potential spike, and is determined via a logistic function on the sum of the inputs to a unit.
- Learning algorithm: different networks modify their connections differently. Generally, any mathematically defined change in connection weights over time is referred to as the "learning algorithm".

Connectionists are in agreement that recurrent neural networks (networks wherein connections of the network can form a directed cycle) are a better model of the brain than feedforward neural networks (networks with no directed cycles). Many recurrent connectionist models also incorporate dynamical systems theory. Many researchers, such as the connectionist Paul Smolensky, have argued that connectionist models will evolve towards fully continuous, high-dimensional, non-linear, dynamic systems approaches.

Biological Realism

The neural network branch of connectionism suggests that the study of mental activity is really the study of neural systems. This links connectionism to neuroscience, and models involve varying degrees of biological realism. Connectionist work in general need not be biologically realistic, but some neural network researchers, computational neuroscientists, try to model the biological aspects of natural neural systems very closely in so-called "neuromorphic networks". Many authors find the clear link between neural activity and cognition to be an appealing aspect of connectionism. This has been criticized as reductionist.

Learning

Connectionists generally stress the importance of learning in their models. Thus, connectionists have created many sophisticated learning procedures for neural networks. Learning always involves modifying the connection weights. These generally involve mathematical formulas to determine the change in weights when given sets of data consisting of activation vectors for some subset of the neural units.

By formalizing learning in such a way, connectionists have many tools. A very common strategy in connectionist learning methods is to incorporate gradient descent over an error surface in a space defined by the weight matrix. All gradient descent learning in connectionist models involves changing each weight by the partial derivative of the error surface with respect to the weight. Backpropagation, first made popular in the 1980s, is probably the most commonly known connectionist gradient descent algorithm today.

History

Connectionism can be traced to ideas more than a century old, which were little more than speculation until the mid-to-late 20th century. It wasn't until the 1980s that connectionism became a popular perspective among scientists.

Parallel Distributed Processing

The prevailing connectionist approach today was originally known as parallel distributed processing(PDP). It was an artificial neural network approach that stressed the parallel nature of neural processing, and the distributed nature of neural representations. It provided a general mathematical framework for researchers to operate in. The framework involved eight major aspects:

- A set of processing units, represented by a set of integers.
- An activation for each unit, represented by a vector of time-dependent functions.
- An output function for each unit, represented by a vector of functions on the activations.
- A pattern of connectivity among units, represented by a matrix of real numbers indicating connection strength.
- A propagation rule spreading the activations via the connections, represented by a function on the output of the units.
- An activation rule for combining inputs to a unit to determine its new activation, represented by a function on the current activation and propagation.
- A learning rule for modifying connections based on experience, represented by a change in the weights based on any number of variables.
- An environment which provides the system with experience, represented by sets of activation vectors for some subset of the units.

These aspects are now the foundation for almost all connectionist models. A perceived limitation of PDP is that it is reductionistic. That is, all cognitive processes can be explained in terms of neural firing and communication.

A lot of the research that led to the development of PDP was done in the 1970s, but PDP became popular in the 1980s with the release of the books Parallel Distributed Processing: Explorations in the Microstructure of Cognition - Volume 1 (foundations) and Volume 2 (Psychological and Biological Models), by James L. McClelland, David E. Rumelhart and the PDP Research Group. The books are now considered seminal connectionist works, and it is now common to fully equate PDP and connectionism, although the term "connectionism" is not used in the books.

Earlier Work

PDP's direct roots were the perceptron theories of researchers such as Frank Rosenblatt from the 1950s and 1960s. But perceptron models were made very unpopular by the book Perceptrons by Marvin Minsky and Seymour Papert, published in 1969. It demonstrated the limits on the sorts of functions which single layered perceptrons can calculate, showing that even simple functions like the exclusive disjunction could not be handled properly. The PDP books overcame this limitation by showing that multi-level, non-linear neural networks were far more robust and could be used for a vast array of functions.

Many earlier researchers advocated connectionist style models, for example in the 1940s and 1950s, Warren McCulloch, Walter Pitts, Donald Olding Hebb, and Karl Lashley. McCulloch and Pitts showed how neural systems could implement first-order logic: their classic paper "A Logical Calculus of Ideas Immanent in Nervous Activity" (1943) is important in this development here. They were influenced by the important work of Nicolas Rashevsky in the 1930s. Hebb contributed greatly to speculations about neural functioning, and proposed a learning principle, Hebbian learning, that is still used today. Lashley argued for distributed representations as a result of his failure to find anything like a localize dengram in years of lesion experiments.

Connectionism apart from PDP

Though PDP is the dominant form of connectionism, other theoretical work should also be classified as connectionist.

Many connectionist principles can be traced to early work in psychology, such as that of William James. Psychological theories based on knowledge about the human brain were fashionable in the late 19th century. As early as 1869, the neurologist John Hughlings Jackson argued for multi-level, distributed systems. Following from this lead, Herbert Spencer's Principles of Psychology, 3rd edition (1872), and Sigmund Freud's Project for a Scientific Psychology (composed 1895) propounded connectionist or proto-connectionist theories. These tended to be speculative theories. But by the early 20th century, Edward Thorndike was experimenting on learning that posited a connectionist type network.

In the 1950s, Friedrich Hayek proposed that spontaneous order in the brain arose out of decentralized networks of simple units. Hayek's work was rarely cited in the PDP literature until recently.

Another form of connectionist model was the relational network framework developed by the linguist Sydney Lamb in the 1960s.

Relational networks have been only used by linguists, and were never unified with the PDP approach. As a result, they are now used by very few researchers.

There are also hybrid connectionist models, mostly mixing symbolic representations with neural network models. The hybrid approach has been advocated by some researchers (such as Ron Sun).

Connectionism vs. Computationalism Debate

As connectionism became increasingly popular in the late 1980s, there was a reaction to it by some researchers, including Jerry Fodor, Steven Pinker and others.

They argued that connectionism, as it was being developed, was in danger of obliterating what they saw as the progress being made in the fields of cognitive science and psychology by the classical approach of computationalism. Computationalism is a specific form of cognitivism which argues that mental activity is computational, that is, that the mind operates by performing purely formal operations on symbols, like a Turing machine. Some researchers argued that the trend in connectionism was a reversion towards associationism and the abandonment of the idea of a language of thought, something they felt was mistaken. In contrast, it was those very tendencies that made connectionism attractive for other researchers.

Connectionism and computationalism need not be at odds, but the debate in the late 1980s and early 1990s led to opposition between the two approaches. Throughout the debate some researchers have argued that connectionism and computationalism are fully compatible, though full consensus on this issue has not been reached. The differences between the two approaches that are usually cited are the following:

- Computationalists posit symbolic models that do not resemble underlying brain structure at all, whereas connectionists engage in "low level" modelling, trying to ensure that their models resemble neurological structures.
- Computationalists generally focus on the structure of explicit symbols (mental models) and syntactical rules for their internal manipulation, whereas connectionists focus on learning from environmental stimuli and storing this information in a form of connections between neurons.

- Computationalists believe that internal mental activity consists of manipulation of explicit symbols, whereas connectionists believe that the manipulation of explicit symbols is a poor model of mental activity.
- Computationalists often posit domain specific symbolic sub-systems designed to support learning in specific areas of cognition (e.g. language, intentionality, number), while connectionists posit one or a small set of very general learning mechanisms.

But despite these differences, some theorists have proposed that the connectionist architecture is simply the manner in which the symbol manipulation system happens to be implemented in the organic brain. This is logically possible, as it is well known that connectionist models can implement symbol manipulation systems of the kind used in computationalist models, as indeed they must be able if they are to explain the human ability to perform symbol manipulation tasks. But the debate rests on whether this symbol manipulation forms the foundation of cognition in general, so this is not a potential vindication of computationalism. Nonetheless, computational descriptions may be helpful high-level descriptions of cognition of logic, for example.

The debate largely centred on logical arguments about whether connectionist networks were capable of producing the syntactic structure observed in this sort of reasoning. This was later achieved, although using processes unlikely to be possible in the brain, thus the debate persisted. Today, progress in neurophysiology, and general advances in the understanding of neural networks, has led to the successful modelling of a great many of these early problems, and the debate about fundamental cognition has thus largely been decided amongst neuroscientists in favour of connectionism. However, these fairly recent developments have yet to reach consensus acceptance amongst those working in other fields, such as psychology or philosophy of mind.

Part of the appeal of computational descriptions is that they are relatively easy to interpret, and thus may be seen as contributing to our understanding of particular mental processes, whereas connectionist models are generally more opaque, to the extent that they may only be describable in very general terms (such as specifying the learning algorithm, the number of units, etc.), or in unhelpfully low-level terms. In this sense connectionist models may instantiate, and thereby provide evidence for, a broad theory of cognition (i.e. connectionism), without representing a helpful theory of the particular process which is being modelled. In this sense the debate might be considered as to some extent reflecting a mere difference in the level of analysis in which particular theories are framed.

The recent popularity of dynamical systems in philosophy of mind have added a new perspective on the debate; some authors now argue that any split between connectionism and computationalism is more conclusively characterised as a split between computationalism and dynamical systems.

The recently proposed Hierarchical temporal memory model may help resolving this dispute, at least to some degree, given that it explains how the neocortex extracts high-level (symbolic) information from low-level sensory input.

Neural Coding

Neural coding is a neuroscience-related field concerned with how sensory and other information is represented in the brain by networks of neurons. The main goal of studying neural coding is to characterize the relationship between the stimulus and the individual or ensemble neuronal responses and the relationship among electrical activity of the neurons in the ensemble. It is thought that neurons can encode both digital and analogue information.

Overview

Neurons are remarkable among the cells of the body in their ability to propagate signals rapidly over large distances. They do this by generating characteristic electrical pulses called action potentials or, more simply, spikes that can travel down nerve fibres. Sensory neurons change their activities by firing sequences of action potentials in various temporal patterns, with the presence of external sensory stimuli, such as light, sound, taste, smell and touch. It is known that information about the stimulus is encoded in this pattern of action potentials and transmitted into and around the brain.

Although action potentials can vary somewhat in duration, amplitude and shape, they are typically treated as identical stereotyped events in neural coding studies. If the brief duration of an action potential (about 1ms) is ignored, an action potential sequence, or spike train, can be characterized simply by a series of all-or-none point events in time. The lengths of interspike intervals (ISIs) between two successive spikes in a spike train often vary, apparently randomly. The study of neural coding involves measuring and characterizing how stimulus attributes, such as light or sound intensity, or motor actions, such as the direction of an arm movement, are represented by neuron action potentials or spikes. In order to describe and analyse neuronal firing, statistical methods and methods of probability theory and stochastic point processes have been widely applied.

Encoding and Decoding

The link between stimulus and response can be studied from two opposite points of view. Neural encoding refers to the map from stimulus to response. The main focus is to understand how neurons respond to a wide variety of stimuli, and to accurately construct models that attempt to predict responses to other stimuli. Neural decoding refers to the reverse map, from response to stimulus, and the challenge is to reconstruct a stimulus, or certain aspects of that stimulus, from the spike sequences it evokes.

Coding Schemes

A sequence, or 'train', of spikes may contain information based on different coding schemes. In motor neurons, for example, the strength at which an innervated muscle is flexed depends solely on the 'firing rate', the average number of spikes per unit time (a 'rate code'). At the other end, a complex 'temporal code' is based on the precise timing of single spikes. They may be locked to an external stimulus such as in the auditory system or be generated intrinsically by the neural circuitry.

Whether neurons use rate coding or temporal coding is a topic of intense debate within the neuroscience community, even though there is no clear definition of what these terms mean.

Rate Coding

Rate coding is a traditional coding scheme, assuming that most, if not all, information about the stimulus is contained in the firing rate of the neuron. Because the sequence of action potentials generated by a given stimulus varies from trial to trial, neuronal responses are typically treated statistically or probabilistically. They may be characterized by firing rates, rather than as specific spike sequences. In most sensory systems, the firing rate increases, generally non-linearly, with increasing stimulus intensity. Any information possibly encoded in the temporal structure of the spike train is ignored. Consequently, rate coding is inefficient but highly robust with respect to the ISI 'noise'.

The concept of firing rates has been successfully applied during the last 80 years. It dates back to the pioneering work of ED Adrian who showed that the firing rate of stretch receptor neurons in the muscles is related to the force applied to the muscle. In the following decades, measurement of firing rates became a standard tool for describing the properties of all types of sensory or cortical neurons, partly due to the relative ease of measuring rates experimentally. However, this approach neglects all the information possibly contained in the exact timing of the spikes. During recent years, more and more experimental evidences have suggested that a straightforward firing rate concept based on temporal averaging may be too simplistic to describe brain activity.

During rate coding, precisely calculating firing rate is very important. In fact, the term "firing rate" has a few different definitions, which refer to different averaging procedures, such as an average over time or an average over several repetitions of experiment.

In rate coding, learning is based on activity-dependent synaptic weight modifications.

Spike-count Rate

The Spike-count rate, also referred to as temporal average, is obtained by counting the number of spikes that appear during a trial and dividing by the duration of trial. The length T of the time window is set by experimenter and depends on the type of neuron recorded from and the stimulus. In practice, to get sensible averages, several spikes should occur within the time window. Typical values are T = 100 ms or T = 500 ms, but the duration may also be longer or shorter.

The spike-count rate can be determined from a single trial, but at the expense of losing all temporal resolution about variations in neural response during the course of the trial. Temporal averaging can work well in cases where the stimulus is constant or slowly varying and does not require a fast reaction of the organism - and this is the situation usually encountered in experimental protocols. Real-world input, however, is hardly stationary, but often changing on a fast time scale. For example, even when viewing a static image, humans perform saccades, rapid changes of the direction of gaze. The image projected onto the retinal photoreceptors changes therefore every few hundred milliseconds.

Despite its shortcomings, the concept of a spike-count rate code is widely used not only in experiments, but also in models of neural networks. It has led to the idea that a neuron transforms information about a single input variable (the stimulus strength) into a single continuous output variable (the firing rate).

Time-dependent Firing Rate

The time-dependent firing rate is defined as the average number of spikes (averaged over trials) appearing during a short interval between times t and t+Ät, divided by the duration of the interval. It works for stationary as well as for time-dependent stimuli. To experimentally measure the time-dependent firing rate, the experimenter records from a neuron while stimulating with some input sequence. The same stimulation sequence is repeated several times and the neuronal response is reported in a Peri-Stimulus-Time Histogram (PSTH). The time t is measured with respect to the start of the stimulation sequence. The Ät must be large enough (typically in the range of one or a few milliseconds) so there are sufficient number of spikes within the interval to obtain a reliable estimate of the average. The number of occurrences of spikes n_K(t;t+Ät) summed over all repetitions of the experiment divided by the number K of repetitions is a measure of the typical activity of the neuron between time t and t+Ät. A further division by the interval length Ät yields time-dependent firing rate r(t) of the neuron, which is equivalent to the spike density of PSTH.

For sufficiently small Ät, r(t)Ät is the average number of spikes occurring between times t and t+Ät over multiple trials. If Ät is small, there will never be more than one spike within the interval between t and t+Ät on any given trial. This means that r(t)Ät is also the fraction of trials on which a spike occurred between those times. Equivalently, r(t)Ät is the probability that a spike occurs during this time interval.

As an experimental procedure, the time-dependent firing rate measure is a useful method to evaluate neuronal activity, in particular in the case of time-dependent stimuli. The obvious problem with this approach is that it can not be the coding scheme used by neurons in the brain. Neurons can not wait for the stimuli to repeatedly present in an exactly same manner before generating response.

Nevertheless, the experimental time-dependent firing rate measure can make sense, if there are large populations of independent neurons that receive the same stimulus. Instead of recording from a population of N neurons in a single run, it is experimentally easier to record from a single neuron and average over N repeated runs. Thus, the time-dependent firing rate coding relies on the implicit assumption that there are always populations of neurons.

Temporal Coding

When precise spike timing or high-frequency firing-rate fluctuations are found to carry information, the neural code is often identified as a temporal code. A number of studies have found that the temporal resolution of the neural code is on a millisecond time scale, indicating that precise spike timing is a significant element in neural coding.

Temporal codes employ those features of the spiking activity that cannot be described by the firing rate. For example, time to first spike after the stimulus onset, characteristics based on the second and higher statistical moments of the ISI probability distribution, spike randomness, or precisely timed groups of spikes (temporal patterns) are candidates for temporal codes. As there is no absolute time reference in the nervous system, the information is carried either in terms of the relative timing of spikes in a population of neurons or with respect to an ongoing brain oscillation.

The temporal structure of a spike train or firing rate evoked by a stimulus is determined both by the dynamics of the stimulus and by the nature of the neural encoding process. Stimuli that change rapidly tend to generate precisely timed spikes and rapidly changing firing rates no matter what neural coding strategy is being used. Temporal coding refers to temporal precision in the response that does not arise solely from the dynamics of the stimulus, but that nevertheless relates to properties of the stimulus. The interplay between stimulus and encoding dynamics makes the identification of a temporal code difficult.

The issue of temporal coding is distinct and independent from the issue of independent-spike coding. If each spike is independent of all the other spikes in the train, the temporal character of the neural code is determined by the behaviour of time-dependent firing rate r(t). If r(t) varies slowly with time, the code is typically called a rate code, and if it varies rapidly, the code is called temporal.

Phase-of-firing code is a type of code which takes into account a time label for each spike according to a time reference based on phase of local ongoing oscillations at low or high frequencies. A feature of this code is that neurons adhere to a preferred order of spiking, resulting in firing sequence.

In temporal coding, learning can be explained by activity-dependent synaptic delay modifications. The modifications can themselves depend non only on spike rates (rate coding) but also on spike timing patterns (temporal coding), i.e., can be a special case of spike-timing-dependent plasticity.

Population Coding

Population coding is a method to represent stimuli by using the joint activities of a number of neurons. In population coding, each neuron has a distribution of responses over some set of inputs, and the responses of many neurons may be combined to determine some value about the inputs.

From the theoretical point of view, population coding is one of a few mathematically well-formulated problems in neuroscience. It grasps the essential features of neural coding and yet, is simple enough for theoretic analysis. Experimental studies have revealed that this coding paradigm is widely used in the sensor and motor areas of the brain.

For example, in the visual area medial temporal (MT), neurons are tuned to the moving direction. In response to an object moving in a particular direction, many neurons in MT fire, with a noise-corrupted and bell-shaped activity pattern across the population. The moving direction of the object is retrieved from the population activity, to be immune from the fluctuation existing in a single neuron's signal.

Population coding has a number of advantages, including reduction of uncertainty due to neuronal variability and the ability to represent a number of different stimulus attributes simultaneously. Population coding is also much faster than rate coding and can reflect changes in the stimulus conditions nearly instantaneously. Individual neurons in such a population typically have different but overlapping selectivities, so that many neurons, but not necessarily all, respond to a given stimulus.

Position Coding

A typical population code involves neurons with a Gaussian tuning curve whose means vary linearly with the stimulus intensity, meaning that the neuron responds most strongly (in terms of spikes per second) to a stimulus near the mean. The actual intensity could be recovered as the stimulus level corresponding to the mean of the neuron with the greatest response. However, the noise inherent in neural responses means that a maximum likelihood estimation function is more accurate.

This type of code is used to encode continuous variables such as joint position, eye position, colour, or sound frequency. Any individual neuron is too noisy to faithfully encode the variable using rate coding, but an entire population ensures greater fidelity and precision.

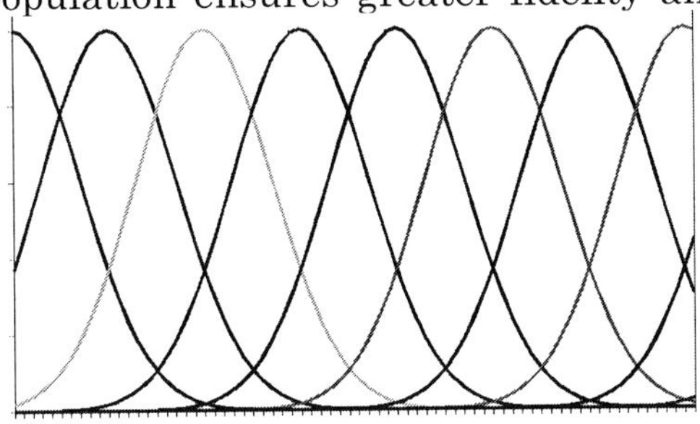

Figure: Plot of typical position coding.

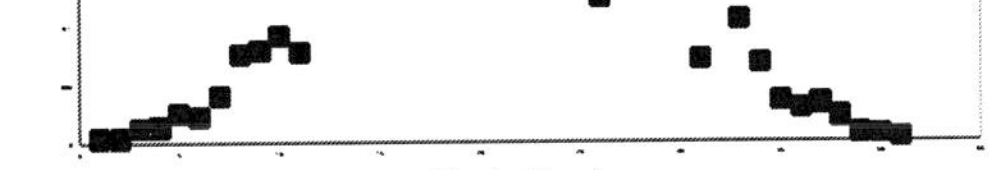

Figure: Neural responses are noisy and unreliable.

Artificial Neuron

An artificial neuron is a mathematical function conceived as a crude model, or abstraction of biological neurons. Artificial neurons are the constitutive units in an artificial neural network. Depending on the specific model used, it can receive different names, such as semi-linear unit, Nv neuron, binary neuron, linear threshold function or McCulloch–Pitts (MCP) neuron . The artificial neuron receives one or more inputs (representing the one or more dendrites) and sums them to produce an output (representing a biological neuron's axon). Usually the sums of each node are weighted, and the sum is passed through a non-linear function known as an activation function or transfer function. The transfer functions usually have a sigmoid shape, but they may also take the form of other non-linear functions, piecewise linear functions, or step functions. They are also often monotonically increasing, continuous, differentiable and bounded.

The artificial neuron transfer function should not be confused with a linear system's transfer function.

Basic Structure

For a given artificial neuron, let there be m + 1 inputs with signals x_0 through x_m and weights w_0t hrough w_m. Usually, the x_0 input is assigned the value +1, which makes it a bias input with $w_{k0} = b_k$. This leaves only m actual inputs to the neuron: from x_1 to x_m.

The output of kth neuron is:

$$y_k = \ell\left(\sum_{j=0}^{m} \omega_{kj} x_j\right)$$

Where φ (phi) is the transfer function.

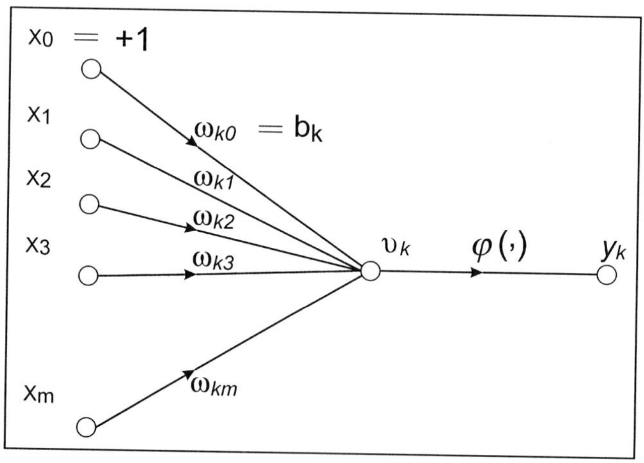

The output is analogous to the axon of a biological neuron, and its value propagates to input of the next layer, through a synapse. It may also exit the system, possibly as part of an output vector.

It has no learning process as such. It cannot decide its own, here weights are calculated and accordingly the threshold value is calculated.

History

The first artificial neuron was the Threshold Logic Unit (TLU) first proposed by Warren McCulloch and Walter Pitts in 1943. As a transfer function, it employed a threshold, equivalent to using the Heaviside step function. Initially, only a simple model was considered, with binary inputs and outputs, some restrictions on the possible weights, and a more flexible threshold value. Since the beginning it was already noticed that any boolean function could be implemented by networks of such devices, what is easily seen from the fact that one can implement the AND and OR functions, and use them in the disjunctive or the conjunctive normal form.

Researchers also soon realized that cyclic networks, with feedbacks through neurons, could define dynamical systems with memory, but most of the research concentrated (and still does) on strictly feed-forward networks because of the smaller difficulty they present.

One important and pioneering artificial neural network that used the linear threshold function was the perceptron, developed by Frank Rosenblatt. This model already considered more flexible weight values in the neurons, and was used in machines with adaptive capabilities. The representation of the threshold values as a bias term was introduced by Widrow in 1960.

In the late 1980s, when research on neural networks regained strength, neurons with more continuous shapes started to be considered. The possibility of differentiating the activation function allows the direct use of the gradient descent and other optimisation algorithms for the adjustment of the weights. Neural networks also started to be used as a general function approximation model.

Types of Transfer Functions

The transfer function of a neuron is chosen to have a number of properties which either enhance or simplify the network containing the neuron. Crucially, for instance, any multilayer perceptron using a linear transfer function has an equivalent single-layer network; a non-linear function is therefore necessary to gain the advantages of a multilayer network. Below, u refers in all cases to the weighted sum of all the inputs to the neuron, i.e. for n inputs,

$$u = \sum_{i=1}^{n} \omega_i x_i$$

where w is a vector of synaptic weights and x is a vector of inputs.

Step Function

The output y of this transfer function is binary, depending on whether the input meets a specified threshold, θ. The "signal" is sent, i.e. the output is set to one, if the activation meets the threshold.

$$y = \begin{cases} 1 & if \quad u \geq \theta \\ 0 & if \quad u < \theta \end{cases}$$

This function is used in perceptrons and often shows up in many other models. It performs a division of the space of inputs by a hyperplane. It is specially useful in the last layer of a network intended to perform binary classification of the inputs. It can be approximated from other sigmoidal functions by assigning large values to the weights.

Linear Combination

In this case, the output unit is simply the weighted sum of its inputs plus a bias term. A number of such linear neurons perform a linear transformation of the input vector. This is usually more useful in the first layers of a network. A number of analysis tools exist based on linear models, such as harmonic analysis, and they can all be used in neural networks with this linear neuron. The bias term allows us to make affine transformations to the data.

Sigmoid

A fairly simple non-linear function, a Sigmoid function such as the logistic function also has an easily calculated derivative, which can be important when calculating the weight updates in the network. It thus makes the network more easily manipulable mathematically, and was attractive to early computer scientists who needed to minimize the computational load of their simulations. It is commonly seen in multilayer perceptrons using a backpropagation algorithm.

Pseudocode algorithm

The following is a simple pseudocode implementation of a single TLU which takes boolean inputs (true or false), and returns a single boolean output when activated. An object-oriented model is used. No method of training is defined, since several exist. If a purely functional model were used, the class TLU below would be replaced with a function TLU with input parameters threshold, weights, and inputs that returned a boolean value.

```
  data member threshold : number
  data member weights : list of numbers of size X
  function member fire( inputs : list of booleans of size
boolean defined as:
    variable T : number
    T ? 0
    for each i in 1 to X :
     if inputs(i) is true :
      T ? T + weights(i)
     end if
    end for each
    if T > threshold :
     return true
    else:
     return false
    end if
   end function
  end class
```

Supervised Neural Network Training for an OR Gate.

Note: Initial weight equals final weight of previous iteration.

Limitations

Artificial neurons of simple types, such as the McCulloch–Pitts model, are sometimes characterized as “caricature models”, in that they are intended to reflect one or more neurophysiological observations, but without regard to realism.

Chapter 6

Applications of Natural and of Artificial Neural Networks

Function Approximation

The need for function approximations arises in many branches of applied mathematics, and computer science in particular. In general, a function approximation problem asks us to select a function among a well-defined class that closely matches ("approximates") a target function in a task-specific way.

One can distinguish two major classes of function approximation problems: First, for known target functions approximation theory is the branch of numerical analysis that investigates how certain known functions (for example, special functions) can be approximated by a specific class of functions (for example, polynomials or rational functions) that often have desirable properties (inexpensive computation, continuity, integral and limit values, etc.).

Second, the target function, call it g, may be unknown; instead of an explicit formula, only a set of points of the form (x, g(x)) is provided.

Depending on the structure of the domain and codomain of g, several techniques for approximating g may be applicable. For example, if g is an operation on the real numbers, techniques of interpolation, extrapolation, regression analysis, and curve fitting can be used. If the codomain (range or target set) of g is a finite set, one is dealing with a classification problem instead.

To some extent the different problems (regression, classification, fitness approximation) have received a unified treatment in statistical learning theory, where they are viewed as supervised learning problems.

Radial basis Function Network

A radial basis function network is an artificial neural network that uses radial basis functions as activation functions. It is a linear combination of radial basis functions. They are used in function approximation, time series prediction, and control.

Network Architecture

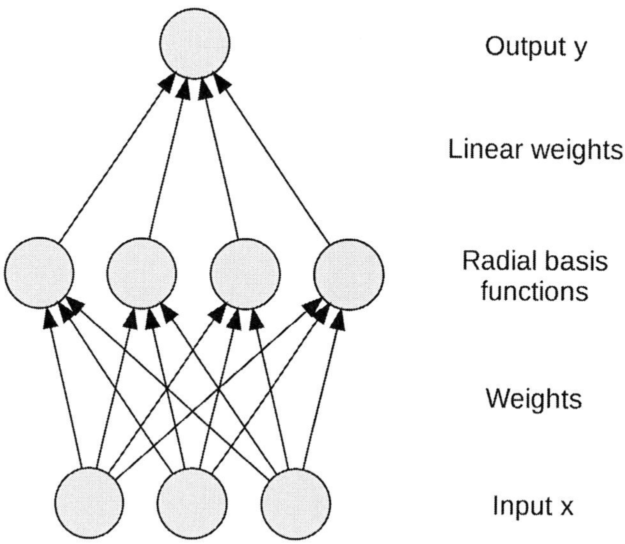

Figure : Architecture of a radial basis function network. An input vector x is used as input to all radial basis functions, each with different parameters. The output of the network is a linear combination of the outputs from radial basis functions.

Radial basis function (RBF) networks typically have three layers: an input layer, a hidden layer with a non-linear RBF activation function and a linear output layer. The output, $\ell : \mathbf{R}^n \to \mathbf{R}$, of the network is thus

$$\ell(x) = \sum_{i=1}^{N} a_i \rho(\|x - c_i\|)$$

where N is the number of neurons in the hidden layer, $\mathbf{c}_i$ is the centre vector for neuron i, and a_i are the weights of the linear output neuron. In the basic form all inputs are connected to each hidden neuron. The norm is typically taken to be the Euclidean distance (though Mahalanobis distance appears to perform better in general) and the basis function is taken to be Gaussian

$$\rho(\|x-c_i\|)=\exp\left[-\beta\|x-c_i\|^2\right].$$

The Gaussian basis functions are local in the sense that

$$\hat{y}_j = h(x_j) \approx y_j$$

i.e. changing parameters of one neuron has only a small effect for input values that are far away from the centre of that neuron.

RBF networks are universal approximators on a compact subset of $\mathbf{R}^n$. This means that a RBF network with enough hidden neurons can approximate any continuous function with arbitrary precision. The weights a_i, , and β are determined in a manner that optimises the fit between ℓ and the data.

Normalized

Normalized Architecture

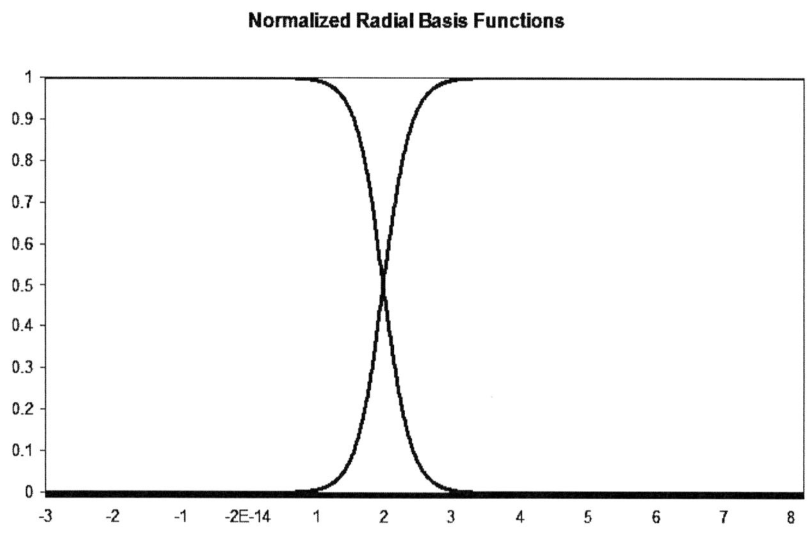

Figure : Two normalized radial basis functions in one input dimension. The basis function centres are located at c_1 = 0.75 andc_2 = 3.25.

In addition to the above unnormalized architecture, RBF networks can be normalized. In this case the mapping is

$$\ell(x) \overset{def}{=} \frac{\sum_{i=1}^{N} a_i \rho(\|x-c_i\|)}{\sum_{i=1}^{N} \rho(\|x-c_i\|)} \sum_{i=1}^{N} a_i u(\|x-c_i\|)$$

where

$$u\left(\left\|x-c_i\right\|\right) \overset{def}{=} \frac{\rho\left(\left\|x-c_i\right\|\right)}{\sum_{i=1}^{N} \rho\left(\left\|x-c_i\right\|\right)}$$

is known as a "normalized radial basis function".

Theoretical Motivation for Normalization

There is theoretical justification for this architecture in the case of stochastic data flow. Assume a stochastic kernel approximation for the joint probability density

$$P(x \wedge y) = \frac{1}{N}\sum_{i=1}^{N} \rho\left(\left\|x-c_i\right\|\right)\sigma\left(\left|y-e_i\right|\right)$$

where the weights C_i and e_i are exemplars from the data and we require the kernels to be normalized

$$\int \rho\left(\left\|x-c_i\right\|\right) d^n x = 1$$

and

$$\int \sigma\left(\left|y-e_i\right|\right) dy = 1$$

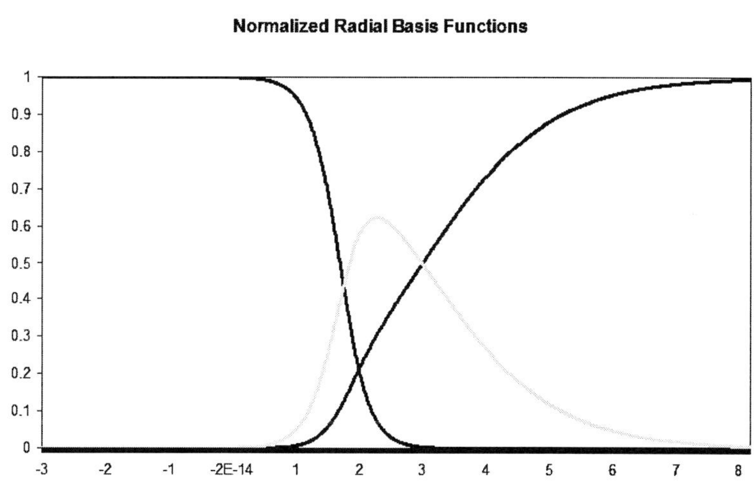

Figure : Three normalized radial basis functions in one input dimension. The additional basis function has centre at $c_3 = 2.75$

The probability densities in the input and output spaces are

$$P(x) = \int P(x \wedge y)\, dy = \frac{1}{N}\sum_{i=1}^{N} \rho\left(\left\|x-c_i\right\|\right)$$

and

The expectation of y given an input X is

$$\ell(x) \overset{def}{=} E(y \mid x) = \int y P(y \mid x)\, dy$$

where

$$P(y \mid x)$$

is the conditional probability of y given x. The conditional probability is related to the joint probability through Bayes theorem

$$P(y \mid x) = \frac{p(x \wedge y)}{P(x)}$$

which yields

$$\varphi(x) = \int y \frac{P(x \wedge y)}{P(x)}\, dy$$

This becomes

$$\ell(x) = \frac{\sum_{i=1}^{N} e_i \rho(\|x - c_i\|)}{\sum_{i=1}^{N} \rho(\|x - c_i\|)} = \sum_{i=1}^{N} e_i u(\|x - c_i\|)$$

when the integrations are performed.

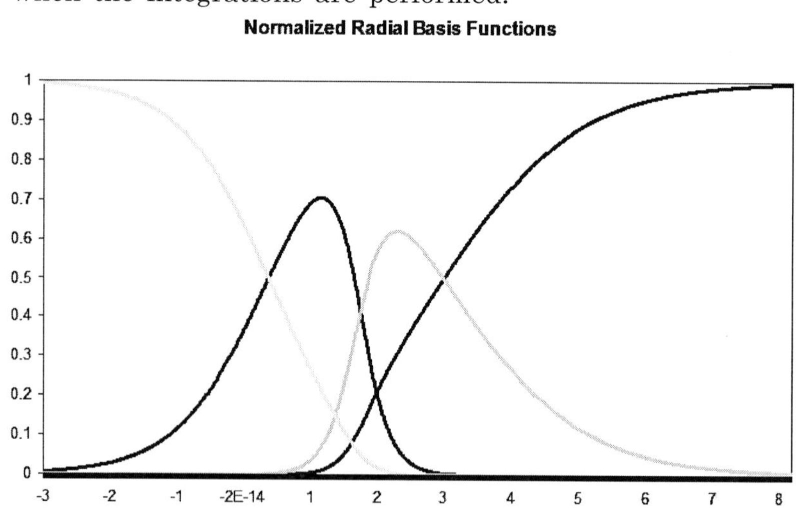

Figure : Four normalized radial basis functions in one input dimension. The fourth basis function has centre at $c_4 = 0$. Note that the first basis function (dark blue) has become localized.

Regression Analysis

In statistics, regression analysis includes many techniques for modelling and analysing several variables, when the focus is on the relationship between a dependent variable and one or more independent variables. More specifically, regression analysis helps one understand how the typical value of the dependent variable changes when any one of the independent variables is varied, while the other independent variables are held fixed. Most commonly, regression analysis estimates the conditional expectation of the dependent variable given the independent variables — that is, the average value of the dependent variable when the independent variables are held fixed. Less commonly, the focus is on a quantile, or other location parameter of the conditional distribution of the dependent variable given the independent variables. In all cases, the estimation target is a function of the independent variables called the regression function. In regression analysis, it is also of interest to characterize the variation of the dependent variable around the regression function, which can be described by a probability distribution.

Regression analysis is widely used for prediction and forecasting, where its use has substantial overlap with the field of machine learning. Regression analysis is also used to understand which among the independent variables are related to the dependent variable, and to explore the forms of these relationships. In restricted circumstances, regression analysis can be used to infer causal relationships between the independent and dependent variables.

A large body of techniques for carrying out regression analysis has been developed. Familiar methods such as linear regression and ordinary least squares regression are parametric, in that the regression function is defined in terms of a finite number of unknown parameters that are estimated from the data. Nonparametric regression refers to techniques that allow the regression function to lie in a specified set of functions, which may be infinite-dimensional.

The performance of regression analysis methods in practice depends on the form of the data generating process, and how it relates to the regression approach being used. Since the true form of the data-generating process is in general not known, regression analysis often depends to some extent on making assumptions about this process. These assumptions are sometimes (but not always) testable if a large amount of data is available. Regression models for prediction are often useful even when the assumptions are moderately violated, although they may not perform optimally. However, in many applications, especially with small effects or questions of causality based on observational data, regression methods give misleading results.

History

The earliest form of regression was the method of least squares (French: méthode des moindres carrés), which was published by Legendre in 1805, and by Gauss in 1809. Legendre and Gauss both applied the method to the problem of determining, from astronomical observations, the orbits of bodies about the Sun. Gauss published a further development of the theory of least squares in 1821, including a version of the Gauss–Markov theorem.

The term "regression" was coined by Francis Galton in the nineteenth century to describe a biological phenomenon. The phenomenon was that the heights of descendants of tall ancestors tend to regress down towards a normal average (a phenomenon also known as regression toward the mean). For Galton, regression had only this biological meaning, but his work was later extended by Udny Yule and Karl Pearson to a more general statistical context. In the work of Yule and Pearson, the joint distribution of the response and explanatory variables is assumed to be Gaussian. This assumption was weakened by R.A. Fisher in his works of 1922 and 1925. Fisher assumed that the conditional distribution of the response variable is Gaussian, but the joint distribution need not be. In this respect, Fisher's assumption is closer to Gauss's formulation of 1821.

In the 1950s and 1960s, economists used electromechanical desk calculators to calculate regressions. Before 1970, it sometimes took up to 24 hours to receive the result from one regression.

Regression methods continue to be an area of active research. In recent decades, new methods have been developed for robust regression, regression involving correlated responses such as time series and growth curves, regression in which the predictor or response variables are curves, images, graphs, or other complex data objects, regression methods accommodating various types of missing data, nonparametric regression, Bayesian methods for regression, regression in which the predictor variables are measured with error, regression with more predictor variables than observations, and causal inference with regression.

Regression Models

Regression models involve the following variables:

- The unknown parameters denoted as β; this may be a scalar or a vector.
- The independent variables, X.
- The dependent variable, Y.

In various fields of application, different terminologies are used in place of dependent and independent variables.

A regression model relates Y to a function of X and β.

$$Y \approx f(X, \beta)$$

The approximation is usually formalized as E(Y | X) = f(X, β). To carry out regression analysis, the form of the function f must be specified. Sometimes the form of this function is based on knowledge about the relationship between Y and X that does not rely on the data. If no such knowledge is available, a flexible or convenient form for f is chosen.

Assume now that the vector of unknown parameters β is of length k. In order to perform a regression analysis the user must provide information about the dependent variable Y:

- If N data points of the form (Y,X) are observed, where N < k, most classical approaches to regression analysis cannot be performed: since the system of equations defining the regression model is underdetermined, there is not enough data to recover β.
- If exactly N = k data points are observed, and the function f is linear, the equations Y = f(X, â) can be solved exactly rather than approximately. This reduces to solving a set of N equations with N unknowns (the elements of β), which has a unique solution as long as the X are linearly independent. If f is nonlinear, a solution may not exist, or many solutions may exist.
- The most common situation is where N > k data points are observed. In this case, there is enough information in the data to estimate a unique value for â that best fits the data in some

sense, and the regression model when applied to the data can be viewed as an overdetermined system in β.

In the last case, the regression analysis provides the tools for:

1. Finding a solution for unknown parameters â that will, for example, minimize the distance between the measured and predicted values of the dependent variable Y (also known as method of least squares).
2. Under certain statistical assumptions, the regression analysis uses the surplus of information to provide statistical information about the unknown parameters â and predicted values of the dependent variable Y.

Necessary Number of Independent Measurements

Consider a regression model which has three unknown parameters, $\hat{a}_0$, $\hat{a}_1$, and $\hat{a}_2$. Suppose an experimenter performs 10 measurements all at exactly the same value of independent variable vectorX (which contains the independent variables X_1, X_2, and X_3). In this case, regression analysis fails to give a unique set of estimated values for the three unknown parameters; the experimenter did not provide enough information.

The best one can do is to estimate the average value and the standard deviation of the dependent variable Y. Similarly, measuring at two different values of X would give enough data for a regression with two unknowns, but not for three or more unknowns.

If the experimenter had performed measurements at three different values of the independent variable vector X, then regression analysis would provide a unique set of estimates for the three unknown parameters in β.

In the case of general linear regression, the above statement is equivalent to the requirement that matrix X^TX is invertible.

Statistical Assumptions

When the number of measurements, N, is larger than the number of unknown parameters, k, and the measurement errors $\mathring{a}_i$ are normally distributed then the excess of information contained in (N - k) measurements is used to make statistical predictions about the unknown parameters. This excess of information is referred to as the degrees of freedom of the regression.

Underlying Assumptions

Classical assumptions for regression analysis include:

- The sample is representative of the population for the inference prediction.
- The error is a random variable with a mean of zero conditional on the explanatory variables.
- The independent variables are measured with no error. (Note: If this is not so, modelling may be done instead using errors-in-variables model techniques).
- The predictors are linearly independent, i.e. it is not possible to express any predictor as a linear combination of the others.
- The errors are uncorrelated, that is, the variance-covariance matrix of the errors is diagonal and each non-zero element is the variance of the error.
- The variance of the error is constant across observations (homoscedasticity). (Note: If not, weighted least squares or other methods might instead be used).

These are sufficient conditions for the least-squares estimator to possess desirable properties, in particular, these assumptions imply that the parameter estimates will be unbiased, consistent, and efficient in the class of linear unbiased estimators. It is important to note that actual data rarely satisfies the assumptions. That is, the method is used even though the assumptions are not true. Variation from the assumptions can sometimes be used as a measure of how far the model is from being useful. Many of these assumptions may be relaxed in more advanced treatments. Reports of statistical analyses usually include analyses of tests on the sample data and methodology for the fit and usefulness of the model.

Assumptions include the geometrical support of the variables (Cressie, 1996). Independent and dependent variables often refer to values measured at point locations. There may be spatial trends and spatial autocorrelation in the variables that violates statistical assumptions of regression. Geographic weighted regression is one technique to deal with such data (Fotheringham et al., 2002). Also, variables may include values aggregated by areas. With aggregated data the Modifiable Areal Unit Problem can cause extreme variation in regression parameters (Fotheringham and Wong, 1991). When analysing data aggregated by political boundaries, postal codes or census areas results may be very different with a different choice of units.

Linear Regression

In linear regression, the model specification is that the dependent variable, y_i is a linear combination of the parameters (but need not be linear in the independent variables). For example, in simple linear regression for modelling n data points there is one independent variable: x_i, and two parameters, β_0 and β_1:

Straight line: $y_i = \beta_0 + \beta_1 x_i + \varepsilon_i, \quad i = 1, \ldots, n.$

In multiple linear regression, there are several independent variables or functions of independent variables. For example, adding a term in x_i to the preceding regression gives:

parabola: $y_i = \beta_0 + \beta_1 x_i + \beta_2 x_i^2 + \varepsilon_i, \quad i = 1, \ldots, n.$

This is still linear regression; although the expression on the right hand side is quadratic in the independent variable x_i, it is linear in the parameters β_0, β_1 and β_2.

In both cases, ε_i is an error term and the subscript i indexes a particular observation. Given a random sample from the population, we estimate the population parameters and obtain the sample linear regression model:

$$\hat{y}_i = \hat{\beta}_0 + \hat{\beta}_1 x_i.$$

The residual, $e_i = y_i - \hat{y}_i$,, is the difference between the value of the dependent variable predicted by the model, and the true value of the dependent variable y_i. One method of estimation is ordinary least squares. This method obtains parameter estimates that minimize the sum of squared residuals, SSE, also sometimes denoted RSS:

$$SSE = \sum_{i=1}^{N} e_i^2.$$

Minimization of this function results in a set of normal equations, a set of simultaneous linear equations in the parameters, which are solved to yield the parameter estimators, $\hat{\beta}_0, \hat{\beta}_1$.

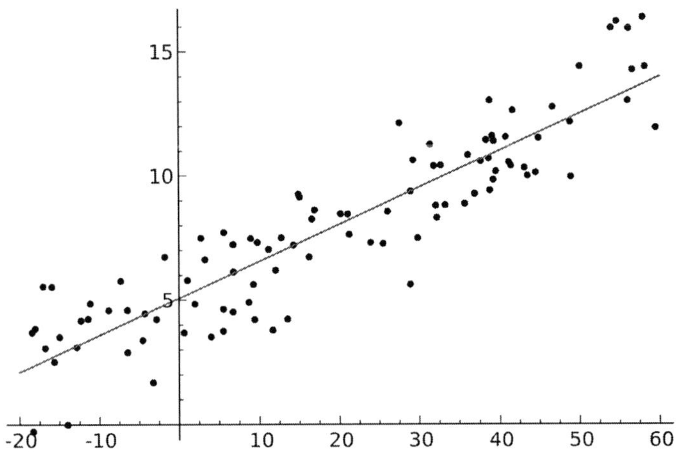

Figure: Illustration of linear regression on a data set.

In the case of simple regression, the formulas for the least squares estimates are

$$\hat{\beta}_1 = \frac{\Sigma(x_i - \bar{x})(y_i - \bar{y})}{\Sigma(x_i - \bar{x})^2} \quad and \quad \hat{\beta}_0 = \bar{y} - \hat{\beta}_1 \bar{x}$$

where $\bar{x}$ is the mean (average) of the x values and $\bar{y}$ is the mean of the y values. Under the assumption that the population error term has a constant variance, the estimate of that variance is given by:

$$\hat{\sigma}_\varepsilon^2 = \frac{SSE}{N-2}.$$

This is called the mean square error (MSE) of the regression. The standard errors of the parameter estimates are given by

$$\hat{\sigma}_{\beta 0} = \hat{\sigma}_\varepsilon \sqrt{\frac{1}{N} + \frac{\bar{x}^2}{\Sigma(x_i - \bar{x})^2}}$$

$$\hat{\sigma}_{\beta_1} = \hat{\sigma}_\varepsilon \sqrt{\frac{1}{\Sigma(x_i - \bar{x})^2}}.$$

Under the further assumption that the population error term is normally distributed, the researcher can use these estimated standard errors to create confidence intervals and conduct hypothesis tests about the population parameters.

General Linear Model

In the more general multiple regression model, there are p independent variables:

$$y_i = \beta_1 x_{i1} + \beta_2 x_{i2} + \cdots + \beta_p x_{ip} + \varepsilon_i,$$

where x_{ij} is the i observation on the j independent variable, and where the first independent variable takes the value 1 for all i (so $\hat{a}_1$ is the regression intercept).

The least squares parameter estimates are obtained from p normal equations. The residual can be written as

$$e_i = y_i - \hat{\beta}_1 x_{i1} - \cdots - \hat{\beta}_p x_{ip}.$$

The normal equations are

$$\sum_{i=1}^{n} \sum_{k=1}^{p} X_{ij} X_{ik} \hat{\beta}_k = \sum_{i=1}^{n} X_{ij} y_i, \; j = 1, \ldots, p.$$

In matrix notation, the normal equations are written as

$$\left(X^T X\right)\hat{\beta} = X^T Y,$$

where the ij element of X is x_{ij}, the i element of the column vector Y is y_i, and the j element of $\hat{\beta}$ is $\hat{\beta}_j$. Thus X is n×p, Y is n×1, and $\hat{\beta}$ is p×1. The solution is

$$\hat{\beta} = \left(X^T X\right)^{-1} X^T Y.$$

Regression Diagnostics

Once a regression model has been constructed, it may be important to confirm the goodness of fit of the model and the statistical significance of the estimated parameters. Commonly used checks of goodness of fit include the R-squared, analyses of the pattern of residuals and hypothesis testing. Statistical significance can be checked by an F-test of the overall fit, followed by t-tests of individual parameters.

Interpretations of these diagnostic tests rest heavily on the model assumptions. Although examination of the residuals can be used to invalidate a model, the results of a t-test or F-test are sometimes more difficult to interpret if the model's assumptions are violated. For example, if the error term does not have a normal distribution, in small samples the estimated parameters will not follow normal distributions and complicate inference. With relatively large samples, however, a central limit theorem can be invoked such that hypothesis testing may proceed using asymptotic approximations.

Regression with "Limited Dependent" Variables

The phrase "limited dependent" is used in econometric statistics for categorical and constrained variables.

The response variable may be non-continuous ("limited" to lie on some subset of the real line). For binary (zero or one) variables, if analysis proceeds with least-squares linear regression, the model is called the linear probability model.

Nonlinear models for binary dependent variables include the probit and logit model. The multivariate probit model is a standard method of estimating a joint relationship between several binary dependent variables and some independent variables.

For categorical variables with more than two values there is the multinomial logit. For ordinal variables with more than two values, there are the ordered logit and ordered probit models. Censored regression models may be used when the dependent variable is only sometimes observed, and Heckman correction type models may be used when the sample is not randomly selected from the population of interest.

An alternative to such procedures is linear regression based on polychoric correlation (or polyserial correlations) between the categorical variables. Such procedures differ in the assumptions made about the distribution of the variables in the population. If the variable is positive with low values and represents the repetition of the occurrence of an event, then count models like the Poisson regression or the negative binomial model may be used.

Interpolation and Extrapolation

Regression models predict a value of the Y variable given known values of the X variables. Prediction within the range of values in the dataset used for model-fitting is known informally as interpolation. Prediction outside this range of the data is known as extrapolation. Performing extrapolation relies strongly on the regression assumptions. The further the extrapolation goes outside the data, the more room there is for the model to fail due to differences between the assumptions and the sample data or the true values. For example, regression model failing the homoskedasticity assumption will make bigger mistakes the further out the extrapolation is.

It is generally advised that when performing extrapolation, one should accompany the estimated value of the dependent variable with a prediction interval that represents the uncertainty. Such intervals tend to expand rapidly as the values of the independent variable(s) moved outside the range covered by the observed data.

For such reasons and others, some tend to say that it might be unwise to undertake extrapolation.

However, this does not cover the full set of modelling errors that may be being made: in particular, the assumption of a particular form for the relation between Y and X. A properly conducted regression analysis will include an assessment of how well the assumed form is matched by the observed data, but it can only do so within the range of values of the independent variables actually available. This means that any extrapolation is particularly reliant on the assumptions being made about the structural form of the regression relationship. Best-practice advice here is that a linear-in-variables and linear-in-parameters relationship should not be chosen simply for computational convenience, but that all available knowledge should be deployed in constructing a regression model. If this knowledge includes the fact that the dependent variable cannot go outside a certain range of values, this can be made use of in selecting the model — even if the observed dataset has no values particularly near such bounds. The implications of this step of choosing an appropriate functional form for the regression can be great when extrapolation is considered. At a minimum, it can ensure that any extrapolation arising from a fitted model is "realistic" (or in accord with what is known).

Nonlinear Regression

When the model function is not linear in the parameters, the sum of squares must be minimized by an iterative procedure. This introduces many complications which are summarized in Differences between linear and non-linear least squares

Power and Sample Size Calculations

There are no generally agreed methods for relating the number of observations versus the number of independent variables in the model. One rule of thumb suggested by Good and Hardin is N = m, where N is the sample size, n is the number of independent variables and m is the number of observations needed to reach the desired precision if the model had only one independent variable.

For example, a researcher is building a linear regression model using a dataset that contains 1000 patients (N). If he decides that five observations are needed to precisely define a straight line (m), then the maximum number of independent variables his model can support is 4, because

$$\frac{\log 1000}{\log 5} = 4.29$$

Other Methods

Although the parameters of a regression model are usually estimated using the method of least squares, other methods which have been used include:

- Bayesian methods, e.g. Bayesian linear regression
- Percentage regression, for situations where reducing percentage errors is deemed more appropriate.
- Least absolute deviations, which is more robust in the presence of outliers, leading to quantile regression
- Nonparametric regression, requires a large number of observations and is computationally intensive
- Distance metric learning, which is learned by the search of a meaningful distance metric in a given input space.

Software

All major statistical software packages perform least squares regression analysis and inference. Simple linear regression and multiple regression using least squares can be done in some spreadsheet applications and on some calculators.

While many statistical software packages can perform various types of nonparametric and robust regression, these methods are less standardized; different software packages implement different methods, and a method with a given name may be implemented differently in different packages. Specialized regression software has been developed for use in fields such as survey analysis and neuroimaging.

Time Series

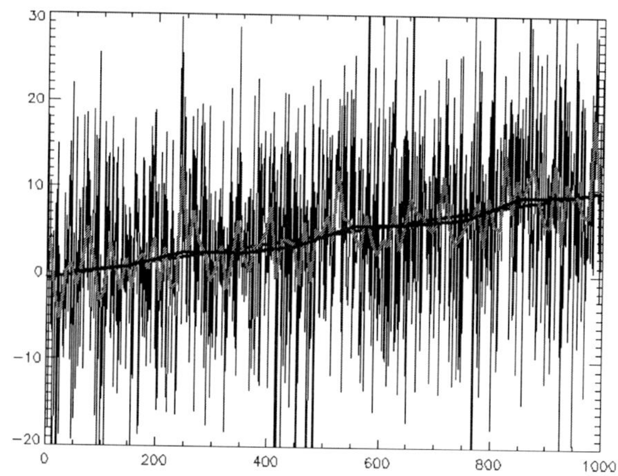

Figure: Time series: random data plus trend, with best-fit line and different smoothings.

In statistics, signal processing, econometrics andmathematical finance, a time series is a sequence of data points, measured typically at successive times spaced at uniform time intervals. Examples of time series are the daily closing value of the Dow Jones index or the annual flow volume of the Nile River at Aswan. Time series analysis comprises methods for analysing time series data in order to extract meaningful statistics and other characteristics of the data. Time series forecasting is the use of a model to predict future values based on previously observed values. Time series are very frequently plotted via line charts.

Time series data have a natural temporal ordering. This makes time series analysis distinct from other common data analysis problems, in which there is no natural ordering of the observations (e.g. explaining people's wages by reference to their education level, where the individuals' data could be entered in any order). Time series analysis is also distinct from spatial data analysis where the observations typically relate to geographical locations (e.g. accounting for house prices by the location as well as the intrinsic characteristics of the houses). A time series model will generally reflect the fact that observations close together in time will be more closely related than observations further apart. In addition, time series models will often make use of the natural one-way ordering of time so that values for a given period will be expressed as deriving in some way from past values, rather than from future values.

Methods for time series analyses may be divided into two classes: frequency-domain methods and time-domain methods. The former include spectral analysis and recently wavelet analysis; the latter include auto-correlation and cross-correlation analysis.

Analysis

There are several types of data analysis available for time series which are appropriate for different purposes.

General Exploration

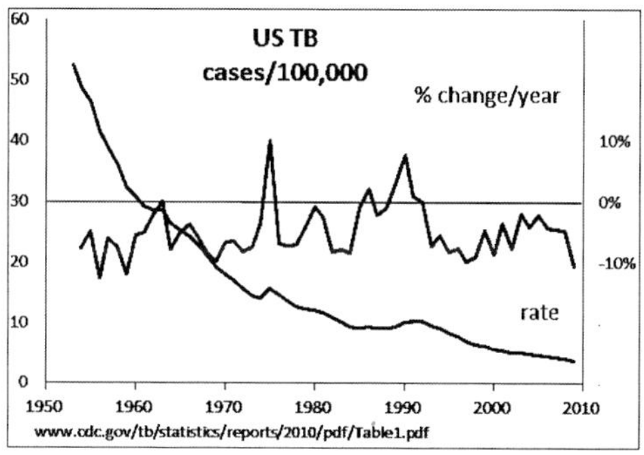

Figure: Tuberculosis incidence US 1953-2009

The clearest way to examine a regular time series is with aline chart such as the one shown for tuberculosis in the United States, made with a spreadsheet program. The number of cases was standardized to a rate per 100,000 and the percent change per year in this rate was calculated. The nearly steadily dropping line shows that the TB incidence was decreasing in most years, but the percent change in this rate varied by as much as +/- 10%, with 'surges' in 1975 and around the early 1990s. The use of both vertical axes allows the comparison of two time series in one graphic. Other techniques include:

- Autocorrelation analysis to examine serial dependence
- Spectral analysis to examine cyclic behaviour which need not be related to seasonality. For example, sun spot activity varies over 11 year cycles. Other common examples include celestial phenomena, weather patterns, neural activity, commodity prices, and economic activity.

Description

- Separation into components representing trend, seasonality, slow and fast variation, cyclical irregular
- Simple properties of marginal distributions.

Prediction and Forecasting

- Fully formed statistical models for stochastic simulation purposes, so as to generate alternative versions of the time series, representing what might happen over non-specific time-periods in the future
- Simple or fully formed statistical models to describe the likely outcome of the time series in the immediate future, given knowledge of the most recent outcomes (forecasting).

Models

Models for time series data can have many forms and represent different stochastic processes. When modelling variations in the level of a process, three broad classes of practical importance are the autoregressive (AR) models, the integrated (I) models, and the moving average (MA) models. These three classes depend linearly on previous data points. Combinations of these ideas produce autoregressive moving average (ARMA) and autoregressive integrated moving average (ARIMA) models.

The autoregressive fractionally integrated moving average (ARFIMA) model generalises the former three. Extensions of these classes to deal with vector-valued data are available under the heading of multivariate time-series models and sometimes the preceding acronyms are extended by including an initial "V" for "vector".

An additional set of extensions of these models is available for use where the observed time-series is driven by some "forcing" time-series (which may not have a causal effect on the observed series): the distinction from the multivariate case is that the forcing series may be deterministic or under the experimenter's control. For these models, the acronyms are extended with a final "X" for "exogenous".

Non-linear dependence of the level of a series on previous data points is of interest, partly because of the possibility of producing a chaotic time series. However, more importantly, empirical investigations can indicate the advantage of using predictions derived from non-linear models, over those from linear models, as for example in nonlinear autoregressive exogenous models.

Among other types of non-linear time series models, there are models to represent the changes of variance along time (heteroskedasticity). These models represent autoregressive conditional heteroskedasticity (ARCH) and the collection comprises a wide variety of representation (GARCH, TARCH, EGARCH, FIGARCH, CGARCH, etc.). Here changes in variability are related to, or predicted by, recent past values of the observed series. This is in contrast to other possible representations of locally varying variability, where the variability might be modelled as being driven by a separate time-varying process, as in a doubly stochastic model.

In recent work on model-free analyses, wavelet transform based methods (for example locally stationary wavelets and wavelet decomposed neural networks) have gained favour. Multiscale (often referred to as multiresolution) techniques decompose a given time series, attempting to illustrate time dependence at multiple scales.

Notation

A number of different notations are in use for time-series analysis. A common notation specifying a time series X that is indexed by the natural numbers is written

$$X = \{X_1, X_2, \ldots\}.$$

Another common notation is

$$Y = \{Y_t : t \in T\},$$

where T is the index set.

Conditions

There are two sets of conditions under which much of the theory is built:

- Stationary process
- Ergodicity.

However, ideas of stationarity must be expanded to consider two important ideas: strict stationarity and second-order stationarity. Both models and applications can be developed under each of these conditions, although the models in the latter case might be considered as only partly specified.

In addition, time-series analysis can be applied where the series are seasonally stationary or non-stationary. Situations where the amplitudes of frequency components change with time can be dealt with in time-frequency analysis which makes use of a time–frequency representation of a time-series or signal.

Models

The general representation of an autoregressive model, well-known as AR(p), is

$$Y_t = \alpha_0 + \alpha_1 Y_{t-1} + \alpha_2 Y_{t-2} + \cdots + \alpha_p Y_{t-p} + \varepsilon_t$$

where the term ε_t is the source of randomness and is called white noise. It is assumed to have the following characteristics:

$$E[\varepsilon_t] = 0,]$$

$$E\left[\varepsilon_t^2\right] = \sigma^2,$$

$$E[\varepsilon_t \varepsilon_s] = 0 \quad \textit{for all } t \neq s.$$

With these assumptions, the process is specified up to second-order moments and, subject to conditions on the coefficients, may be second-order stationary.

If the noise also has a normal distribution, it is called normal or Gaussian white noise. In this case, the AR process may be strictly stationary, again subject to conditions on the coefficients.

Tools for investigating time-series data include:

- Consideration of the autocorrelation function and the spectral density function (also cross-correlation functions and cross-spectral density functions)
- Performing a Fourier transform to investigate the series in the frequency domain
- Use of a filter to remove unwanted noise
- Principal components analysis (or empirical orthogonal function analysis)
- Singular spectrum analysis
- Artificial neural networks
- Hidden Markov model
- Dynamic time warping
- Dynamic Bayesian network
- Time-frequency analysis techniques:
- Fast Fourier Transform
- Continuous wavelet transform

- Short-time Fourier transform
- Chirplet transform
- Fractional Fourier transform.
- Chaotic analysis
- Correlation dimension
- Recurrence plots
- Recurrence quantification analysis
- Lyapunov exponents
- Entropy encoding.

Statistical Classification

In machine learning, statistical classification is the problem of identifying the sub-population to which new observations belong, where the identity of the sub-population is unknown, on the basis of a training set of data containing observations whose sub-population is known. Therefore these classifications will show a variable behaviour which can be studied by statistics.

Thus the requirement is that new individual items are placed into groups based on quantitative information on one or more measurements, traits or characteristics, etc. and based on the training set in which previously decided groupings are already established.

The problem here may be contrasted with that for cluster analysis, where the problem is to analyse a single data-set and decide how and whether the observations in the data-set can be divided into groups. In certain terminology, particularly that of machine learning, the classification problem is known as supervised learning, while clustering is known as unsupervised learning.

Unfortunately, terminology can be different in various fields of application. For example, in community ecology, the term "classification" is synonymous with cluster analysis.

Learning Classifiers. Problem Statement

A learning classifier is able to learn based on a sample. The data-set used for training consists of information x and y for each data-point, where x denotes what is generally a vector of observed characteristics for the data-item and y denotes a group-label. The label y can take only a finite number of values.

The classification problem can be stated as follows: given training data $\{(x_1, y_1),...,(x_n, y_n)\}$ produce a rule (or "classifier") h, such that h(x) can be evaluated for any possible value of x (not just those included in the training data) and such that the group attributed to any new observation, specifically

$$\bar{y} = h(x),$$

is as close as possible to the true group label y. For the training data-set, the true labels y_i are known but will not necessarily match their in-sample approximations

$$\hat{y}_i = h(x_i).$$

For new observations, the true labels y_j are unknown, but it is a prime target for the classification procedure that the approximation

$$\hat{y}_j = h(x_j) \approx y_j$$

as well as possible, where the quality of this approximation needs to be judged on the basis of the statistical or probabilistic properties of the overall population from which future observations will be drawn.

Frequentist Procedures

Early work on statistical classification was undertaken by Fisher, in the context of two-group problems, leading to Fisher's linear discriminant function as the rule for assigning a group to a new observation. This early work assumed that data-values within each of the two groups had a multivariate normal distribution. The extension of this same context to more than two-groups has also been considered with a restriction imposed that the classification rule should be linear. Later work for the multivariate normal distribution allowed the classifier to be nonlinear: several classification rules can be derived based on slight different adjustments of the Mahalanobis distance, with a new observation being assigned to the group whose centre has the lowest adjusted distance from the observation.

Bayesian Procedures

Unlike frequentist procedures, Bayesian classification procedures provide a natural way of taking into account any available information about the relative sizes of the sub-populations associated with the different groups within the overall population. Bayesian procedures tend to be computationally expensive and, in the days before Markov chain Monte Carlo computations were developed, approximations for Bayesian clustering rules were devised.

Some Bayesian procedures involve the calculation of group membership probabilities: these can be viewed as providing a more informative outcome of a data analysis than a simple attribution of a single group-label to each new observation.

Binary and Multiclass Classification

Classification can be thought of as two separate problems - binary classification and multiclass classification. In binary classification, a better understood task, only two classes are involved, whereas in multiclass classification involves assigning an object to one of several classes. Since many classification methods have been developed specifically for binary classification, multiclass classification often requires the combined use of multiple binary classifiers.

Algorithms

The most widely used classifiers are the neural network (multi-layer perceptron), support vector machines, k-nearest neighbours, Gaussian mixture model, Gaussian, naive Bayes, decision tree and RBF classifiers.

Examples of classification algorithms include:

- Linear classifiers
- Fisher's linear discriminant
- Logistic regression
- Naive Bayes classifier
- Perceptron
- Support vector machines
- Least squares support vector machines
- Quadratic classifiers
- Kernel estimation
- k-nearest neighbour
- Boosting
- Decision trees
- Random forests
- Neural networks

- Bayesian networks
- Hidden Markov models
- Learning vector quantization.

Evaluation

Classifier performance depends greatly on the characteristics of the data to be classified. There is no single classifier that works best on all given problems (a phenomenon that may be explained by the no-free-lunch theorem). Various empirical tests have been performed to compare classifier performance and to find the characteristics of data that determine classifier performance. Determining a suitable classifier for a given problem is however still more an art than a science.

The measures precision and recall are popular metrics used to evaluate the quality of a classification system. More recently, receiver operating characteristic (ROC) curves have been used to evaluate the tradeoff between true- and false-positive rates of classification algorithms.

As a performance metric, the uncertainty coefficient has the advantage over simple accuracy in that it is not affected by the relative sizes of the different classes. Further, it will not penalize an algorithm for simply rearranging the classes.

An intriguing problem in pattern recognition yet to be solved is the relationship between the problem to be solved (data to be classified) and the performance of various pattern recognition algorithms (classifiers).

Application Domains

Classification problems has many applications. In some of these it is employed as a data mining procedure, while in others more detailed statistical modelling is undertaken.

- Computer vision
- Medical imaging and medical image analysis
- Optical character recognition
- Video tracking
- Drug discovery and development
- Toxicogenomics

- Quantitative structure-activity relationship
- Geostatistics
- Speech recognition
- Handwriting recognition
- Biometric identification
- Biological classification
- Statistical natural language processing
- Document classification
- Internet search engines
- Credit scoring
- Pattern recognition.

Pattern Recognition

In machine learning, pattern recognition is the assignment of some sort of output value (or label) to a given input value (or instance). An example of pattern recognition is classification, which attempts to assign each input value to one of a given set of classes (for example, determine whether a given email is "spam" or "non-spam"). However, pattern recognition is a more general problem that encompasses other types of output as well. Other examples are regression, which assigns a real-valued output to each input; sequence labelling, which assigns a class to each member of a sequence of values (for example, part of speech tagging, which assigns a part of speech to each word in an input sentence); and parsing, which assigns a parse tree to an input sentence, describing the syntactic structure of the sentence.

Pattern recognition algorithms generally aim to provide a reasonable answer for all possible inputs and to do "fuzzy" matching of inputs. This is opposed to pattern matching algorithms, which look for exact matches in the input with pre-existing patterns. A common example of a pattern-matching algorithm is regular expression matching, which looks for patterns of a given sort in textual data and is included in the search capabilities of many text editors and word processors. In contrast to pattern recognition, pattern matching is generally not considered a type of machine learning, although pattern-matching algorithms (especially with fairly general, carefully tailored patterns) can sometimes succeed in providing similar-quality output to the sort provided by pattern-recognition algorithms.

Pattern recognition is studied in many fields, including psychology, psychiatry, ethology, cognitive science, traffic flow and computer science.

Overview

Pattern recognition is generally categorized according to the type of learning procedure used to generate the output value. Supervised learning assumes that a set of training data (the training set) has been provided, consisting of a set of instances that have been properly labelled by hand with the correct output. A learning procedure then generates a model that attempts to meet two sometimes conflicting objectives: Perform as well as possible on the training data, and generalise as well as possible to new data (usually, this means being as simple as possible, for some technical definition of "simple", in accordance with Occam's Razor). Unsupervised learning, on the other hand, assumes training data that has not been hand-labelled, and attempts to find inherent patterns in the data that can then be used to determine the correct output value for new data instances. A combination of the two that has recently been explored is semi-supervised learning, which uses a combination of labelled and unlabelled data (typically a small set of labelled data combined with a large amount of unlabelled data). Note that in cases of unsupervised learning, there may be no training data at all to speak of; in other words, the data to be labelled is the training data.

Note that sometimes different terms are used to describe the corresponding supervised and unsupervised learning procedures for the same type of output. For example, the unsupervised equivalent of classification is normally known as clustering, based on the common perception of the task as involving no training data to speak of, and of grouping the input data into clusters based on some inherent similarity measure (e.g. the distance between instances, considered as vectors in a multidimensional vector space), rather than assigning each input instance into one of a set of pre-defined classes. Note also that in some fields, the terminology is different: For example, in community ecology, the term "classification" is used to refer to what is commonly known as "clustering".

The piece of input data for which an output value is generated is formally termed an instance. The instance is formally described by a vector of features, which together constitute a description of all known characteristics of the instance. (These feature vectors can be seen as defining points in an appropriate multidimensional space, and methods for manipulating vectors in vector spaces can be correspondingly applied to them, such as computing the dot product or the angle between two vectors.) Typically, features are either categorical (also known as nominal, i.e. consisting of one of a set of unordered items, such as a gender of "male" or "female", or a blood type of "A", "B", "AB" or "O"), ordinal (consisting of one of a set of ordered items, e.g. "large", "medium" or "small"), integer-valued (e.g. a count of the number of occurrences of a particular word in an email) or real-valued (e.g. a measurement of blood pressure). Often, categorical and ordinal data are grouped together; likewise for integer-valued and real-valued data. Furthermore, many algorithms work only in terms of categorical data and require that real-valued or integer-valued data be discretized into groups (e.g. less than 5, between 5 and 10, or greater than 10).

Many common pattern recognition algorithms are probabilistic in nature, in that they use statistical inference to find the best label for a given instance. Unlike other algorithms, which simply output a "best" label, oftentimes probabilistic algorithms also output a probability of the instance being described by the given label. In addition, many probabilistic algorithms output a list of the N-best labels with associated probabilities, for some value of N, instead of simply a single best label. When the number of possible labels is fairly small (e.g. in the case of classification), N may be set so that the probability of all possible labels is output. Probabilistic algorithms have many advantages over non-probabilistic algorithms:

- They output a confidence value associated with their choice. (Note that some other algorithms may also output confidence values, but in general, only for probabilistic algorithms is this value mathematically grounded in probability theory. Non-probabilistic confidence values can in general not be given any specific meaning, and only used to compare against other confidence values output by the same algorithm.)
- Correspondingly, they can abstain when the confidence of choosing any particular output is too low.
- Because of the probabilities output, probabilistic pattern-recognition algorithms can be more effectively incorporated into larger machine-learning tasks, in a way that partially or completely avoids the problem of error propagation.

Techniques to transform the raw feature vectors are sometimes used prior to application of the pattern-matching algorithm. For example, feature extraction algorithms attempt to reduce a large-dimensionality feature vector into a smaller-dimensionality vector that is easier to work with and encodes less redundancy, using mathematical techniques such as principal components analysis(PCA). Feature selection algorithms, attempt to directly prune out redundant or irrelevant features.

The distinction between the two is that the resulting features after feature extraction has taken place are of a different sort than the original features and may not easily be interpretable, while the features left after feature selection are simply a subset of the original features.

Problem Statement (Supervised Version)

Formally, the problem of supervised pattern recognition can be stated as follows: Given an unknown function $g : X \rightarrow y$ the ground truth) that maps input instances $x \in x$ to output labels $y \in y$, along with training data $D = \{(x_1, y_1), \ldots, (x_n, y_n)\}$ assumed to represent accurate examples of the mapping, produce a function that approximates as closely as possible the correct mapping g. (For example, if the problem is filtering spam, then x_i is some representation of an email and y is either "spam" or "non-spam"). In order for this to be a well-defined problem, "approximates as closely as possible" needs to be defined rigorously. In decision theory, this is defined by specifying a loss function that assigns a specific value to "loss" resulting from producing an incorrect label.

The goal then is to minimize the expected loss, with the expectation taken over the probability distribution of . In practice, neither the distribution of nor the ground truth function are known exactly, but can be computed only empirically by collecting a large number of samples of and hand-labelling them using the correct value of (a time-consuming process, which is typically the limiting factor in the amount of data of this sort that can be collected). The particular loss function depends on the type of label being predicted.

For example, in the case of classification, the simple zero-one loss function is often sufficient. This corresponds simply to assigning a loss of 1 to any incorrect labelling and is equivalent to computing the accuracy of the classification procedure over the set of test data (i.e. counting up the fraction of instances that the learned function $h:\chi \rightarrow y$ labels correctly. The goal of the learning procedure is to maximize this test accuracy on a "typical" test set.

For a probabilistic pattern recognizer, the problem is instead to estimate the probability of each possible output label given a particular input instance, i.e. to estimate a function of the form

$$p(label \mid x,\theta) = f(x;\theta)$$

where the feature vector input is x , and the function f is typically parameterized by some parameters θ . In a discriminative approach to the problem, f is estimated directly. In a generative approach, however, the inverse probability $(px \mid label)$ is instead estimated and combined with the prior probability $p(label \mid \theta)$ using Bayes' rule, as follows:

$$p(label \mid x,\theta) = \frac{p(x \mid label)\,p(label \mid \theta)}{\sum_{L \in all\ labels} p(x \mid L)\,p(L \mid \theta)}.$$

When the labels are continuously distributed (e.g. in regression analysis), the denominator involves integration rather than summation:

$$p(label \mid x,\theta) = \frac{p(x \mid label)\,p(label \mid \theta)}{\int_{L \in all\ lables} p(x \mid L)\,p(L \setminus \theta)\,dL}.$$

The value of θ is typically learned using maximum a posteriori (MAP) estimation.

This finds the best value that simultaneously meets two conflicting objects: To perform as well as possible on the training data and to find the simplest possible model. Essentially, this combines maximum likelihood estimation with a regularization procedure that favours simpler models over more complex models. In a Bayesian context, the regularization procedure can be viewed as placing a prior probability $p(\theta)$ on different values of θ. Mathematically:

$$\theta^{*} = \arg\max p(\theta \mid D)$$

where θ^{*} is the value used for θ in the subsequent evaluation procedure, and $p(\theta \mid D)$,, the posterior probability of θ , is given by

$$p(\theta | D) = \left[\prod_{i=1}^{n} p(y_i | x_i, \theta) \right] p(\theta)$$

In the Bayesian approach to this problem, instead of choosing a single parameter vector θ^*, the probability of a given label for a new instance x is computed by integrating over all possible values of θ, weighted according to the posterior probability:

Uses

Within medical science, pattern recognition is the basis for computer-aided diagnosis (CAD) systems. CAD describes a procedure that supports the doctor's interpretations and findings.

Typical applications are automatic speech recognition, classification of text into several categories (e.g. spam/non-spam email messages), the automatic recognition of handwritten postal codes on postal envelopes, automatic recognition of images of human faces, or handwriting image extraction from medical forms. The last two examples form the subtopic image analysis of pattern recognition that deals with digital images as input to pattern recognition systems.

The method of signing one's name was captured with stylus and overlay starting 1990. The strokes, speed, relative min, relative max, acceleration and pressure is used to uniquely identify and confirm identity. Banks were first offered this technology, but were content to collect from the FDIC for any bank fraud and didn't want to inconvenience customers..

Algorithms

Algorithms for pattern recognition depend on the type of label output, on whether learning is supervised or unsupervised, and on whether the algorithm is statistical or non-statistical in nature. Statistical algorithms can further be categorized as generative or discriminative.

Classification Algorithms (Supervised Algorithms Predicting Categoricallabels)

- Maximum entropy classifier (aka logistic regression, multinomial logistic regression): Note that logistic regression is an algorithm for classification, despite its name. (The name comes from the fact that logistic regression uses an extension of a linear regression model to model the probability of an input being in a particular class.)

- Naive Bayes classifier
- Decision trees, decision lists
- Support vector machines
- Kernel estimation and K-nearest-neighbour algorithms
- Perceptrons
- Neural networks (multi-level perceptrons)

Clustering Algorithms (Unsupervised Algorithms Predicting Categoricallabels)

- Categorical mixture models
- K-means clustering
- Hierarchical clustering (agglomerative or divisive)
- Kernel principal component analysis (Kernel PCA).

Regression Algorithms (Predicting Real-valued Labels)

Supervised:

- Linear regression and extensions
- Neural networks
- Gaussian process regression (kriging)

Unsupervised:

- Principal components analysis (PCA)
- Independent component analysis (ICA).

Categorical Sequence Labelling Algorithms (Predicting Sequences of Categorical Labels)

Supervised:

- Hidden Markov models (HMMs)
- Maximum entropy Markov models (MEMMs)
- Conditional random fields (CRFs).

Unsupervised:

- Hidden Markov models (HMMs).

Real-valued sequence labelling algorithms (predicting sequences of real-valued labels)

Supervised (?):

- Kalman filters
- Particle filters.

Parsing Algorithms (Predicting Tree Structured Labels)

Supervised and unsupervised:

- Probabilistic context free grammars (PCFGs).

General Algorithms for Predicting Arbitrarily-Structured Labels

- Bayesian networks
- Markov random fields.

Ensemble learning algorithms (supervised meta-algorithms for combining multiple learning algorithms together)

- Bootstrap aggregating ("bagging")
- Boosting
- Ensemble averaging
- Mixture of experts, hierarchical mixture of experts.

Computer Data Processing

Computer data processing is any process that a computer program does to enter data and summarise, analyse or otherwise convert data into usable information. The process may be automated and run on a computer.

It involves recording, analysing, sorting, summarising, calculating, disseminating and storing data. Because data are most useful when well-presented and actually informative, data-processing systems are often referred to as information systems. Nevertheless, the terms are roughly synonymous, performing similar conversions; data-processing systems typically manipulate raw data into information, and likewise information systems typically take raw data as input to produce information as output.

Data processing may or may not be distinguished from data conversion, when the process is merely to convert data to another format, and does not involve any data manipulation.

Data Analysis

Data Analysis is the domain from which the data are harvested is a science or an engineering field. Data processing and information systems are considered terms that are too broad and the more specialized term data analysis is typically used. This is a focus on the highly-specialized and highly-accurate algorithmic derivations and statistical calculations that are less often observed in the typical general business environment.

In these contexts data analysis packages like DAP, gretl or PSPP are often used. This divergence of culture is exhibited in the typical numerical representations used in data processing versus numerical; data processing's measurements are typically represented by integersor by fixed-point or binary-coded decimal representations of numbers whereas the majority of data analysis's measurements are often represented by floating-point representation of rational numbers.

Processing

Basically, data are nothing but facts (organized or unorganized) which can be converted into other forms to make it useful, clear and pratically used. This process of converting facts to information is Processing. Practically all naturally occurring processes can be viewed as examples of data processing systems where "observable" information in the form of pressure, light, etc. are converted by human observers into electrical signals in the nervous system as the senses we recognize as touch, sound, and vision. Even the interaction of non-living systems may be viewed in this way as rudimentary information processing systems.

Conventional usage of the terms data processing and information systems restricts their use to refer to the algorithmic derivations, logical deductions, and statistical calculations that recur perennially in general business environments, rather than in the more expansive sense of all conversions of real-world measurements into real-world information in, say, an organic biological system or even a scientific or engineering system.

Elements of Data Processing

In order to be processed by a computer, data needs first be converted into a machine readable format. Once data are in digital format, various procedures can be applied on the data to get useful information. Data processing may involve various processes, including:

- Data summarization
- Data aggregation

- Data validation
- Data tabulation
- Statistical analysis.

Blind Signal Separation

Blind signal separation, also known as blind source separation, is the separation of a set of signals from a set of mixed signals, without the aid of information (or with very little information) about the source signals or the mixing process.

Blind signal separation relies on the assumption that the source signals do not correlate with each other. For example, the signals may be mutually statistically independent or decorrelated. Blind signal separation thus separates a set of signals into a set of other signals, such that the regularity of each resulting signal is maximized, and the regularity between the signals is minimized (i.e. statistical independence is maximized).

Because temporal redundancies (statistical regularities in the time domain) are "clumped" in this way into the resulting signals, the resulting signals can be more effectively deconvolved than the original signals.

There are different methods of blind signal separation:

- Principal components analysis
- Singular value decomposition
- Independent component analysis
- Dependent component analysis
- Non-negative matrix factorization
- Low-Complexity Coding and Decoding
- Stationary Subspace Analysis.

Data Mining

Data mining (the analysis step of the knowledge discovery in databases process, or KDD), a relatively young and interdisciplinary field of computer science is the process of discovering new patterns from large data sets involving methods at the intersection of artificial intelligence, machine learning, statistics and database systems. The goal of data mining is to extract knowledge from a data set in a human-understandable structure and involves database and data management, data preprocessing, model and inference considerations, interestingness metrics, complexity considerations, post-processing of found structure, visualization and online updating.

The term is a buzzword, and is frequently misused to mean any form of large scale data or information processing (collection, extraction, warehousing, analysis and statistics) but also generalised to any kind of computer decision support system including artificial intelligence, machine learning and business intelligence. In the proper use of the word, the key term is discovery, commonly defined as "detecting something new". Even the popular book "Data mining: Practical machine learning tools and techniques with Java" (which covers mostly machine learning material) was originally to be named just "Practical machine learning", and the term "data mining" was only added for marketing reasons. Often the more general terms "(large scale) data analysis" or "analytics" or when referring to actual methods, artificial intelligence and machine learning are more appropriate.

The actual data-mining task is the automatic or semi-automatic analysis of large quantities of data to extract previously unknown interesting patterns such as groups of data records (cluster analysis), unusual records (anomaly detection) and dependencies (association rule mining). This usually involves using database techniques such as spatial indexes. These patterns can then be seen as a kind of summary of the input data, and used in further analysis or for example in machine learning and predictive analytics. For example, the data mining step might identify multiple groups in the data, which can then be used to obtain more accurate prediction results by a decision support system. Neither the data collection, data preparation nor result interpretation and reporting are part of the data mining step, but do belong to the overall KDD process as additional steps.

The related terms data dredging, data fishing and data snooping refer to the use of data mining methods to sample parts of a larger population data set that are (or may be) too small for reliable statistical inferences to be made about the validity of any patterns discovered. These methods can, however, be used in creating new hypotheses to test against the larger data populations.

Background

The manual extraction of patterns from data has occurred for centuries. Early methods of identifying patterns in data include Bayes' theorem (1700s) and regression analysis (1800s). The proliferation, ubiquity and increasing power of computer technology has increased data collection, storage and manipulations. As data sets have grown in size and complexity, direct hands-on data analysis has increasingly been augmented with indirect, automatic data processing. This has been aided by other discoveries in computer science, such as neural networks, cluster analysis, genetic algorithms (1950s), decision trees (1960s) and support vector machines (1990s). Data mining is the process of applying these methods to data with the intention of uncovering hidden patterns in large data sets. It bridges the gap from applied statistics and artificial intelligence (which usually provide the mathematical background) to database management by exploiting the way data is stored and indexed in databases to execute the actual learning and discovery algorithms more efficiently, allowing such methods to be applied to larger data sets.

Research and Evolution

The premier professional body in the field is the Association for Computing Machinery's Special Interest Group on knowledge discovery and Data Mining (SIGKDD). Since 1989 they have hosted an annual international conference and published its proceedings, and since 1999 have published a biannual academic journal titled "SIGKDD Explorations".

Computer science conferences on data mining include:

- CIKM – ACM Conference on Information and Knowledge Management
- DMIN – International Conference on Data Mining
- DMKD – Research Issues on Data Mining and Knowledge Discovery
- ECDM – European Conference on Data Mining
- ECML-PKDD – European Conference on Machine Learning and Principles and Practice of Knowledge Discovery in Databases
- EDM – International Conference on Educational Data Mining
- ICDM – IEEE International Conference on Data Mining
- KDD – ACM SIGKDD Conference on Knowledge Discovery and Data Mining

- MLDM – Machine Learning and Data Mining in Pattern Recognition
- PAKDD – The annual Pacific-Asia Conference on Knowledge Discovery and Data Mining
- PAW – Predictive Analytics World
- SDM – SIAM International Conference on Data Mining (SIAM)
- SSTD – Symposium on Spatial and Temporal Databases

Data mining topics are present on most data management/database conferences.

Process

The knowledge discovery in databases (KDD) process is commonly defined with the stages (1) Selection (2) Preprocessing (3) Transformation (4) Data Mining (5) Interpretation/Evaluation.

It exists however in many variations of this theme such as the CRoss Industry Standard Process for Data Mining (CRISP-DM) which defines six phases: (1) Business Understanding, (2) Data Understanding, (3) Data Preparation, (4) Modelling, (5) Evaluation, and (6) Deployment or a simplified process such as (1) Pre-processing, (2) Data mining, and (3) Results validation.

Pre-processing

Before data mining algorithms can be used, a target data set must be assembled.

As data mining can only uncover patterns actually present in the data, the target dataset must be large enough to contain these patterns while remaining concise enough to be mined in an acceptable timeframe. A common source for data is a data mart or data warehouse. Pre-process is essential to analyse the multivariate datasets before data mining.

The target set is then cleaned. Data cleaning removes the observations with noise and missing data.

Data Mining

Data mining involves six common classes of tasks:

- Anomaly detection (Outlier/change/deviation detection) – The identification of unusual data records, that might be interesting or data errors and require further investigation.

- Association rule learning (Dependency modelling) – Searches for relationships between variables. For example a supermarket might gather data on customer purchasing habits. Using association rule learning, the supermarket can determine which products are frequently bought together and use this information for marketing purposes. This is sometimes referred to as market basket analysis.
- Clustering – is the task of discovering groups and structures in the data that are in some way or another "similar", without using known structures in the data.
- Classification – is the task of generalising known structure to apply to new data. For example, an email program might attempt to classify an email as legitimate or spam.
- Regression – Attempts to find a function which models the data with the least error.
- Summarization – providing a more compact representation of the data set, including visualization and report generation.

Results Validation

The final step of knowledge discovery from data is to verify the patterns produced by the data mining algorithms occur in the wider data set. Not all patterns found by the data mining algorithms are necessarily valid. It is common for the data mining algorithms to find patterns in the training set which are not present in the general data set. This is called overfitting. To overcome this, the evaluation uses a test set of data on which the data mining algorithm was not trained. The learned patterns are applied to this test set and the resulting output is compared to the desired output. For example, a data mining algorithm trying to distinguish spam from legitimate emails would be trained on a training set of sample emails. Once trained, the learned patterns would be applied to the test set of emails on which it had not been trained. The accuracy of these patterns can then be measured from how many emails they correctly classify. A number of statistical methods may be used to evaluate the algorithm such as ROC curves. If the learned patterns do not meet the desired standards, then it is necessary to re-evaluate and change the pre-processing and data mining. If the learned patterns do meet the desired standards then the final step is to interpret the learned patterns and turn them into knowledge.

Standards

There have been some efforts to define standards for the data mining process, for example the 1999 European Cross Industry Standard Process for Data Mining (CRISP-DM 1.0) and the 2004 Java Data Mining standard (JDM 1.0). Development on successors of these processes (CRISP-DM 2.0 and JDM 2.0) was active in 2006, but has stalled since. JDM 2.0 was withdrawn without reaching a final draft.

For exchanging the extracted models – in particular for the use in predictive analytics – the key standard is the Predictive Model Markup Language (PMML), which is an XML-based language developed by the Data Mining Group (DMG) and supported as exchange format by many data mining applications. As the name suggests it only covers prediction models, a particular data mining task of high importance to business applications, however extensions to for example cover subspace clustering have been proposed independently of the DMG.

Notable Uses

Games

Since the early 1960s, with the availability of oracles for certain combinatorial games, also called tablebases (e.g. for 3x3-chess) with any beginning configuration, small-board dots-and-boxes, small-board-hex, and certain endgames in chess, dots-and-boxes, and hex; a new area for data mining has been opened. This is the extraction of human-usable strategies from these oracles. Current pattern recognition approaches do not seem to fully acquire the high level of abstraction required to be applied successfully. Instead, extensive experimentation with the tablebases, combined with an intensive study of tablebase-answers to well designed problems and with knowledge of prior art, i.e. pre-tablebase knowledge, is used to yield insightful patterns. Berlekamp in dots-and-boxes etc. and John Nunn in chess endgames are notable examples of researchers doing this work, though they were not and are not involved in tablebase generation.

Business

Data mining in customer relationship management applications can contribute significantly to the bottom line. Rather than randomly contacting a prospect or customer through a call centre or sending mail, a company can concentrate its efforts on prospects that are predicted to have a high likelihood of responding to an offer. More sophisticated methods may be used to optimise resources across campaigns so that one may predict to which channel and to which offer an individual is most likely to respond—across all potential offers. Additionally, sophisticated applications could be used to automate the mailing. Once the results from data mining (potential prospect/customer and channel/offer) are determined, this "sophisticated application" can either automatically send an e-mail or regular mail. Finally, in cases where many people will take an action without an offer, uplift modelling can be used to determine which people will have the greatest increase in responding if given an offer. Data clustering can also be used to automatically discover the segments or groups within a customer data set.

Businesses employing data mining may see a return on investment, but also they recognize that the number of predictive models can quickly become very large. Rather than one model to predict how many customers will churn, a business could build a separate model for each region and customer type. Then instead of sending an offer to all people that are likely to churn, it may only want to send offers to loyal customers. Finally, it may want to determine which customers are going to be profitable over a window of time and only send the offers to those that are likely to be profitable. In order to maintain this quantity of models, they need to manage model versions and move to automated data mining.

Data mining can also be helpful to human-resources departments in identifying the characteristics of their most successful employees. Information obtained, such as universities attended by highly successful employees, can help HR focus recruiting efforts accordingly. Additionally, Strategic Enterprise Management applications help a company translate corporate-level goals, such as profit and margin share targets, into operational decisions, such as production plans and workforce levels.

Another example of data mining, often called the market basket analysis, relates to its use in retail sales. If a clothing store records the purchases of customers, a data-mining system could identify those customers who favour silk shirts over cotton ones. Although some explanations of relationships may be difficult, taking advantage of it is easier. The example deals with association rules within transaction-based data. Not all data are transaction based and logical or inexact rules may also be present within a database.

Market basket analysis has also been used to identify the purchase patterns of the Alpha consumer. Alpha Consumers are people that play a key role in connecting with the concept behind a product, then adopting that product, and finally validating it for the rest of society. Analysing the data collected on this type of user has allowed companies to predict future buying trends and forecast supply demands.

Data Mining is a highly effective tool in the catalogue marketing industry. Catalogers have a rich history of customer transactions on millions of customers dating back several years. Data mining tools can identify patterns among customers and help identify the most likely customers to respond to upcoming mailing campaigns.

Data Mining for business applications is a component which needs to be integrated into a complex modelling and decision making process. Reactive Business Intelligence (RBI) advocates a holistic approach that integrates data mining, modelling and interactive visualization, into an end-to-end discovery and continuous innovation process powered by human and automated learning. In the area of decision making the RBI approach has been used to mine the knowledge which is progressively acquired from the decision maker and self-tune the decision method accordingly.

Related to an integrated-circuit production line, an example of data mining is described in the paper "Mining IC Test Data to Optimise VLSI Testing." In this paper the application of data mining and decision analysis to the problem of die-level functional test is described. Experiments mentioned in this paper demonstrate the ability of applying a system of mining historical die-test data to create a probabilistic model of patterns of die failure. These patterns are then utilized to decide in real time which die to test next and when to stop testing. This system has been shown, based on experiments with historical test data, to have the potential to improve profits on mature IC products.

Science and Engineering

In recent years, data mining has been used widely in the areas of science and engineering, such as bioinformatics, genetics, medicine, education and electrical power engineering.

In the study of human genetics, an important goal is to understand the mapping relationship between the inter-individual variation in human DNA sequences and variability in disease susceptibility. In lay terms, it is to find out how the changes in an individual's DNA sequence affect the risk of developing common diseases such as cancer. This is very important to help improve the diagnosis, prevention and treatment of the diseases. The data mining method that is used to perform this task is known as multifactor dimensionality reduction.

In the area of electrical power engineering, data mining methods have been widely used for condition monitoring of high voltage electrical equipment. The purpose of condition monitoring is to obtain valuable information on the insulation's health status of the equipment. Data clustering such as self-organizing map (SOM) has been applied on the vibration monitoring and analysis of transformer on-load tap-changers (OLTCS).

Using vibration monitoring, it can be observed that each tap change operation generates a signal that contains information about the condition of the tap changer contacts and the drive mechanisms. Obviously, different tap positions will generate different signals. However, there was considerable variability amongst normal condition signals for exactly the same tap position. SOM has been applied to detect abnormal conditions and to estimate the nature of the abnormalities.

Data mining methods have also been applied for dissolved gas analysis (DGA) on power transformers. DGA, as a diagnostics for power transformer, has been available for many years. Methods such as SOM has been applied to analyse data and to determine trends which are not obvious to the standard DGA ratio methods such as Duval Triangle.

A fourth area of application for data mining in science/engineering is within educational research, where data mining has been used to study the factors leading students to choose to engage in behaviours which reduce their learning and to understand the factors influencing university student retention.

A similar example of the social application of data mining is its use in expertise finding systems, whereby descriptors of human expertise are extracted, normalized and classified so as to facilitate the finding of experts, particularly in scientific and technical fields.

In this way, data mining can facilitate Institutional memory. Other examples of applying data mining method applications are biomedical data facilitated by domain on tologies, mining clinical trial data, traffic analysis using SOM, et cetera. In adverse drug reaction surveillance, the Uppsala Monitoring Centre has, since 1998, used data mining methods to routinely screen for reporting patterns indicative of emerging drug safety issues in the WHO global database of 4.6 million suspected adverse drug reaction incidents. Recently, similar methodology has been developed to mine large collections of electronic health records for temporal patterns associating drug prescriptions to medical diagnoses.

Spatial Data Mining

Spatial data mining is the application of data mining methods to spatial data. Spatial data mining follows along the same functions in data mining, with the end objective to find patterns in geography. So far, data mining and Geographic Information Systems (GIS) have existed as two separate technologies, each with its own methods, traditions and approaches to visualization and data analysis. Particularly, most contemporary GIS have only very basic spatial analysis functionality.

The immense explosion in geographically referenced data occasioned by developments in IT, digital mapping, remote sensing, and the global diffusion of GIS emphasizes the importance of developing data driven inductive approaches to geographical analysis and modelling.

Data mining, which is the partially automated search for hidden patterns in large databases, offers great potential benefits for applied GIS-based decision-making. Recently, the task of integrating these two technologies has become critical, especially as various public and private sector organizations possessing huge databases with thematic and geographically referenced data begin to realize the huge potential of the information hidden there. Among those organizations are:

- offices requiring analysis or dissemination of geo-referenced statistical data
- public health services searching for explanations of disease clusters
- environmental agencies assessing the impact of changing land-use patterns on climate change

- geo-marketing companies doing customer segmentation based on spatial location.

Challenges

Geospatial data repositories tend to be very large. Moreover, existing GIS datasets are often splintered into feature and attribute components, that are conventionally archived in hybrid data management systems. Algorithmic requirements differ substantially for relational (attribute) data management and for topological (feature) data management. Related to this is the range and diversity of geographic data formats, that also presents unique challenges. The digital geographic data revolution is creating new types of data formats beyond the traditional "vector" and "raster" formats. Geographic data repositories increasingly include ill-structured data such as imagery and geo-referenced multimedia.

There are several critical research challenges in geographic knowledge discovery and data mining. Miller and Han offer the following list of emerging research topics in the field:

- Developing and supporting geographic data warehouses – Spatial properties are often reduced to simple a spatial attributes in mainstream data warehouses. Creating an integrated GDW requires solving issues in spatial and temporal data interoperability, including differences in semantics, referencing systems, geometry, accuracy and position.
- Better spatio-temporal representations in geographic knowledge discovery – Current geographic knowledge discovery (GKD) methods generally use very simple representations of geographic objects and spatial relationships. Geographic data mining methods should recognize more complex geographic objects (lines and polygons) and relationships (non-Euclidean distances, direction, connectivity and interaction through attributed geographic space such as terrain). Time needs to be more fully integrated into these geographic representations and relationships.
- Geographic knowledge discovery using diverse data types – GKD methods should be developed that can handle diverse data types beyond the traditional raster and vector models, including imagery and geo-referenced multimedia, as well as dynamic data types (video streams, animation).

In four annual surveys of data miners, data mining practitioners consistently identified that they faced three key challenges more than any others:

- Dirty Data
- Explaining Data Mining to Others
- Unavailability of Data/Difficult Access to Data.

In the 2010 survey data miners also shared their experiences in overcoming these challenges.

Visual Data Mining

The process of turning from analogical into digital, large data sets have been generated, collected and stored discovering statistical patterns, trends and information which is hidden in data, in order to build predictive patterns. A study found that Visual Data Mining is faster and much more intuitive than traditional data mining.

Surveillance

Prior data mining to stop terrorist programs under the U.S. government include the Total Information Awareness (TIA) program, Secure Flight (formerly known as Computer-Assisted Passenger Prescreening System (CAPPS II)), Analysis, Dissemination, Visualization, Insight, Semantic Enhancement (ADVISE), and the Multi-state Anti-Terrorism Information Exchange (MATRIX). These programs have been discontinued due to controversy over whether they violate the US Constitution's 4th amendment, although many programs that were formed under them continue to be funded by different organizations, or under different names.

Two plausible data mining methods in the context of combating terrorism include "pattern mining" and "subject-based data mining".

Pattern Mining

"Pattern mining" is a data mining method that involves finding existing patterns in data. In this context patterns often means association rules. The original motivation for searching association rules came from the desire to analyse supermarket transaction data, that is, to examine customer behaviour in terms of the purchased products. For example, an association rule "beer Ò! potato chips (80%)" states that four out of five customers that bought beer also bought potato chips.

In the context of pattern mining as a tool to identify terrorist activity, the National Research Council provides the following definition: "Pattern-based data mining looks for patterns (including anomalous data patterns) that might be associated with terrorist activity — these patterns might be regarded as small signals in a large ocean of noise."

Pattern Mining includes new areas such a Music Information Retrieval (MIR) where patterns seen both in the temporal and non temporal domains are imported to classical knowledge discovery search methods.

Subject-based Data Mining

"Subject-based data mining" is a data mining method involving the search for associations between individuals in data. In the context of combating terrorism, the National Research Council provides the following definition: "Subject-based data mining uses an initiating individual or other datum that is considered, based on other information, to be of high interest, and the goal is to determine what other persons or financial transactions or movements, etc., are related to that initiating datum."

Knowledge Grid

Researchers at the University of Calabria developed a Knowledge Grid architecture for distributed knowledge discovery, based on grid computing.

Privacy Concerns and Ethics

Some people believe that data mining itself is ethically neutral. It is important to note that the term data mining has no ethical implications. The term is often associated with the mining of information in relation to peoples' behaviour.

However, data mining is a statistical method that is applied to a set of information, or a data set. Associating these data sets with people is an extreme narrowing of the types of data that are available in today's technological society.

Examples could range from a set of crash test data for passenger vehicles, to the performance of a group of stocks. These types of data sets make up a great proportion of the information available to be acted on by data mining methods, and rarely have ethical concerns associated with them. However, the ways in which data mining can be used can raise questions regarding privacy, legality, and ethics. In particular, data mining government or commercial data sets for national security or law enforcement purposes, such as in the Total Information Awareness Program or in ADVISE, has raised privacy concerns.

Data mining requires data preparation which can uncover information or patterns which may compromise confidentiality and privacy obligations. A common way for this to occur is through data aggregation.

Data aggregation is when the data are accrued, possibly from various sources, and put together so that they can be analysed. This is not data mining per se, but a result of the preparation of data before and for the purposes of the analysis. The threat to an individual's privacy comes into play when the data, once compiled, cause the data miner, or anyone who has access to the newly compiled data set, to be able to identify specific individuals, especially when originally the data were anonymous.

It is recommended that an individual is made aware of the following before data are collected:

- the purpose of the data collection and any data mining projects,
- how the data will be used,
- who will be able to mine the data and use them,
- the security surrounding access to the data, and in addition,
- how collected data can be updated.

In the United States, privacy concerns have been somewhat addressed by their congress via the passage of regulatory controls such as the Health Insurance Portability and Accountability Act (HIPAA). The HIPAA requires individuals to be given "informed consent" regarding any information that they provide and its intended future uses by the facility receiving that information. According to an article in Biotech Business Week, "In practice, HIPAA may not offer any greater protection than the longstanding regulations in the research arena, says the AAHC. More importantly, the rule's goal of protection through informed consent is undermined by the complexity of consent forms that are required of patients and participants, which approach a level of incomprehensibility to average individuals." This underscores the necessity for data anonymity in data aggregation practices.

One may additionally modify the data so that they are anonymous, so that individuals may not be readily identified. However, even de-identified data sets can contain enough information to identify individuals, as occurred when journalists were able to find several individuals based on a set of search histories that were inadvertently released by AOL.

Software

Free libre open-source data-mining software and applications

1. Carrot2 – Text and search results clustering framework.
2. Chemicalize.org – A chemical structure miner and web search engine.
3. ELKI – A university research project with advanced cluster analysis and outlier detection methods written in the Java language.
4. GATE – Natural language processing and language engineering tool.
5. JHepWork – Java cross-platform data analysis framework developed at ANL.
6. KNIME – The Konstanz Information Miner, a user friendly and comprehensive data analytics framework.
7. NLTK or Natural Language Toolkit – A suite of libraries and programs for symbolic and statistical natural language processing (NLP) for the Python language.
8. Orange – A component-based data mining and machine learning software suite written in the Python language.
9. R – A programming language and software environment for statistical computing, data mining and graphics. It is part of the GNU project.
10. RapidMiner – An environment for machine learning and data mining experiments.
11. UIMA – The UIMA (Unstructured Information Management Architecture) is a component framework for analysing unstructured content such as text, audio and video, originally developed by IBM.
12. Weka – A suite of machine learning software written in the Java language.

In 2010, the open source R language overtook other tools to become the tool used by more data miners (43%) than any other.

Commercial Data-Mining Software and Applications

- Microsoft Analysis Services data mining software provided by Microsoft
- SAS Enterprise Miner – data mining software provided by the SAS Institute.
- SPSS Modeler – data mining software provided by IBM SPSS.
- STATISTICA Data Miner – data mining software provided by StatSoft.

According to Rexer's Annual Data Miner Survey in 2010, IBM SPSS Modeler, STATISTICA Data Miner and R received the strongest satisfaction ratings.

Marketplace Surveys

Several researchers and organizations have conducted reviews of data mining tools and surveys of data miners. These identify some of the strengths and weaknesses of the software packages. They also provide an overview of the behaviours, preferences and views of data miners. Some of these reports include:

- Annual Rexer Analytics Data Miner Surveys.
- Forrester Research 2010 Predictive Analytics and Data Mining Solutions report.
- Gartner 2008 "Magic Quadrant" report.
- Haughton et al.'s 2003 Review of Data Mining Software Packages in The American Statistician.
- Robert A. Nisbet's 2006 Three Part Series of articles "Data Mining Tools: Which One is Best For CRM?"
- 2011 Wiley Interdisciplinary Reviews: Data Mining and Knowledge Discovery.

Email Spam

Email spam, also known as junk email or unsolicited bulk email (UBE), is a subset of spam that involves nearly identical messages sent to numerous recipients by email. Definitions of spam usually include the aspects that email is unsolicited and sent in bulk. One subset of UBE is UCE (unsolicited commercial email). The opposite of "spam", email which one wants, is called "ham", usually when referring to a message's automated analysis (such as Bayesian filtering).

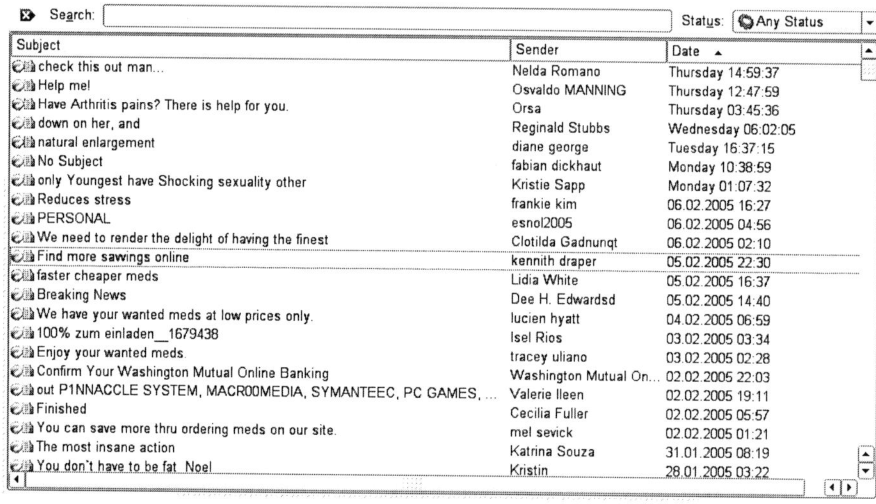

Figure: An email box folder filled with spam messages.

Email spam has steadily grown since the early 1990s. Botnets, networks of virus-infected computers, are used to send about 80% of spam. Since the expense of the spam is borne mostly by the recipient, it is effectively postage due advertising.

The legal status of spam varies from one jurisdiction to another. In the United States, spam was declared to be legal by the CAN-SPAM Act of 2003 provided the message adheres to certain specifications. ISPs have attempted to recover the cost of spam through lawsuits against spammers, although they have been mostly unsuccessful in collecting damages despite winning in court.

Spammers collect email addresses from chatrooms, customer lists, newsgroups, and viruses which harvest users' address books, and are sold to other spammers. They also use a practice known as "email appending" or "epending" in which they use known information about their target (such as a postal address) to search for the target's email address. Much of spam is sent to invalid email addresses. Spam averages 78% of all email sent. According to the Message Anti-Abuse Working Group, the amount of spam email was between 88–92% of email messages sent in the first half of 2010.

From the beginning of the Internet (the ARPANET), sending of junk email has been prohibited, enforced by the Terms of Service/

Acceptable Use Policy (ToS/AUP) of internet service providers (ISPs) and peer pressure. Even with a thousand users junk email for advertising is not tenable, and with a million users it is not only impractical, but also expensive. It is estimated that spam cost businesses on the order of $100 billion in 2007. As the scale of the spam problem has grown, ISPs and the public have turned to government for relief from spam, which has failed to materialize.

Types

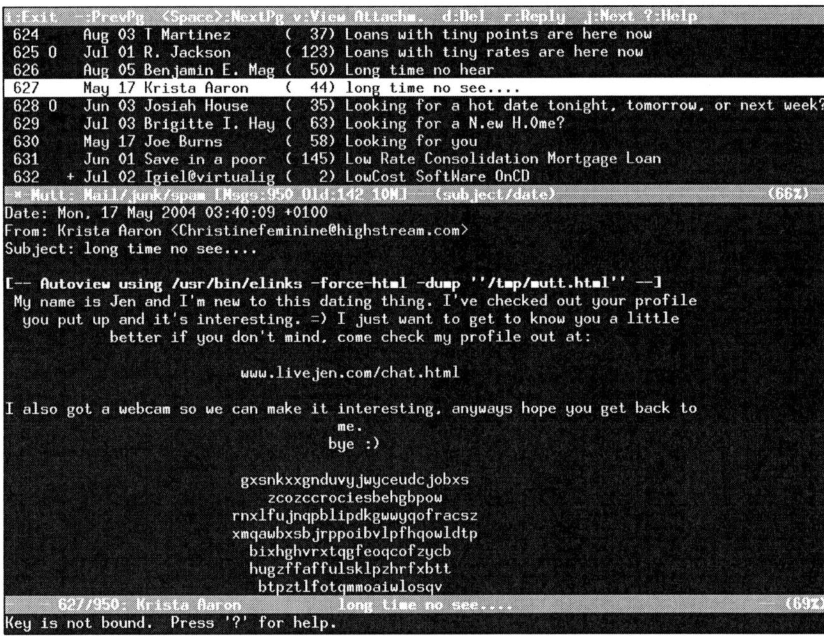

Mutt in Action

Spam has several definitions varying by source.

- Unsolicited bulk email (UBE)—unsolicited email, sent in large quantities.
- Unsolicited commercial email (UCE)—this more restrictive definition is used by regulators whose mandate is to regulate commerce, such as the U.S. Federal Trade Commission.

Spamvertised Sites

According to a Commtouch report in the first quarter of 2010, there are "...183 billion spam messages" sent every day. The most popular spam topic is "pharmacy ads" which make up 81% of email spam messages.

Most Common Products Advertised

According to information compiled by Commtouch Software Ltd., email spam for the first quarter of 2010 can be broken down as follows.

EMail Spam by Topic	
Pharmacy	81%
Replica	5.40%
Enhancers	2.30%
Phishing	2.30%
Degrees	1.30%
Casino	1%
Weight Loss	0.40%
Other	m30%

419 Scams

Advance fee fraud spam such as the Nigerian "419" scam may be sent by a single individual from a cyber cafe in a developing country. Organized "spam gangs" operating from Russia or eastern Europeshare many features in common with other forms of organized crime, including turf battles and revenge killings.

Phishing

Spam is also a medium for fraudsters to scam users into entering personal information on fake Web sites using emails forged to look like they are from banks or other organizations, such as PayPal. This is known as phishing. Targeted phishing, where known information about the recipient is used to created forged emails, is known as spear-phishing.

Spam Techniques

Appending

If a marketer has one database containing names, addresses, and telephone numbers of prospective customers, they can pay to have their database matched against an external database containing email addresses.

The company then has the means to send email to persons who have not requested email, which may include persons who have deliberately withheld their email address.

Image Spam

Image spam is an obfuscating method in which the text of the message is stored as a GIF or JPEGimage and displayed in the email. This prevents text based spam filters from detecting and blocking spam messages. Image spam was reportedly used in the mid 2000s to advertise "pump and dump" stocks.

Often, image spam contains nonsensical, computer-generated text which simply annoys the reader. However, new technology in some programs try to read the images by attempting to find text in these images. They are not very accurate, and sometimes filter out innocent images of products like a box that has words on it.

A newer technique, however, is to use an animated GIF image that does not contain clear text in its initial frame, or to contort the shapes of letters in the image (as in CAPTCHA) to avoid detection by OCR tools.

Blank Spam

Blank spam is spam lacking a payload advertisement. Often the message body is missing altogether, as well as the subject line. Still, it fits the definition of spam because of its nature as bulk and unsolicited email. Blank spam may be originated in different ways, either intentional or unintentionally:

1. Blank spam can have been sent in a directory harvest attack, a form of dictionary attack for gathering valid addresses from an email service provider. Since the goal in such an attack is to use the bounces to separate invalid addresses from the valid ones, spammers may dispense with most elements of the header and the entire message body, and still accomplish their goals.
2. Blank spam may also occur when a spammer forgets or otherwise fails to add the payload when he or she sets up the spam run.
3. Often blank spam headers appear truncated, suggesting that computer glitches may have contributed to this problem—from poorly-written spam software to malfunctioning relay servers, or any problems that may truncate header lines from the message body.
4. Some spam may appear to be blank when in fact it is not. An example of this is the VBS. Davinia.B email worm which

propagates through messages that have no subject line and appears blank, when in fact it uses HTML code to download other files.

Backscatter Spam

Backscatter is a side-effect of email spam, viruses and worms, where email servers receiving spam and other mail send bounce messages to an innocent party. This occurs because the original message's envelope sender is forged to contain the email address of the victim. A very large proportion of such email is sent with a forged From: header, matching the envelope sender.

Since these messages were not solicited by the recipients, are substantially similar to each other, and are delivered in bulk quantities, they qualify as unsolicited bulk email or spam. As such, systems that generate email backscatter can end up being listed on various DNSBLs and be in violation of internet service providers' Terms of Service.

Legality

Sending spam violates the Acceptable use policy (AUP) of almost all Internet service providers. Providers vary in their willingness or ability to enforce their AUP. Some actively enforce their terms and terminate spammers' accounts without warning. Some ISPs lack adequate personnel or technical skills for enforcement, while others may be reluctant to enforce restrictive terms against profitable customers.

As the recipient directly bears the cost of delivery, storage, and processing, one could regard spam as the electronic equivalent of "postage-due" junk mail. Due to the low cost of sending unsolicited email and the potential profit entailed, some believe that only strict legal enforcement can stop junk email. The Coalition Against Unsolicited Commercial Email (CAUCE) argues "Today, much of the spam volume is sent by career criminals and malicious hackers who won't stop until they're all rounded up and put in jail."

European Union

All the countries of the European Union have passed laws that specifically target spam.

Article 13 of the European Union Directive on Privacy and Electronic Communications (2002/58/EC) provides that the EU member states shall take appropriate measures to ensure that unsolicited communications for the purposes of direct marketing are not allowed either without the consent of the subscribers concerned or in respect of subscribers who do not wish to receive these communications, the choice between these options to be determined by national legislation.

In the United Kingdom, for example, unsolicited emails cannot be sent to an individual subscriber unless prior permission has been obtained or unless there is a previous relationship between the parties. The regulations can be enforced against an offending company or individual anywhere in the European Union. The Information Commissioner's Office has responsibility for the enforcement of unsolicited emails and considers complaints about breaches. A breach of an enforcement notice is a criminal offence subject to a fine of up to £5000.

Canada

The Government of Canada has passed anti-spam legislation called the Fighting Internet and Wireless Spam Act to fight spam.

Australia

In Australia, the relevant legislation is the Spam Act 2003 which covers some types of email and phone spam, which took effect on 11 April 2004. The Spam Act provides that "Unsolicited commercial electronic messages must not be sent." Whether an email is unsolicited depends on whether you have consent. Consent can be express or inferred. Express consent is when someone directly instructs you to send them emails, e.g. if they opt-in. Consent can also be inferred from the business relationship between the sender and recipient or if the recipient conspicuously publishes their email address in a public place. Penalties are up to 10,000 penalty units, or 2,000 penalty units for a person other than a body corporate.

United States

In the United States, most states enacted anti-spam laws during the late 1990s and early 2000s. Many of these have since been pre-empted by the less restrictive CAN-SPAM Act of 2003.

Spam is legally permissible according to the CAN-SPAM Act of 2003 provided it follows certain criteria: a "truthful" subject line, no forged information in the technical headers or sender address, and other minor requirements. If the spam fails to comply with any of these requirements it is illegal. Aggravated or accelerated penalties apply if the spammer harvested the email addresses using methods described earlier.

A review of the effectiveness of CAN-SPAM in 2005 by the Federal Trade Commission (the agency charged with CAN-SPAM enforcement) stated that the amount of sexually explicit spam had significantly decreased since 2003 and the total volume had begun to level off. Senator Conrad Burns, a principal sponsor, noted that "Enforcement is key regarding the CAN-SPAM legislation." In 2004, less than 1% of spam complied with the CAN-SPAM Act of 2003. In contrast to the FTC evaluation, many observers view the CAN-SPAM act as having failed in its purpose of reducing spam.

Other Laws

Accessing privately owned computer resources without the owner's permission counts as illegal undercomputer crime statutes in most nations. Deliberate spreading of computer viruses is also illegal in the United States and elsewhere. Thus, some common behaviours of spammers are criminal regardless of the legality of spamming per se. Even before the advent of laws specifically banning or regulating spamming, spammers were successfully prosecuted under computer fraud and abuse laws for wrongfully using others' computers.

The use of botnets can be perceived as theft. The spammer consumes a zombie owner's bandwidth and resources without any cost. In addition, spam is perceived as theft of services. The receiving SMTP servers consume significant amounts of system resources dealing with this unwanted traffic. As a result, service providers have to spend large amounts of money to make their systems capable of handling these amounts of email. Such costs are inevitably passed on to the service providers' customers.

Other laws, not only those related to spam, have been used to prosecute alleged spammers. For example, Alan Ralsky was indicted on stock fraud charges in January 2008, and Robert Solowayplead guilty to charges of mail fraud, fraud in connection with email, and failing to file a tax return in March 2008.

Deception and Fraud

Spammers may engage in deliberate fraud to send out their messages. Spammers often use false names, addresses, phone numbers, and other contact information to set up "disposable" accounts at various Internet service providers. They also often use falsified or stolen credit card numbers to pay for these accounts. This allows them to move quickly from one account to the next as the host ISPs discover and shut down each one.

Senders may go to great lengths to conceal the origin of their messages. Large companies may hire another firm to send their messages so that complaints or blocking of email falls on a third party. Others engage in spoofing of email addresses (much easier than IP address spoofing). The email protocol (SMTP) has no authentication by default, so the spammer can pretend to originate a message apparently from any email address. To prevent this, some ISPs and domains require the use of SMTP-AUTH, allowing positive identification of the specific account from which an email originates.

Senders cannot completely spoof email delivery chains (the 'Received' header), since the receiving mailserver records the actual connection from the last mailserver's IP address. To counter this, some spammers forge additional delivery headers to make it appear as if the email had previously traversed many legitimate servers.

Spoofing can have serious consequences for legitimate email users. Not only can their email in boxes get clogged up with "undeliverable" emails in addition to volumes of spam, they can mistakenly be identified as a spammer. Not only may they receive irate email from spam victims, but (if spam victims report the email address owner to the ISP, for example) a naive ISP may terminate their service for spamming.

Theft of Service

Spammers frequently seek out and make use of vulnerable third-party systems such as open mail relays and open proxy servers. SMTP forwards mail from one server to another—mail servers that ISPs run commonly require some form of authentication to ensure that the user is a customer of that ISP. Open relays, however, do not properly check who is using the mail server and pass all mail to the destination address, making it harder to track down spammers.

Increasingly, spammers use networks of malware-infected PCs (zombies) to send their spam. Zombie networks are also known as Botnets (such zombifying malware is known as a bot, short for robot). In June 2006, an estimated 80% of email spam was sent by zombie PCs, an increase of 30% from the prior year. An estimated 55 billion email spam were sent each day in June 2006, an increase of 25 billion per day from June 2005. For Q1 2010, an estimated 305,000 newly activated zombie PCs were brought online each day for malicious activity. This number is slightly lower than the 312,000 of Q4 2009.

Brazil produced the most zombies in the first quarter of 2010. Brazil was the source of 20% of all zombies, which is down from 14% from the fourth quarter 2009. India had 10%, with Vietnam at 8%, and the Russian Federation at 7%.

Side Effects

To combat the problems posed by botnets, open relays and proxy servers many email server administrators pre-emptively block dynamic IP ranges and impose stringent requirements on other servers wishing to deliver mail. Forward-confirmed reverse DNS must be correctly set for the outgoing mail server and large swaths of IP addresses are blocked sometimes pre-emptively to prevent spam. These measures can pose problems for people wanting to run a small email server off an inexpensive domestic connection. Blacklisting of IP ranges due to spam eminating from them also causes problems for legitimate email servers in the same IP range.

Statistics and Estimates

The total volume of email spam has been consistently growing, but in 2011 the trend seems to have reversed. The amount of spam users see in their mailboxes is only a portion of total spam sent, since spammers' lists often contain a large percentage of invalid addresses and many spam filters simply delete or reject "obvious spam."

The first known spam email, advertising a DEC product presentation, was sent in 1978 by Gary Thuerk to 600 addresses, which was all the users of ARPANET at the time, though software limitations meant only slightly more than half of the intended recipients actually received it. As of August 2010, the amount of spam was estimated to be around 200 billion spam messages sent per day. More than 97% of all emails sent over the net are unwanted, according to a Microsoft security report. MAAWG estimates that 85% of incoming mail is "abusive email", as of the second half of 2007. The sample size for the MAAWG's study was over 100 million mailboxes. A 2010 survey of US and European email users showed that 46% of the respondents had opened spam messages, although only 11% had clicked on a link.

Highest Amount of Spam Received

According to Steve Ballmer, Microsoft founder Bill Gates receives four million emails per year, most of them spam. This was originally incorrectly reported as "per day".

At the same time Jef Poskanzer, owner of the domain name acme.com, was receiving over one million spam emails per day.

Cost of Spam

A 2004 survey estimated that lost productivity costs Internet users in the United States $21.58 billion annually, while another reported the cost at $17 billion, up from $11 billion in 2003. In 2004, the worldwide productivity cost of spam has been estimated to be $50 billion in 2005. An estimate of the percentage cost borne by the sender of marketing junk mail (snail mail) is 88%, whereas in 2001 one spam was estimated to cost $0.10 for the receiver and $0.00001 (0.01% of the cost) for the sender.

Origin of Spam

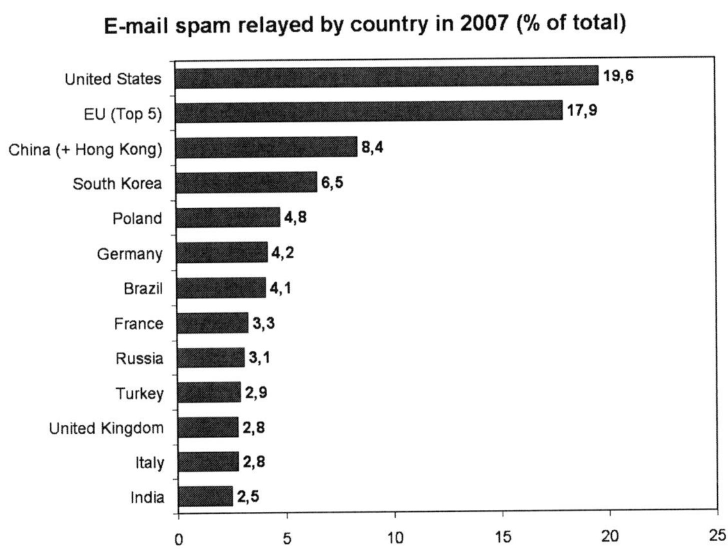

Figure: Email spam relayed by country in Q2/2007.

Origin or source of spam refers to the geographical location of the computer from which the spam is sent; it is not the country where the spammer resides, nor the country that hosts the spamvertised site. Because of the international nature of spam, the spammer, the hijacked spam-sending computer, the spamvertised server, and the user target of the spam are all often located in different countries. As much as 80% of spam received by Internet users in North America and Europe can be traced to fewer than 200 spammers. In terms of volume of spam: According to Sophos, the major sources of spam in the fourth quarter of 2008 (October to December) were:

- The United States (the origin of 19.8% of spam messages, up from 18.9% in Q3)
- China (9.9%, up from 5.4%)
- Russia (6.4%, down from 8.3%)
- Brazil (6.3%, up from 4.5%)
- Turkey (4.4%, down from 8.2%).

When grouped by continents, spam comes mostly from:

- Asia (37.8%, down from 39.8%)
- North America (23.6%, up from 21.8%)
- Europe (23.4%, down from 23.9%)
- South America (12.9%, down from 13.2%).

In terms of number of IP addresses: the Spamhaus Project (which measures spam sources in terms of number of IP addresses used for spamming, rather than volume of spam sent) ranks the top three as the United States, China, and Russia, followed by Japan, Canada, and South Korea. In terms of networks: As of 5 June 2007, the three networks hosting the most spammers are Verizon, AT&T, and VSNL International. Verizon inherited many of these spam sources from its acquisition of MCI, specifically through the UUNet subsidiary of MCI, which Verizon subsequently renamed Verizon Business.

Anti-spam Techniques

The U.S. Department of Energy Computer Incident Advisory Capability (CIAC) has provided specific countermeasures against email spamming.

Some popular methods for filtering and refusing spam include email filtering based on the content of the email, DNS-based blackhole lists (DNSBL), greylisting, spamtraps, Enforcing technical requirements of email (SMTP), checksumming systems to detect bulk email, and by putting some sort of cost on the sender via a Proof-of-work system or a micropayment. Each method has strengths and weaknesses and each is controversial because of its weaknesses. For example, one company's offer to "remove some spamtrap and honeypot addresses" from email lists, defeats the ability for those methods to identify spammers. In one study, 95% of revenues (in the study) cleared through just three banks.

How Spammers Operate

Gathering of Addresses

In order to send spam, spammers need to obtain the email addresses of the intended recipients. To this end, both spammers themselves and list merchants gather huge lists of potential email addresses. Since spam is, by definition, unsolicited, this address harvesting is done without the consent (and sometimes against the expressed will) of the address owners. As a consequence, spammers' address lists are inaccurate. A single spam run may target tens of millions of possible addresses – many of which are invalid, malformed, or undeliverable.

Sometimes, if the sent spam is "bounced" or sent back to the sender by various programs that eliminate spam, or if the recipient clicks on an unsubscribe link, that may cause that email address to be marked as "valid", which is interpreted by the spammer as "send me more".

Delivering Spam Messages

Obfuscating Message Content

Many spam-filtering techniques work by searching for patterns in the headers or bodies of messages. For instance, a user may decide that all email they receive with the word "Viagra" in the subject line is spam, and instruct their mail program to automatically delete all such messages. To defeat such filters, the spammer may intentionally misspell commonly filtered words or insert other characters, often in a style similar to leetspeak, as in the following examples: V1agra, Via'gra, Vi@graa,vi*gra, \/iagra. This also allows for many different ways to express a given word, making identifying them all more difficult for filter software. The principle of this method is to leave the word readable to humans (who can easily recognize the intended word for such misspellings), but not likely to be recognized by a literal computer program. This is only somewhat effective, because modern filter patterns have been designed to recognize blacklisted terms in the various iterations of misspelling. Other filters target the actual obfuscation methods, such as the non-standard use of punctuation or numerals into unusual places. Similarly, HTML-based email gives the spammer more tools to obfuscate text. Inserting HTML comments between letters can foil some filters, as can including text made invisible by setting the font colour to white on a white background, or shrinking the font size to the smallest fine print. Another common ploy involves presenting the text as an image, which is either sent along or loaded from a remote server. This can be foiled by not permitting an email-program to load images.

As Bayesian filtering has become popular as a spam-filtering technique, spammers have started using methods to weaken it. To a rough approximation, Bayesian filters rely on word probabilities. If a message contains many words which are only used in spam, and few which are never used in spam, it is likely to be spam. To weaken Bayesian filters, some spammers, alongside the sales pitch, now include lines of irrelevant, random words, in a technique known as Bayesian poisoning. A variant on this tactic may be borrowed from the Usenet abuser known as "Hipcrime" — to include passages from books taken from Project Gutenberg, or nonsense sentences generated with "dissociated press" algorithms. Randomly generated phrases can create spoetry (spam poetry) or spam art.

Another method used to masquerade spam as legitimate messages is the use of autogenerated sender names in the From: field, ranging from realistic ones such as "Jackie F. Bird" to (either by mistake or intentionally) bizarre attention-grabbing names such as "Sloppiest U. Epiglottis" or "Attentively E. Behavioural". Return addresses are also routinely auto-generated, often using unsuspecting domain owners' legitimate domain names, leading some users to blame the innocent domain owners. Blocking lists use IP addresses rather than sender domain names, as these are more accurate. A mail purporting to be from example.com can be seen to be faked by looking for the originating IP address in the email's headers; also Sender Policy Framework, for example, helps by stating that a certain domain will only send email from certain IP addresses. Spam can also be hidden inside a fake "Undelivered mail notification" which looks like the failure notices sent by a mail transfer agent (a "MAILER-DAEMON") when it encounters an error.

Spam-support Services

A number of other online activities and business practices are considered by anti-spam activists to be connected to spamming. These are sometimes termed spam-support services: business services, other than the actual sending of spam itself, which permit the spammer to continue operating. Spam-support services can include processing orders for goods advertised in spam, hosting Web sites or DNS records referenced in spam messages, or a number of specific services as follows: Some Internet hosting firms advertise bulk-friendly or bulletproof hosting. This means that, unlike most ISPs, they will not terminate a customer for spamming. These hosting firms operate as clients of larger ISPs, and many have eventually been taken offline by these larger ISPs as a result of complaints regarding spam activity. Thus, while a firm may advertise bulletproof hosting, it is ultimately unable to deliver without the connivance of its upstream ISP. However, some spammers have managed to get what is called a pink contract – a contract with the ISP that allows them to spam without being disconnected.

A few companies produce spamware, or software designed for spammers. Spamware varies widely, but may include the ability to import thousands of addresses, to generate random addresses, to insert fraudulent headers into messages, to use dozens or hundreds of mail servers simultaneously, and to make use of open relays. The sale of spamware is illegal in eight U.S. states.

So-called millions CDs are commonly advertised in spam. These are CD-ROMs purportedly containing lists of email addresses, for use in sending spam to these addresses. Such lists are also sold directly online, frequently with the false claim that the owners of the listed addresses have requested (or "opted in") to be included. Such lists often contain invalid addresses. In recent years, these have fallen almost entirely out of use due to the low quality email addresses available on them, and because some email lists exceed 20GB in size. The amount you can fit on a CD is no longer substantial.

A number of DNS blacklists (DNSBLs), including the MAPS RBL, Spamhaus SBL, SORBS and SPEWS, target the providers of spam-support services as well as spammers. DNSBLs blacklist IPs or ranges of IPs to persuade ISPs to terminate services with known customers who are spammers or resell to spammers.

Related Vocabulary

Unsolicited Bulk Email (UBE)

A synonym for email spam.

Unsolicited Commercial Email (UCE)

Spam promoting a commercial service or product. This is the most common type of spam, but it excludes spam which are hoaxes (e.g. virus warnings), political advocacy, religious messages and chain letters sent by a person to many other people. The term UCE may be most common in the USA.

Pink Contract

A pink contract is a service contract offered by an ISP which offers bulk email service to spamming clients, in violation of that ISP's publicly posted acceptable use policy.

Spamvertising

Spamvertising is advertising through the medium of spam.

Opt-in, Confirmed Opt-in, Double opt-in, opt-out

Opt-in, confirmed opt-in, double opt-in, opt-out refers to whether the people on a mailing list are given the option to be put in, or taken out, of the list. Confirmation (and "double", in marketing speak) refers to an email address transmitted eg. through a web form being confirmed to actually request joining a mailing list, instead of being added to the list without verification.

Final, Ultimate Solution for the Spam Problem (FUSSP)

An ironic reference to naïve developers who believe they have invented the perfect spam filter, which will stop all spam from reaching users' inboxes while deleting no legitimate email accidentally.

Bacn

Bacn is an infrequently-used term to refer to email sent to a user who at one time subscribed to a mailing list - not unsolicited, but also not personal.

Chapter 7

Parents Fields of Genetic Algorithms

Evolutionary Algorithm

In artificial intelligence, an evolutionary algorithm (EA) is a subset of evolutionary computation, a generic population-based metaheuristic optimisation algorithm. An EA uses some mechanisms inspired by biological evolution: reproduction, mutation, recombination, and selection. Candidate solutions to the optimisation problem play the role of individuals in a population, and the fitness function determines the environment within which the solutions "live". Evolution of the population then takes place after the repeated application of the above operators. Artificial evolution (AE) describes a process involving individual evolutionary algorithms; EAs are individual components that participate in an AE.

Evolutionary algorithms often perform well approximating solutions to all types of problems because they ideally do not make any assumption about the underlying fitness landscape; this generality is shown by successes in fields as diverse as engineering, art, biology, economics, marketing, genetics, operations research, robotics, social sciences, physics, politics and chemistry.

Apart from their use as mathematical optimisers, evolutionary computation and algorithms have also been used as an experimental framework within which to validate theories about biological evolution and natural selection, particularly through work in the field of artificial life. Techniques from evolutionary algorithms applied to the modelling of biological evolution are generally limited to explorations of microevolutionary processes, however some computer simulations, such as Tierra and Avida, attempt to model macroevolutionary dynamics. In most of real applications of EAs, computational complexity is a prohibiting factor. In fact, this computational complexity is due to fitness function evaluation. Fitness approximation is one of the solutions to overcome this difficulty. However, seemingly simple EA can solve often complex problems; therefore, there may be no direct link between algorithm complexity and problem complexity.

Another possible limitation of many evolutionary algorithms is their lack of a clear genotype-phenotype distinction. In nature, the fertilized egg cell undergoes a complex process known as embryogenesis to become a mature phenotype. This indirect encoding is believed to make the genetic search more robust (i.e. reduce the probability of fatal mutations), and also may improve the evolvability of the organism. Such indirect (aka generative or developmental) encodings also enable evolution to exploit the regularity in the environment. Recent work in the field of artificial embryogeny, or artificial developmental systems, seeks to address these concerns.

Implementation of Biological Processes

Usually, an initial population of randomly generated candidate solutions comprise the first generation. The fitness function is applied to the candidate solutions and any subsequent offspring.

In selection, parents for the next generation are chosen with a bias towards higher fitness. The parents reproduce one or two offsprings (new candidates) by copying their genes, with two possible changes: crossover recombines the parental genes and mutation alters the genotype of an individual in a random way. These new candidates compete with old candidates for their place in the next generation (survival of the fittest). This process can be repeated until a candidate with sufficient quality (a solution) is found or a previously defined computational limit is reached.

Evolutionary Algorithm Techniques

Similar techniques differ in the implementation details and the nature of the particular applied problem.

- Genetic algorithm - This is the most popular type of EA. One seeks the solution of a problem in the form of strings of numbers (traditionally binary, although the best representations are usually those that reflect something about the problem being solved), by applying operators such as recombination and mutation (sometimes one, sometimes both). This type of EA is often used in optimisation problems;

- Genetic programming - Here the solutions are in the form of computer programs, and their fitness is determined by their ability to solve a computational problem.
- Evolutionary programming - Similar to genetic programming, but the structure of the program is fixed and its numerical parameters are allowed to evolve;
- Evolution strategy - Works with vectors of real numbers as representations of solutions, and typically uses self-adaptive mutation rates;
- Neuroevolution - Similar to genetic programming but the genomes represent artificial neural networks by describing structure and connection weights. The genome encoding can be direct or indirect.

Related Techniques

Swarm algorithms, including:

- Ant colony optimisation - Based on the ideas of ant foraging by pheromone communication to form paths. Primarily suited for combinatorial optimisation and graph problems.
- Bees algorithm is based on the foraging behaviour of honey bees. It has been applied in many applications such as routing and scheduling.
- Cuckoo search is inspired by the brooding parasitism of some cuckoo species. It also uses Lévy flights, and thus it suits for global optimisation problems.
- Particle swarm optimisation - Based on the ideas of animal flocking behaviour. Also primarily suited for numerical optimisation problems.

Other population-based metaheuristic methods:

- Differential evolution - Based on vector differences and is therefore primarily suited for numerical optimisation problems.
- Firefly algorithm is inspired by the behaviour of fireflies, attracting each other by flashing light. This is especially useful for multimodal optimisation.
- Invasive weed optimisation algorithm - Based on the ideas of weed colony behaviour in searching and finding a suitable place for growth and reproduction.

- Harmony search - Based on the ideas of musicians' behaviour in searching for better harmonies. This algorithm is suitable for combinatorial optimisation as well as parameter optimisation.
- Gaussian adaptation - Based on information theory. Used for maximization of manufacturing yield, mean fitness or average information.

Evolutionary Computation

In computer science, evolutionary computation is a subfield of artificial intelligence (more particularly computational intelligence) that involves combinatorial optimisation problems.

Evolutionary computation uses iterative progress, such as growth or development in a population. This population is then selected in a guided random search using parallel processing to achieve the desired end. Such processes are often inspired by biological mechanisms of evolution.

As evolution can produce highly optimised processes and networks, it has many applications in computer science. Here, simulations of evolution using evolutionary algorithms and artificial life started with the work of Nils Aall Barricelli in the 1960s, and was extended by Alex Fraser, who published a series of papers on simulation of artificial selection. Artificial evolution became a widely recognised optimisation method as a result of the work of Ingo Rechenberg in the 1960s and early 1970s, who used evolution strategies to solve complex engineering problems. Genetic algorithms in particular became popular through the writing of John Holland. As academic interest grew, dramatic increases in the power of computers allowed practical applications, including the automatic evolution of computer programs. Evolutionary algorithms are now used to solve multidimensional problems more efficiently than software produced by human designers, and also to optimise the design of systems.

History

The use of Darwinian principles for automated problem solving originated in the fifties. It was not until the sixties that three distinct interpretations of this idea started to be developed in three different places. Evolutionary programming was introduced by Lawrence J. Fogel in the USA, while John Henry Holland called his method a genetic algorithm. In Germany Ingo Rechenberg and Hans-Paul Schwefel introduced evolution strategies. These areas developed separately for about 15 years. From the early nineties on they are unified as different representatives ("dialects") of one technology, called evolutionary computing. Also in the early nineties, a fourth stream following the general ideas had emerged – genetic programming. Since the 1990s, evolutionary computation has largely become swarm-based computation, and nature-inspired algorithms are becoming an increasingly significant part.

These terminologies denote the field of evolutionary computing and consider evolutionary programming, evolution strategies, genetic algorithms, and genetic programming as sub-areas.

Techniques

Evolutionary computing techniques mostly involve metaheuristic optimisation algorithms. Broadly speaking, the field includes:

Evolutionary algorithms:

- Genetic algorithms
- Evolutionary programming
- Evolution strategy
- Eagle strategy
- Swarm intelligence
- Ant colony optimisation
- Particle swarm optimisation

and in a lesser extent also:

- Artificial life
- Artificial immune systems
- Cuckoo search
- Cultural algorithms
- Differential evolution
- Firefly algorithm
- Harmony search
- Learning classifier systems
- Learnable Evolution Model
- Parallel simulated annealing

- Self-organization such as self-organizing maps, competitive learning
- Self-Organizing Migrating Genetic Algorithm
- Swarm-based computing

Evolutionary Algorithms

Evolutionary algorithms form a subset of evolutionary computation in that they generally only involve techniques implementing mechanisms inspired by biological evolution such as reproduction, mutation, recombination, natural selection and survival of the fittest. Candidate solutions to the optimisation problem play the role of individuals in a population, and the cost function determines the environment within which the solutions "live". Evolution of the population then takes place after the repeated application of the above operators.

In this process, there are two main forces that form the basis of evolutionary systems: Recombination and mutation create the necessary diversity and thereby facilitate novelty, while selection acts as a force increasing quality.

Many aspects of such an evolutionary process are stochastic. Changed pieces of information due to recombination and mutation are randomly chosen. On the other hand, selection operators can be either deterministic, or stochastic. In the latter case, individuals with a higher fitness have a higher chance to be selected than individuals with a lower fitness, but typically even the weak individuals have a chance to become a parent or to survive.

Metaheuristic

In computer science, metaheuristic designates a computational method that optimises a problem by iteratively trying to improve a candidate solution with regard to a given measure of quality. Metaheuristics make few or no assumptions about the problem being optimised and can search very large spaces of candidate solutions. However, metaheuristics do not guarantee an optimal solution is ever found. Many metaheuristics implement some form of stochastic optimisation. Other terms having a similar meaning as metaheuristic, are: derivative-free, direct search, black-box, or indeed just heuristic optimiser. Several books and survey papers have been published on the subject.

Applications

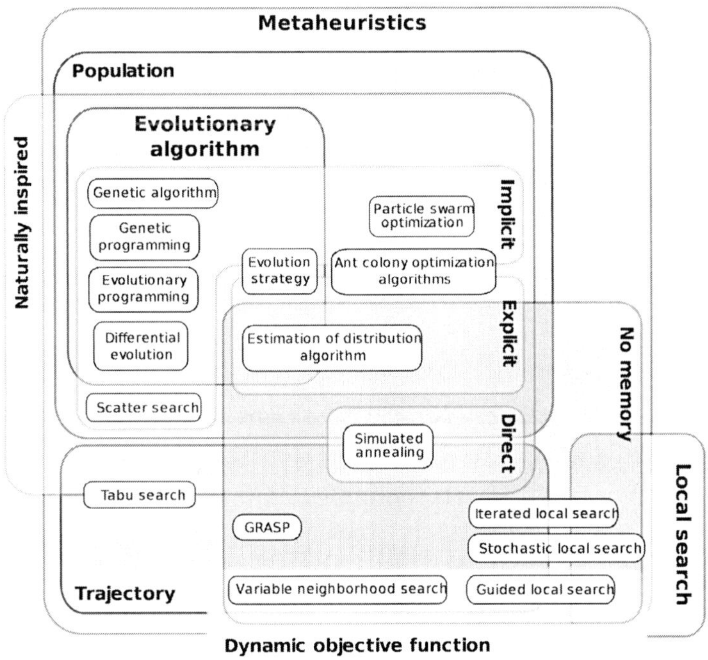

Figure: Different classifications of metaheuristics.

Metaheuristics are used for combinatorial optimisation in which an optimal solution is sought over a discrete search-space. An example problem is the travelling salesman problem where the search-space of candidate solutions grows more than exponentially as the size of the problem increases, which makes an exhaustive search for the optimal solution infeasible. Additionally, multidimensional combinatorial problems, including most design problems in engineering such as form-finding and behaviour-finding, suffer from the curse of dimensionality, which also makes them infeasible for exhaustive search or analytical methods. Popular metaheuristics for combinatorial problems include simulated annealing by Kirkpatrick et al., genetic algorithms by Holland et al., ant colony optimisation by Dorigo, scatter search and tabu search by Glover.

Metaheuristics are also used for problems over real-valued search-spaces, where the classic way of optimisation is to derive the gradient of the function to be optimised and then employ gradient descentor a quasi-Newton method. Metaheuristics do not use the gradient or Hessian matrix so their advantage is that the function to be optimised need not be continuous or differentiable and it can also have constraints. Popular metaheuristic optimisers for real-valued search-spaces include particle swarm optimisation by Eberhart and Kennedy, differential evolution by Storn and Price and evolution strategies by Rechenberg and Schwefel.

Metaheuristics based on decomposition techniques have also been proposed for tackling hard combinatorial problems of large size.

Main Contributions

Many different metaheuristics are in existence and new variants are continually being proposed. Some of the most significant contributions to the field are:

- 1952: Robbins and Monro work on stochastic optimisation methods.
- 1952: Fermi and Metropolis develop an early form of pattern search as described belatedly by Davidon.
- 1954: Barricelli carry out the first simulations of the evolution process and use them on general optimisation problems.
- 1963: Rastrigin proposes random search.
- 1965: Matyas proposes random optimisation.
- 1965: Rechenberg proposes evolution strategies.
- 1965: Nelder and Mead propose a simplex heuristic, which was shown by Powell to converge to non-stationary points on some problems.
- 1966: Fogel et al. propose evolutionary programming.
- 1970: Hastings proposes the Metropolis-Hastings algorithm.
- 1970: Cavicchio proposes adaptation of control parameters for an optimiser.
- 1970: Kernighan and Lin propose a graph partitioning method, related to variable-depth search and prohibition-based (tabu) search.
- 1975: Holland proposes the genetic algorithm.
- 1977: Glover proposes Scatter Search.
- 1978: Mercer and Sampson propose a metaplan for tuning an optimiser's parameters by using another optimiser.
- 1980: Smith describes genetic programming.

- 1983: Kirkpatrick et al. propose simulated annealing.
- 1986: Glover proposes tabu search, first mention of the term metaheuristic.
- 1986: Farmer et al. work on the artificial immune system.
- 1986: Grefenstette proposes another early form of metaplan for tuning an optimiser's parameters by using another optimiser.
- 1988: First conference on genetic algorithms is organized at the University of Illinois at Urbana-Champaign.
- 1988: Koza registers his first patent on genetic programming.
- 1989: Goldberg publishes a well known book on genetic algorithms.
- 1989: Evolver, the first optimisation software using the genetic algorithm.
- 1989: Moscato proposes the memetic algorithm.
- 1991: Interactive evolutionary computation.
- 1992: Dorigo proposes the ant colony algorithm.
- 1993: The journal, Evolutionary Computation, begins publication by the Massachusetts Institute of Technology.
- 1993: Fonseca and Fleming propose MOGA for multiobjective optimisation.
- 1994: Battiti and Tecchiolli propose Reactive Search Optimisation(RSO) principles for the online self-tuning of heuristics.
- 1994: Srinivas and Deb propose NSGA for multiobjective optimisation.
- 1995: Kennedy and Eberhart propose particle swarm optimisation.
- 1995: Wolpert and Macready prove the no free lunch theorems.
- 1996: Mühlenbein and Paaß work on the estimation of distribution algorithm.
- 1996: Hansen and Ostermeier propose CMA-ES.
- 1997: Storn and Price propose differential evolution.
- 1997: Rubinstein proposes the cross entropy method.
- 1999: Taillard and Voss propose POPMUSIC.

- 2001: Geem et al. propose harmony search.
- 2002: Deb et al. propose NSGA-II for multiobjective optimisation.
- 2004: Nakrani and Tovey propose bee colony optimisation.
- 2005: Krishnanand and Ghose propose Glowworm swarm optimisation.
- 2005: Karaboga proposes Artificial Bee Colony Algorithm (ABC).
- 2006: Haddad et al. introduces honey-bee mating optimisation.
- 2007: Hamed Shah-Hosseini introduces Intelligent Water Drops.
- 2008: Wierstra et al. propose natural evolution strategies based on the natural gradient.
- 2008: Yang introduces firefly algorithm.
- 2008: Mucherino and Seref propose the Monkey Search
- 2009: Yang and Deb introduce cuckoo search.
- 2011: Hamed Shah-Hosseini proposes the Galaxy-based Search Algorithm.
- 2011: Tamura and Yasuda propose spiral optimisation.

Criticism

Mathematical analyses of metaheuristics have been presented in the literature, the work by Trelea, amongst others, for analysis of particle swarm optimisation, and Zaharie for analysis of differential evolution. These analyses make a number of assumptions in regard to the optimiser variants and the simplicity of the optimisation problems which limit their validity in real-world optimisation scenarios. Performance and convergence aspects of metaheuristic optimisers are therefore often demonstrated empirically in the research literature. This has been criticized in the no free lunch set of theorems by Wolpert and Macready, which, among other things, prove that all optimisers perform equally well when averaged over all problems. The practical relevance of the no free lunch theorems however is minor, because they will generally not hold on the collection of problems a practitioner is facing.

For the practitioner the most relevant issue is that metaheuristics are not guaranteed to find the optimum or even a satisfactory near-optimal solution. All metaheuristics will eventually encounter problems on which they perform poorly and the practitioner must gain experience in which optimisers work well on different classes of problems.

Stochastic Optimisation

Stochastic optimisation (SO) methods are optimisation methods that generate and use random variables. For stochastic problems, the random variables appear in the formulation of the optimisation problem itself, which involve random objective functions or random constraints, for example.

Stochastic optimisation methods also include methods with random iterates. Some stochastic optimisation methods use random iterates to solve stochastic problems, combining both meanings of stochastic optimisation. Stochastic optimisation methods generalise deterministic methods for deterministic problems.

Methods for Stochastic Functions

Partly random input data arise in such areas as real-time estimation and control, simulation-based optimisation where Monte Carlo simulations are run as estimates of an actual system, and problems where there is experimental (random) error in the measurements of the criterion. In such cases, knowledge that the function values are contaminated by random "noise" leads naturally to algorithms that use statistical inference tools to estimate the "true" values of the function and/or make statistically optimal decisions about the next steps. Methods of this class include

- stochastic approximation (SA), by Robbins and Monro (1951)
- stochastic gradient descent
- finite-difference SA by Kiefer and Wolfowitz (1952)
- simultaneous perturbation SA by Spall (1992)

Randomized Search Methods

On the other hand, even when the data set consists of precise measurements, some methods introduce randomness into the search-process to accelerate progress. Such randomness can also make the method less sensitive to modelling errors. Further, the injected randomness may enable the method to escape a local minimum and eventually to approach a global optimum. Indeed, this randomization principle is known to be a simple and effective way to obtain algorithms with almost certain good performance uniformly across many data sets, for many sorts of problems. Stochastic optimisation methods of this kind include:

- simulated annealing by S. Kirkpatrick, C. D. Gelatt and M. P. Vecchi (1983)
- reactive search optimisation (RSO) by Roberto Battiti, G. Tecchiolli (1994), recently reviewed in the reference book
- cross-entropy method by Rubinstein and Kroese (2004)
- random search by Anatoly Zhigljavsky (1991)
- stochastic tunnelling
- parallel tempering a.k.a. replica exchange
- stochastic hill climbing
- swarm algorithms
- evolutionary algorithms
- genetic algorithms by Holland (1975)
- evolution strategies

Mathematical Optimisation

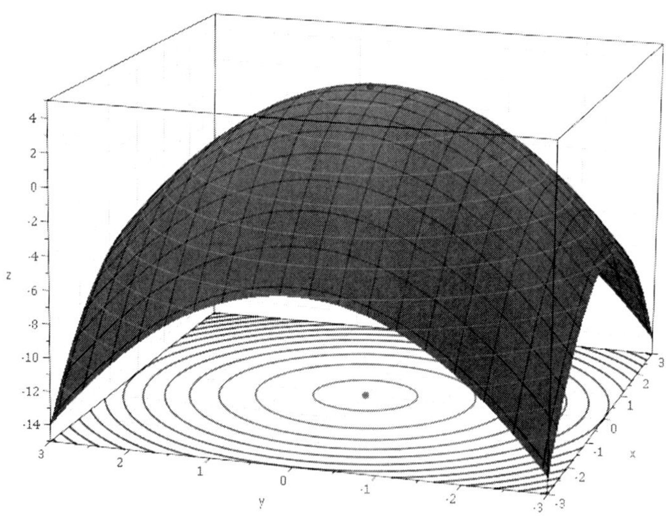

Figure: The maximum of a paraboloid (red dot)

In mathematics, computational science, or management science, mathematical optimisation (alternatively, optimisation or mathematical programming) refers to the selection of a best element from some set of available alternatives.

In the simplest case, an optimisation problem consists of maximizing or minimizing a real function by systematically choosing input values from within an allowed set and computing the value of the function. The generalisation of optimisation theory and techniques to other formulations comprises a large area of applied mathematics. More generally, optimisation includes finding "best available" values of some objective function given a defined domain, including a variety of different types of objective functions and different types of domains.

Optimisation Problems

An optimisation problem can be represented in the following way

Given: a function f : A R from some set A to the real numbers

Sought: an element x_0 in A such that $f(x_0) \leq f(x)$ for all x in A ("minimization") or such that $f(x_0) \geq f(x)$ for all x in A ("maximization").

Such a formulation is called an optimisation problem or a mathematical programming problem (a term not directly related to computer programming, but still in use for example in linear programming). Many real-world and theoretical problems may be modelled in this general framework. Problems formulated using this technique in the fields of physics and computer vision may refer to the technique as energy minimization, speaking of the value of the function f as representing the energy of the system being modelled.

Typically, A is some subset of the Euclidean space R, often specified by a set of constraints, equalities or inequalities that the members of A have to satisfy. The domain A of f is called the search space or the choice set, while the elements of A are called candidate solutions or feasible solutions.

The function f is called, variously, an objective function, cost function (minimization), utility function (maximization), or, in certain fields, energy function, or energy functional. A feasible solution that minimizes (or maximizes, if that is the goal) the objective function is called an optimal solution.

By convention, the standard form of an optimisation problem is stated in terms of minimization. Generally, unless both the objective function and the feasible region are convex in a minimization problem, there may be several local minima, where a local minimum x is defined as a point for which there exists some $\delta > 0$ so that for all x such that

$$\|x - x^*\| \leq \delta;$$

the expression

$$f(x^*) \leq f(x)$$

holds; that is to say, on some region around x all of the function values are greater than or equal to the value at that point. Local maxima are defined similarly.

A large number of algorithms proposed for solving non-convex problems – including the majority of commercially available solvers – are not capable of making a distinction between local optimal solutions and rigorous optimal solutions, and will treat the former as actual solutions to the original problem. The branch of applied mathematics and numerical analysis that is concerned with the development of deterministic algorithms that are capable of guaranteeing convergence in finite time to the actual optimal solution of a non-convex problem is called global optimisation.

Notation

Optimisation problems are often expressed with special notation. Here are some examples.

Minimum and Maximum Value of a Function

Consider the following notation:

$$\min_{x \in \mathbf{R}} \left(x^2 + 1\right)$$

This denotes the minimum value of the objective function x + 1, when choosing x from the set of real numbers $\mathbf{R}$. The minimum value in this case is 1, occurring at x = 0.

Similarly, the notation

$$\max_{x \in \mathbf{R}} 2x$$

asks for the maximum value of the objective function 2x, where x may be any real number. In this case, there is no such maximum as the objective function is unbounded, so the answer is "infinity" or "undefined".

Optimal Input Arguments

Consider the following notation:

$$\underset{x\in(-\infty,-1)}{\arg\min}\ x^2+1,$$

or equivalently

$$\underset{x}{\arg\min}\, x^2+1, subject\ to: x\in(-\infty,-1).$$

This represents the value (or values) of the argument x in the interval $(-\infty,-1]$ that minimizes (or minimize) the objective function x + 1 (the actual minimum value of that function is not what the problem asks for). In this case, the answer is x = –1, since x = 0 is infeasible, i.e. does not belong to the feasible set.

Similarly,

$$\underset{x\varepsilon[-5,5],y\in\mathbf{R}}{\arg\max}\quad x\cos(y)$$

or equivalently

$$\underset{x,y}{\arg\max}\ x\cos(y), subject\ to: x\in[-5,5],\quad y\in\mathbf{R}$$

represents the (x,y) pair (or pairs) that maximizes (or maximize) the value of the objective function xcos(y), with the added constraint that x lie in the interval [– 5,5] (again, the actual maximum value of the expression does not matter). In this case, the solutions are the pairs of the form (5, 2kπ) and (–5,(2k+1)π), where k ranges over all integers.

Arg min and arg max are sometimes also written argmin and argmax, and stand for argument of the minimum and argument of the maximum.

History

Fermat and Lagrange found calculus-based formulas for identifying optima, while Newton and Gaussproposed iterative methods for moving towards an optimum. Historically, the first term for optimisation was "linear programming", which was due to George B. Dantzig, although much of the theory had been introduced by Leonid Kantorovich in 1939. Dantzig published the Simplex algorithm in 1947, and John von Neumann developed the theory of duality in the same year.

The term programming in this context does not refer to computer programming. Rather, the term comes from the use of program by the United States military to refer to proposed training and logistics schedules, which were the problems Dantzig studied at that time. Later important researchers in mathematical optimisation include the following:

- Richard Bellman
- Ronald A. Howard
- Narendra Karmarkar
- William Karush
- Leonid Khachiyan
- Bernard Koopman
- Harold Kuhn
- Joseph Louis Lagrange
- László Lovász
- Arkadii Nemirovskii
- Yurii Nesterov
- Boris Polyak
- Lev Pontryagin
- James Renegar
- R. Tyrrell Rockafellar
- Cornelis Roos
- Naum Z. Shor
- Michael J. Todd
- Albert Tucker.

Major Subfields

- Convex programming studies the case when the objective function is convex (minimization) or concave (maximization) and the constraint set is convex. This can be viewed as a particular case of nonlinear programming or as generalisation of linear or convex quadratic programming.
- Linear programming (LP), a type of convex programming, studies the case in which the objective function f is linear and the set of constraints is specified using only linear equalities and inequalities. Such a set is called a polyhedron or a polytope if it is bounded.

- Second order cone programming (SOCP) is a convex program, and includes certain types of quadratic programs.
- Semidefinite programming (SDP) is a subfield of convex optimisation where the underlying variables are semidefinite matrices. It is generalisation of linear and convex quadratic programming.
- Conic programming is a general form of convex programming. LP, SOCP and SDP can all be viewed as conic programs with the appropriate type of cone.
- Geometric programming is a technique whereby objective and inequality constraints expressed as posynomials and equality constraints as monomials can be transformed into a convex program.
- Integer programming studies linear programs in which some or all variables are constrained to take on integer values. This is not convex, and in general much more difficult than regular linear programming.
- Quadratic programming allows the objective function to have quadratic terms, while the feasible set must be specified with linear equalities and inequalities. For specific forms of the quadratic term, this is a type of convex programming.
- Fractional programming studies optimisation of ratios of two nonlinear functions. The special class of concave fractional programs can be transformed to a convex optimisation problem.
- Nonlinear programming studies the general case in which the objective function or the constraints or both contain nonlinear parts. This may or may not be a convex program. In general, whether the program is convex affects the difficulty of solving it.
- Stochastic programming studies the case in which some of the constraints or parameters depend on random variables.
- Robust programming is, like stochastic programming, an attempt to capture uncertainty in the data underlying the optimisation problem. This is not done through the use of random variables, but instead, the problem is solved taking into account inaccuracies in the input data.
- Combinatorial optimisation is concerned with problems where the set of feasible solutions is discrete or can be reduced to a discrete one.

- Infinite-dimensional optimisation studies the case when the set of feasible solutions is a subset of an infinite-dimensional space, such as a space of functions.
- Metaheuristics make few or no assumptions about the problem being optimised and can search very large spaces of candidate solutions. However, metaheuristics do not guarantee an optimal solution is ever found.
- Constraint satisfaction studies the case in which the objective function f is constant (this is used in artificial intelligence, particularly in automated reasoning).
- Constraint programming.
- Disjunctive programming is used where at least one constraint must be satisfied but not all. It is of particular use in scheduling.

In a number of subfields, the techniques are designed primarily for optimisation in dynamic contexts (that is, decision making over time):

- Calculus of variations seeks to optimise an objective defined over many points in time, by considering how the objective function changes if there is a small change in the choice path.
- Optimal control theory is a generalisation of the calculus of variations.
- Dynamic programming studies the case in which the optimisation strategy is based on splitting the problem into smaller subproblems. The equation that describes the relationship between these subproblems is called the Bellman equation.
- Mathematical programming with equilibrium constraints is where the constraints include variational inequalities or complementarities.

Multi-objective Optimisation

Adding more than one objective to an optimisation problem adds complexity. For example, to optimise a structural design, one would want a design that is both light and rigid. Because these two objectives conflict, a trade-off exists. There will be one lightest design, one stiffest design, and an infinite number of designs that are some compromise of weight and stiffness. The set of trade-off designs that cannot be improved upon according to one criterion without hurting another criterion is known as the Pareto set. The curve created plotting weight against stiffness of the best designs is known as the Pareto frontier.

A design is judged to be "Pareto optimal" (equivalently, "Pareto efficient" or in the Pareto set) if it is not dominated by any other design: If it is worse than another design in some respects and no better in any respect, then it is dominated and is not Pareto optimal.

Multi-modal Optimisation

Optimisation problems are often multi-modal; that is they possess multiple good solutions. They could all be globally good (same cost function value) or there could be a mix of globally good and locally good solutions. Obtaining all (or at least some of) the multiple solutions is the goal of a multi-modal optimiser. Classical optimisation techniques due to their iterative approach do not perform satisfactorily when they are used to obtain multiple solutions, since it is not guaranteed that different solutions will be obtained even with different starting points in multiple runs of the algorithm. Evolutionary Algorithmsare however a very popular approach to obtain multiple solutions in a multi-modal optimisation task.

Classification of Critical Points and Extrema

Feasibility Problem

The satisfiability problem, also called the feasibility problem, is just the problem of finding any feasible solution at all without regard to objective value. This can be regarded as the special case of mathematical optimisation where the objective value is the same for every solution, and thus any solution is optimal.

Many optimisation algorithms need to start from a feasible point. One way to obtain such a point is to relax the feasibility conditions using a slack variable; with enough slack, any starting point is feasible. Then, minimize that slack variable until slack is null or negative.

Existence

The extreme value theorem of Karl Weierstrass states that a continuous real-valued function on a compact set attains its maximum and minimum value. More generally, a lower semi-continuous function on a compact set attains its minimum; an upper semi-continuous function on a compact set attains its maximum.

Necessary Conditions for Optimality

One of Fermat's theorems states that optima of unconstrained problems are found at stationary points, where the first derivative or the gradient of the objective function is zero. More generally, they may be found at critical points, where the first derivative or gradient of the objective function is zero or is undefined, or on the boundary of the choice set. An equation (or set of equations) stating that the first derivative(s) equal(s) zero at an interior optimum is called a 'first-order condition' or a set of first-order conditions.

Optima of inequality-constrained problems are instead found by the Lagrange multiplier method. This method calculates a system of inequalities called the 'Karush–Kuhn–Tucker conditions' or 'complementary slackness conditions', which may then be used to calculate the optimum.

Sufficient Conditions for Optimality

While the first derivative test identifies points that might be optima, this test does not distinguish a point which is a minimum from one that is a maximum or one that is neither. When the objective function is twice differentiable, these cases can be distinguished by checking the second derivative or the matrix of second derivatives (called the Hessian matrix) in unconstrained problems, or the matrix of second derivatives of the objective function and the constraints called the bordered Hessian in constrained problems. The conditions that distinguish maxima, or minima, from other stationary points are called 'second-order conditions'. If a candidate solution satisfies the first-order conditions, then satisfaction of the second-order conditions as well is sufficient to establish at least local optimality.

Sensitivity and Continuity of Optima

The envelope theorem describes how the value of an optimal solution changes when an underlying parameter changes. The process of computing this change is called comparative statics.

The maximum theorem of Claude Berge (1963) describes the continuity of an optimal solution as a function of underlying parameters.

Calculus of Optimisation

For unconstrained problems with twice-differentiable functions, some critical points can be found by finding the points where the gradient of the objective function is zero (that is, the stationary points). More generally, a zero subgradient certifies that a local minimum has been found for minimization problems with convex functions and other locally Lipschitz functions.

Further, critical points can be classified using the definiteness of the Hessian matrix: If the Hessian is positive definite at a critical point, then the point is a local minimum; if the Hessian matrix is negative definite, then the point is a local maximum; finally, if indefinite, then the point is some kind of saddle point.

Constrained problems can often be transformed into unconstrained problems with the help of Lagrange multipliers. Lagrangian relaxation can also provide approximate solutions to difficult constrained problems.

When the objective function is convex, then any local minimum will also be a global minimum. There exist efficient numerical techniques for minimizing convex functions, such as interior-point methods.

Computational Optimisation Techniques

To solve problems, researchers may use algorithms that terminate in a finite number of steps, oriterative methods that converge to a solution (on some specified class of problems), or heuristics that may provide approximate solutions to some problems (although their iterates need not converge).

Optimisation Algorithms

- Simplex algorithm of George Dantzig, designed for linear programming.
- Extensions of the simplex algorithm, designed for quadratic programming and for linear-fractional programming.
- Variants of the simplex algorithm that are especially suited for network optimisation.
- Combinatorial algorithms

Iterative Methods

The iterative methods used to solve problems of nonlinear programming differ according to whether they evaluate Hessians, gradients, or only function values. While evaluating Hessians (H) and gradients (G) improves the rate of convergence, such evaluations increase the computational complexity (or computational cost) of each iteration. In some cases, the computational complexity may be excessively high.

One major criterion for optimisers is just the number of required function evaluations as this often is already a large computational effort, usually much more effort than within the optimiser itself, which mainly has to operate over the N variables. The derivatives provide detailed information for such optimisers, but are even harder to calculate, e.g. approximating the gradient takes at least N+1 function evaluations. For approximations of the 2nd derivatives (collected in the Hessian matrix) the number of function evaluations is in the order of N^2. Newton's method requires the 2nd order derivates, so for each iteration the number of function calls is in the order of N^2, but for a simpler pure gradient optimiser it is only N. However, gradient optimisers need usually more iterations than Newton's algorithm. Which one is best wrt. number of function calls depends on the problem itself.

- Methods that evaluate Hessians (or approximate Hessians, using finite differences):
- Newton's method
- Sequential quadratic programming: A method for small-medium scale constrained problems. Some versions can handle large-dimensional problems.
- Methods that evaluate gradients or approximate gradients using finite differences (or even subgradients):
- Quasi-Newton methods: Iterative methods for medium-large problems (e.g. N<1000).
- Conjugate gradient methods: Iterative methods for large problems. (In theory, these methods terminate in a finite number of steps with quadratic objective functions, but this finite termination is not observed in practice on finite–precision computers.)
- Interior point methods: This is a large class of methods for constrained optimisation. Some interior-point methods use only (sub)gradient information, and others of which require the evaluation of Hessians.
- Gradient descent (alternatively, "steepest descent" or "steepest ascent"): A (slow) method of historical and theoretical interest,

which has had renewed interest for finding approximate solutions of enormous problems.

- Subgradient methods - An iterative method for large locally Lipschitz functions using generalised gradients. Following Boris T. Polyak, subgradient–projection methods are similar to conjugate–gradient methods.
- Bundle method of descent: An iterative method for small–medium sized problems with locally Lipschitz functions, particularly for convex minimization problems. (Similar to conjugate gradient methods)
- Ellipsoid method: An iterative method for small problems with quasiconvex objective functions and of great theoretical interest, particularly in establishing the polynomial time complexity of some combinatorial optimisation problems. It has similarities with Quasi-Newton methods.
- Reduced gradient method (Frank–Wolfe) for approximate minimization of specially structured problems with linear constraints, especially with traffic networks. For general unconstrained problems, this method reduces to the gradient method, which is regarded as obsolete (for almost all problems).
- Methods that evaluate only function values: If a problem is continuously differentiable, then gradients can be approximated using finite differences, in which case a gradient-based method can be used. Usually such non-gradient methods work only fine for problems with few parameter only.
- Interpolation methods
- Pattern search methods, which have better convergence properties than the Nelder–Mead simplicial heuristic (listed below, under heuristics).

Global Convergence

More generally, if the objective function is not a quadratic function, then many optimisation methods use other methods to ensure that some subsequence of iterations converges to an optimal solution. The first and still popular method for ensuring convergence relies on-line searches, which optimise a function along one dimension. A second and increasingly popular method for ensuring convergence uses trust regions. Both line searches and trust regions are used in modern methods of non-differentiable optimisation. Usually a global optimiser is much slower than advanced local optimisers (such as BFGS), so often an efficient global optimiser can be constructed by starting the local optimiser from different starting points.

Heuristics

Besides (finitely terminating) algorithms and (convergent) iterative methods, there are heuristics that can provide approximate solutions to some optimisation problems:

- Memetic algorithm
- Differential evolution
- Dynamic relaxation
- Genetic algorithms
- Hill climbing
- Nelder-Mead simplicial heuristic: A popular heuristic for approximate minimization (without calling gradients)
- Particle swarm optimisation
- Simulated annealing
- Tabu search

Applications

Mechanics and Engineering

Problems in rigid body dynamics (in particular articulated rigid body dynamics) often require mathematical programming techniques, since you can view rigid body dynamics as attempting to solve an ordinary differential equation on a constraint manifold; the constraints are various nonlinear geometric constraints such as "these two points must always coincide", "this surface must not penetrate any other", or "this point must always lie somewhere on this curve". Also, the problem of computing contact forces can be done by solving a linear complementarity problem, which can also be viewed as a QP (quadratic programming) problem. Many design problems can also be expressed as optimisation programs. This application is called design optimisation. One subset is the engineering optimisation, and another recent and growing subset of this field is multidisciplinary design optimisation, which, while useful in many problems, has in particular been applied to aerospace engineering problems.

Economics

Economics is closely enough linked to optimisation of agents that an influential definition relatedly describes economics qua science as the "study of human behaviour as a relationship between ends and scarce means" with alternative uses. Modern optimisation theory includes traditional optimisation theory but also overlaps with game theory and the study of economic equilibria. The Journal of Economic Literature codes classify mathematical programming, optimisation techniques, and related topics under JEL:C61-C63.

In microeconomics, the utility maximization problem and its dual problem, the expenditure minimization problem, are economic optimisation problems. Insofar as they behave consistently, consumers are assumed to maximize their utility, while firms are usually assumed to maximize their profit. Also, agents are often modelled as being risk-averse, thereby preferring to avoid risk. Asset prices are also modelled using optimisation theory, though the underlying mathematics relies on optimising stochastic processes rather than on static optimisation. Trade theory also uses optimisation to explain trade patterns between nations.

Since the 1970s, economists have modelled dynamic decisions over time using control theory. For example, microeconomists use dynamic search models to study labour-market behaviour. A crucial distinction is between deterministic and stochastic models. Macroeconomists build dynamic stochastic general equilibrium (DSGE) models that describe the dynamics of the whole economy as the result of the interdependent optimising decisions of workers, consumers, investors, and governments.

Operations Research

Another field that uses optimisation techniques extensively is operations research. Operations research also uses stochastic modelling and simulation to support improved decision-making. Increasingly, operations research uses stochastic programming to model dynamic decisions that adapt to events; such problems can be solved with large-scale optimisation and stochastic

Chapter 8

Genetic Algorithms

A genetic algorithm (GA) is a search heuristic that mimics the process of natural evolution. This heuristic is routinely used to generate useful solutions to optimisation and search problems. Genetic algorithms belong to the larger class of evolutionary algorithms (EA), which generate solutions to optimisation problems using techniques inspired by natural evolution, such as inheritance, mutation, selection, and crossover.

Methodology

In a genetic algorithm, a population of strings (called chromosomes or the genotype of the genome), which encode candidate solutions (called individuals, creatures, or phenotypes) to an optimisation problem, evolves toward better solutions. Traditionally, solutions are represented in binary as strings of 0s and 1s, but other encodings are also possible. The evolution usually starts from a population of randomly generated individuals and happens in generations. In each generation, the fitness of every individual in the population is evaluated, multiple individuals are stochastically selected from the current population (based on their fitness), and modified (recombined and possibly randomly mutated) to form a new population. The new population is then used in the next iteration of the algorithm. Commonly, the algorithm terminates when either a maximum number of generations has been produced, or a satisfactory fitness level has been reached for the population. If the algorithm has terminated due to a maximum number of generations, a satisfactory solution may or may not have been reached.

Genetic algorithms find application in bioinformatics, phylogenetics, computational science, engineering, economics, chemistry, manufacturing, mathematics, physics and other fields.

A typical genetic algorithm requires:

Genetic Representation

Genetic representation is a way of representing solutions/ individuals in evolutionary computation methods. Genetic representation can encode appearance, behaviour, physical qualities of individuals. Designing a good genetic representation that is expressive and evolvable is a hard problem in evolutionary computation. Difference in genetic representations is one of the major criteria drawing a line between known classes of evolutionary computation.

Genetic algorithms use linear binary representations. The most standard one is an array of bits. Arrays of other types and structures can be used in essentially the same way. The main property that makes these genetic representations convenient is that their parts are easily aligned due to their fixed size. This facilitates simple crossover operation. Variable length representations were also explored in Genetic algorithms, but crossover implementation is more complex in this case. Evolution strategy uses linear real-valued representations, e.g. an array of real values. It uses mostly gaussian mutation and blending/averaging crossover.

Genetic programming (GP) pioneered tree-like representations and developed genetic operators suitable for such representations. Tree-like representations are used in GP to represent and evolve functional programs with desired properties.

Human-based genetic algorithm (HBGA) offers a way to avoid solving hard representation problems by outsourcing all genetic operators to outside agents, in this case, humans. The algorithm has no need for knowledge of a particular fixed genetic representation as long as there are enough external agents capable of handling those representations, allowing for free-form and evolving genetic representations.

Fitness Function

A fitness function is a particular type of objective function that is used to summarise, as a singlefigure of merit, how close a given design solution is to achieving the set aims.

In particular, in the fields of genetic programming and genetic algorithms, each design solution is represented as a string of numbers (referred to as a chromosome). After each round of testing, or simulation, the idea is to delete the 'n' worst design solutions, and to breed 'n' new ones from the best design solutions. Each design solution, therefore, needs to be awarded a figure of merit, to indicate how close it came to meeting the overall specification, and this is generated by applying the fitness function to the test, or simulation, results obtained from that solution.

The reason that genetic algorithms are not a lazy way of performing design work is precisely because of the effort involved in designing a workable fitness function. Even though it is no longer the human designer, but the computer, that comes up with the final design, it is the human designer who has to design the fitness function. If this is designed wrongly, the algorithm will either converge on an inappropriate solution, or will have difficulty converging at all. Moreover, the fitness function must not only correlate closely with the designer's goal, it must also be computed quickly. Speed of execution is very important, as a typical genetic algorithm must be iterated many times in order to produce a usable result for a non-trivial problem. Fitness approximation may be appropriate, especially in the following cases:

- Fitness computation time of a single solution is extremely high
- Precise model for fitness computation is missing
- The fitness function is uncertain or noisy.

Two main classes of fitness functions exist: one where the fitness function does not change, as in optimising a fixed function or testing with a fixed set of test cases; and one where the fitness function is mutable, as in niche differentiation or co-evolving the set of test cases.

Another way of looking at fitness functions is in terms of a fitness landscape, which shows the fitness for each possible chromosome.

Definition of the fitness function is not straightforward in many cases and often is performed iteratively if the fittest solutions produced by GA are not what is desired. In some cases, it is very hard or impossible to come up even with a guess of what fitness function definition might be. Interactive genetic algorithms address this difficulty by outsourcing evaluation to external agents (normally humans). A standard representation of the solution is as an array of bits. Arrays of other types and structures can be used in essentially the same way. The main property that makes these genetic representations convenient is that their parts are easily aligned due to their fixed size, which facilitates simple crossover operations.

Variable length representations may also be used, but crossover implementation is more complex in this case. Tree-like representations are explored in genetic programming and graph-form representations are explored in evolutionary programming.

The fitness function is defined over the genetic representation and measures the quality of the represented solution. The fitness function is always problem dependent. For instance, in the knapsack problem one wants to maximize the total value of objects that can be put in a knapsack of some fixed capacity. A representation of a solution might be an array of bits, where each bit represents a different object, and the value of the bit (0 or 1) represents whether or not the object is in the knapsack. Not every such representation is valid, as the size of objects may exceed the capacity of the knapsack. The fitness of the solution is the sum of values of all objects in the knapsack if the representation is valid, or 0 otherwise. In some problems, it is hard or even impossible to define the fitness expression; in these cases, interactive genetic algorithms are used. Once the genetic representation and the fitness function are defined, a GA proceeds to initialize a population of solutions (usually randomly) and then to improve it through repetitive application of the mutation, crossover, inversion and selection operators.

Initialization

Initially many individual solutions are (usually) randomly generated to form an initial population. The population size depends on the nature of the problem, but typically contains several hundreds or thousands of possible solutions. Traditionally, the population is generated randomly, allowing the entire range of possible solutions (the search space). Occasionally, the solutions may be "seeded" in areas where optimal solutions are likely to be found

Selection (Genetic Algorithm)

Selection is the stage of a genetic algorithm in which individual genomes are chosen from a population for later breeding (recombination or crossover). A generic selection procedure may be implemented as follows:

1. The fitness function is evaluated for each individual, providing fitness values, which are then normalized. Normalization means dividing the fitness value of each individual by the sum of all fitness values, so that the sum of all resulting fitness values equals 1.

2. The population is sorted by descending fitness values.
3. Accumulated normalized fitness values are computed (the accumulated fitness value of an individual is the sum of its own fitness value plus the fitness values of all the previous individuals). The accumulated fitness of the last individual should be 1 (otherwise something went wrong in the normalization step).
4. A random number R between 0 and 1 is chosen.
5. The selected individual is the first one whose accumulated normalized value is greater than R.

If this procedure is repeated until there are enough selected individuals, this selection method is called fitness proportionate selection or roulette-wheel selection. If instead of a single pointer spun multiple times, there are multiple, equally spaced pointers on a wheel that is spun once, it is called stochastic universal sampling. Repeatedly selecting the best individual of a randomly chosen subset is tournament selection. Taking the best half, third or another proportion of the individuals is truncation selection. There are other selection algorithms that do not consider all individuals for selection, but only those with a fitness value that is higher than a given (arbitrary) constant. Other algorithms select from a restricted pool where only a certain percentage of the individuals are allowed, based on fitness value. Retaining the best individuals in a generation unchanged in the next generation, is called elitism orelitist selection. It is a successful (slight) variant of the general process of constructing a new population.

Crossover (Genetic Algorithm)

In genetic algorithms, crossover is a genetic operator used to vary the programming of a chromosome or chromosomes from one generation to the next. It is analogous to reproduction and biological crossover, upon which genetic algorithms are based. Cross over is a process of taking more than one parent solutions and producing a child solution from them. There are methods for selection of the chromosomes. Those are also given below.

Methods of Selection of Chromosomes for Crossover

- Roulette wheel selection: It is also known as fitness proportionate selection. The individual is selected on the basis of fitness. The probability of an individual to be selected increases with the fitness of the individual greater or less than its competitor's fitness.

- Boltzmann selection
- Tournament selection
- Rank selection
- Steady state selection.

Crossover Techniques

Many crossover techniques exist for organisms which use different data structures to store themselves.

One-point Crossover

A single crossover point on both parents' organism strings is selected. All data beyond that point in either organism string is swapped between the two parent organisms. The resulting organisms are the children:

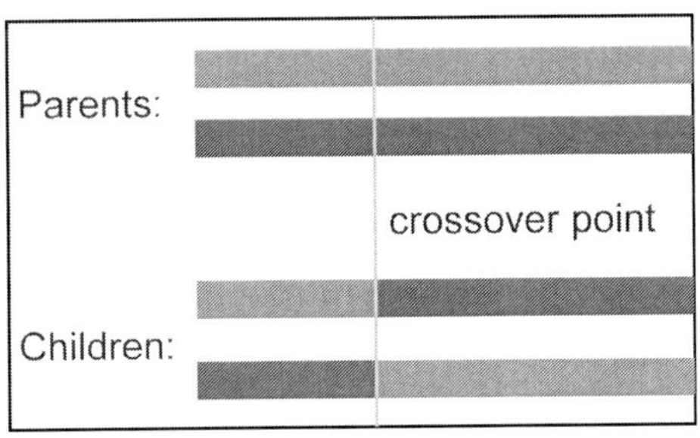

Two-point Crossover

Two-point crossover calls for two points to be selected on the parent organism strings. Everything between the two points is swapped between the parent organisms, rendering two child organisms:

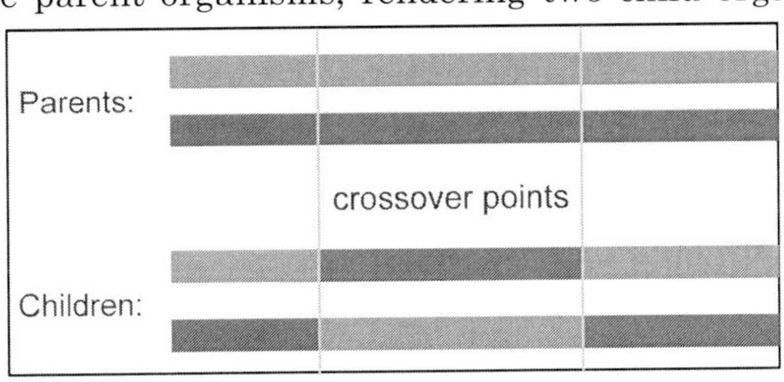

"Cut and Splice"

Another crossover variant, the "cut and splice" approach, results in a change in length of the children strings. The reason for this difference is that each parent string has a separate choice of crossover point.

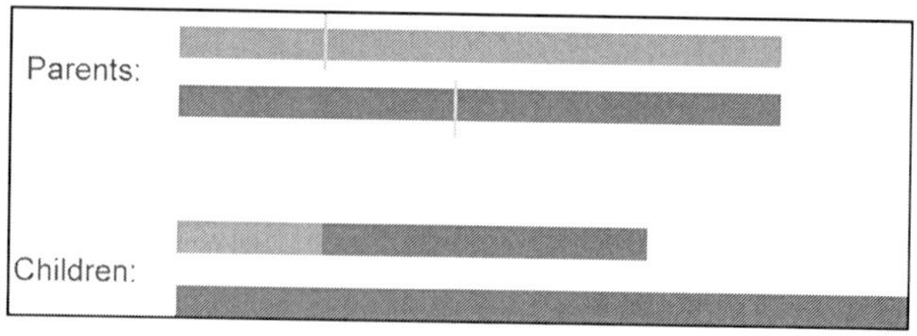

Uniform Crossover and Half Uniform Crossover

The Uniform Crossover uses a fixed mixing ratio between two parents. Unlike one- and two-point crossover, the Uniform Crossover enables the parent chromosomes to contribute the gene level rather than the segment level. If the mixing ratio is 0.5, the offspring has approximately half of the genes from first parent and the other half from second parent, although cross over points can be randomly chosen.

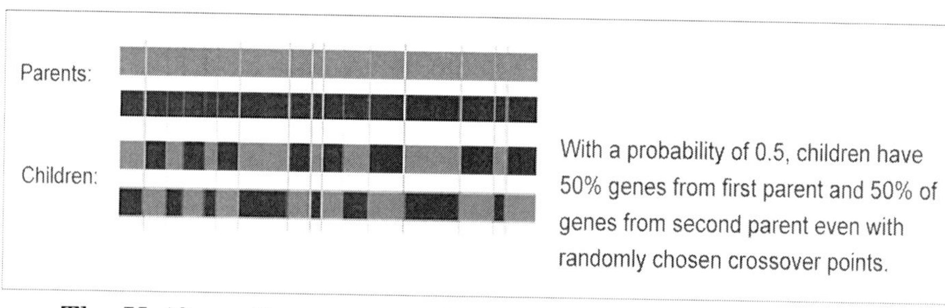

The Uniform Crossover evaluates each bit in the parent strings for exchange with a probability of 0.5. Even though the uniform crossover is a poor method, empirical evidence suggest that it is a more exploratory approach to crossover than the traditional exploitative approach that maintains longer schemata.

This results in a more complete search of the design space with maintaining the exchange of good information. Unfortunately, no satisfactory theory exists to explain the discrepancies between the Uniform Crossover and the traditional approaches.

In the uniform crossover scheme (UX) individual bits in the string are compared between two parents. The bits are swapped with a fixed probability, typically 0.2. In the half uniform crossover scheme (HUX), exactly half of the nonmatching bits are swapped.

Thus first the Hamming distance (the number of differing bits) is calculated. This number is divided by two. The resulting number is how many of the bits that do not match between the two parents will be swapped.

Three Parent Crossover

In this technique, the child is derived from three parents. They are randomly chosen. Each bit of first parent is checked with bit of second parent whether they are same. If same then the bit is taken for the offspring otherwise the bit from the third parent is taken for the offspring.

parent1 1 1 0 1 0 0 0 1 0

parent2 0 1 1 0 0 1 0 0 1

parent3 1 1 0 1 1 0 1 0 1

offspring 1 1 0 1 0 0 0 0 1

Crossover for Ordered Chromosomes

Depending on how the chromosome represents the solution, a direct swap may not be possible. One such case is when the chromosome is an ordered list, such as an ordered list of the cities to be travelled for the travelling salesman problem. There are many crossover methods for ordered chromosomes.

The already mentioned N-point crossover can be applied for ordered chromosomes also, but this always need a corresponding repair process, actually, some ordered crossover method are derived from the idea. However, sometimes a crossover of chromosomes produces recombinations which violate the constraint of ordering and thus need to be repaired. Several examples for crossover operators (also mutation operator) preserving a given order are given in :

1. partially-matched crossover (PMX): In this method, two crossover points are selected at random and PMX proceeds by position wise exchanges. The two crossover points give matching selection. It affects cross by position-by-position exchange operations. In this method parents are mapped to each other hence we can also call it partially mapped crossover.
2. cycle crossover (CX): Beginning at any gene i in parent 1, the i-th gene in parent 2 becomes replaced by it. The same is repeated for the displaced gene until the gene which is equal to the first inserted gene becomes replaced (cycle).
3. order crossover operator (OX1): A portion of one parent is mapped to a portion of the other parent. From the replaced portion on, the rest is filled up by the remaining genes, where already present genes are omitted and the order is preserved.

4. order-based crossover operator (OX2)
5. position-based crossover operator (POS)
6. voting recombination crossover operator (VR)
7. alternating-position crossover operator (AP)
8. sequential constrictive crossover operator (SCX)

Other possible methods include the edge recombination operator and partially mapped crossover.

Crossover Biases

For crossover operators which exchange contiguous sections of the chromosomes (e.g. k-point) the ordering of the variables may become important. This is particularly true when good solutions contain building blocks which might be disrupted by a non-respectful crossover operator.

Mutation (Genetic Algorithm)

In genetic algorithms of computing, mutation is a genetic operator used to maintain genetic diversity from one generation of a population of algorithm chromosomes to the next. It is analogous to biological mutation. Mutation alters one or more gene values in a chromosome from its initial state.

In mutation, the solution may change entirely from the previous solution. Hence GA can come to better solution by using mutation, mutation occurs during evolution according to a user-definable mutation probability. This probability should be set low. If it is set to high, the search will turn into a primitive random search.

The classic example of a mutation operator involves a probability that an arbitrary bit in a genetic sequence will be changed from its original state. A common method of implementing the mutation operator involves generating a random variable for each bit in a sequence. This random variable tells whether or not a particular bit will be modified. This mutation procedure, based on the biological point mutation, is called single point mutation. Other types are inversion and floating point mutation. When the gene encoding is restrictive as in permutation problems, mutations are swaps, inversions and scrambles.

The purpose of mutation in GAs is preserving and introducing diversity. Mutation should allow the algorithm to avoid local minima by preventing the population of chromosomes from becoming too similar to each other, thus slowing or even stopping evolution. This reasoning also explains the fact that most GA systems avoid only taking the fittest of the population in generating the next but rather a random (or semi-random) selection with a weighting toward those that are fitter.

For different genome types, different mutation types are suitable:

- Bit string mutation: The mutation of bit strings ensue through bit flips at random positions.

Example:

1 0 1 0 0 1 0

↓

1 0 1 0 1 1 0

The probability of a mutation of a bits is $\frac{1}{l}$, where l is the length of the binary vector. Thus, a mutation rate of 1 per mutation and individual selected for mutation is reached.

- Flip Bit: This mutation operator takes the chosen genome and invert the bits. (i.e. if the genome bit is 1,it is changed to 0 and vice versa)
- Boundary: This mutation operator replaces the genome with either lower or upper bound randomly. This can be used for integer and float genes.
- Non-Uniform: The probability that amount of mutation will go to 0 with the next generation is increased by using non-uniform mutation operator. It keeps the population from stagnating in the early stages of the evolution. It tunes solution in later stages of evolution. This mutation operator can only be used for integer and float genes.
- Uniform: This operator replaces the value of the chosen gene with a uniform random value selected between the user-specified upper and lower bounds for that gene. This mutation operator can only be used for integer and float genes.
- Gaussian: This operator adds a unit Gaussian distributed random value to the chosen gene. If it falls outside of the user-specified lower or upper bounds for that gene, the new gene value is clipped. This mutation operator can only be used for integer and float genes.

Chapter 9

Applications of Genetic Algorithms

Computational Creativity

Computational creativity (also known as artificial creativity, mechanical creativity or creative computation) is a multidisciplinary endeavour that is located at the intersection of the fields of artificial intelligence, cognitive psychology, philosophy, and the arts. The goal of computational creativity is to model, simulate or replicate creativity using a computer, to achieve one of several ends:

- to construct a program or computer capable of human-level creativity
- to better understand human creativity and to formulate an algorithmic perspective on creative behaviour in humans
- to design programs that can enhance human creativity without necessarily being creative themselves

The field of computational creativity concerns itself with theoretical and practical issues in the study of creativity. Theoretical work on the nature and proper definition of creativity is performed in parallel with practical work on the implementation of systems that exhibit creativity, with one strand of work informing the other.

Theoretical Issues

As measured by the amount of activity in the field (e.g., publications, conferences and workshops), computational creativity is a growing area of research. But the field is still hampered by a number of fundamental problems:

- Creativity is very difficult, perhaps even impossible, to define in objective terms.
- Creativity takes many forms in human activity, some eminent (meaning "recognized" or "ingenious", e.g., Einstein's creativity;

sometimes referred to as "Creativity" with a capital C) and some mundane.

- Creativity can mean different things in different contexts: Is it a state of mind, a talent or ability, or a process? Does it describe a person, an activity or an end-product? Can collaborative work in which exceptional products emerge from simple interactions be considered creative?

These are problems that complicate the study of creativity in general, but certain problems attach themselves specifically to computational creativity:

- Can creativity be hard-wired? In existing systems to which creativity is attributed, is the creativity that of the system or that of the system's programmer or designer?
- How do we evaluate computational creativity? What counts as creativity in a computational system? Are natural language generation systems creative? Are machine translation systems creative? What distinguishes research in computational creativity from research in artificial intelligence generally?
- If eminent creativity is about rule-breaking or the disavowal of convention, how is it possible for an algorithmic system to be creative? In essence, this is a variant of the Ada Lovelace objection to machine intelligence, as recapitulated by modern theorists such as Teresa Amabile: If a machine can do only what it was programmed to do, how can its behaviour ever be called creative?

Defining Creativity in Computational Terms

Since no single perspective or definition seems to offer a complete picture of creativity, the AI researchers Newell, Shaw and Simon developed the combination of novelty and usefulness into the cornerstone of a multi-pronged view of creativity, one that uses the following four criteria to categorize a given answer or solution as creative:

1. The answer is novel and useful (either for the individual or for society)
2. The answer demands that we reject ideas we had previously accepted

3. The answer results from intense motivation and persistence
4. The answer comes from clarifying a problem that was originally vague

Notice how these criteria touch on many of the stereotypical themes that are typically associated with creativity: newness and value (1), transformation and revolution (2), passion and drive (3), vision and insight (4). These four criteria also combine elements of the producer-perspective and the product-perspective described earlier: criterion (1) characterizes the two most important qualities of a creative product, while criteria (2) – (4) characterize the attitude and actions of the producer of such a product. A given product may satisfy all or none of these criteria, but we should expect products that exhibit all four to be widely perceived as creative, while products that exhibit just some of these criteria will be judged with greater subjectivity and variation. Though no criterion is likely to be either necessary or sufficient, criterion (1) is perhaps the most common hallmark of creativity and thus serves to anchor the others. From a computational perspective, then, one can consider (1) to be a must-have feature, and (2) – (4) as desirable extras.

Newell and Simon are best known for their contribution to the search-in-a-state-space paradigm of AI, sometimes caricatured as Good Old Fashioned AI (GOFAI), and it is interesting to consider how the GOFAI paradigm can incorporate these criteria. From a search perspective, criterion (1) characterizes the goal or end-state of a computational search, criterion (4) characterizes the starting state from which the search is launched, criterion (3) characterizes the scale of the search, suggesting that many dead-ends are likely to be encountered, while criterion (2) suggests that well-worn pathways through the search space are best avoided if a creative end-state is to be reached.

Key Ideas

Some high-level and philosophical themes recur throughout the field of computational creativity.

P-creativity and H-creativity

Margaret Boden refers to creativity that is novel merely to the agent that produces it as "P-creativity" (or "psychological creativity"), and refers to creativity that is recognized as novel by society at large as "H-creativity" (or "historical creativity").

Exploratory and Transformational Creativity

Boden also distinguishes between the creativity that arises from an exploration within an established conceptual space, and the creativity that arises from a deliberate transformation or transcendence of this space. She labels the former as "exploratory creativity" and the latter as "transformational creativity", seeing the latter as a form of creativity far more radical, challenging, and rarer than the former. Following Newell and Simon's criteria, we can see that both forms of creativity should produce results that are appreciably novel and useful (criterion 1), but exploratory creativity is more likely to arise from a thorough and persistent search of a well-understood space (criterion 3) while transformational creativity should involve the rejection of some of the constraints that define this space (criterion 2) or some of the assumptions that define the problem itself (criterion 4).

Boden's insights have guided work in computational creativity at a very general level, providing more an inspirational touchstone for development work than a technical framework of algorithmic substance. However, Boden's insights are the subject of formalization, most notably in the work by Geraint Wiggins.

Generation and Evaluation

The criterion that creative products should be novel and useful means that creative computational systems are typically structured into two phases, generation and evaluation. In the first phase, novel (to the system itself, thus P-Creative) constructs are generated; unoriginal constructs that are already known to the system are filtered at this stage. This body of potentially creative constructs are then evaluated, to determine which are meaningful and useful and which are not. This two-phase structure conforms to the Geneplore model of Finke, Ward and Smith, which is a psychological model of creative generation based on empirical observation of human creativity.

Combinatorial Creativity

A great deal, perhaps all, of human creativity can be understood as a novel combination of pre-existing ideas or objects. Common strategies for combinatorial creativity include:

- placing a familiar object in an unfamiliar setting (e.g., Marcel Duchamp's Fountain) or an unfamiliar object in a familiar setting (e.g., a fish-out-of-water story such as The Beverly Hillbillies)

- Blending two superficially different objects or genres (e.g., a sci-fi story set in the Wild West, with robot cowboys, as in Westworld, or the reverse, as in Firefly; Japanese haiku poems, etc.)
- Comparing a familiar object to a superficially unrelated and semantically distant concept (e.g., "Makeup is the Western burka"; "A zoo is a gallery with living exhibits")
- Adding a new and unexpected feature to an existing concept (e.g., adding a scalpel to a Swiss Army knife; adding a camera to a mobile phone)
- Compressing two incongruous scenarios into the same narrative to get a joke (e.g., the Emo Philips joke "Women are always using me to advance their careers. Damned anthropologists!")
- Using an iconic image from one domain in a domain for an unrelated or incongruous idea or product (e.g., using the Marlboro Man image to sell cars, or to advertise the dangers of smoking-related impotence).

The combinatorial perspective allows us to model creativity as a search process through the space of possible combinations. The combinations can arise from composition or concatenation of different representations, or through a rule-based or stochastic transformation of initial and intermediate representations. Genetic algorithms and neural networks can be used to generate blended or crossover representations that capture a combination of different inputs.

Bisociation

Arthur Koestler proposes a very general model of creative combination in his 1964 book The Act of Creation, claiming that scientific discovery, art and humour are all linked by a common mechanism called "bisociation". Koestler lacked a formal, computational vocabulary for describing bisociation, which he defined as a reconciliation of two orthogonal matrices of thought (conceptual structures, mental spaces).

Conceptual Blending

Mark Turner and Gilles Fauconnier propose a model called Conceptual Integration Networks that elaborates upon the ideas of Koestler by synthesizing ideas from Cognitive Linguistic research into mental spaces and conceptual metaphors. Their basic model defines an integration network as four connected spaces:

- A first input space (contains one conceptual structure or mental space)
- A second input space (to be blended with the first input)
- A generic space of stock conventions and image-schemas that allow the input spaces to be understood from an integrated perspective
- A blend space in which a selected projection of elements from both input spaces are combined; inferences arising from this combination also reside here, sometimes leading to emergent structures that conflict with the inputs.

Fauconnier and Turner describe a collection of optimality principles that are claimed to guide the construction of a well-formed integration network. In essence, they see blending as a compression mechanism in which two or more input structures are compressed into a single blend structure. This compression operates on the level of conceptual relations. For example, a series of similarity relations between the input spaces can be compressed into a single identity relationship in the blend.

Blending theory is an elaborate framework that provides a rich terminology for describing the products of creative thinking, from metaphors to jokes to neologisms to adverts. It is most typically applied retrospectively, to describe how a blended conceptual structure could have arisen from a particular pair of input structures. These conceptual structures are often good examples of human creativity, but blending theory is not a theory of creativity, nor – despite its authors' claims – does it describe a mechanism for creativity. The theory lacks an explanation for how a creative individual chooses the input spaces that should be blended to generate a desired result.

Nonetheless, some computational success has been achieved with the blending model by extending pre-existing computational models of analogical mapping that are compatible by virtue of their emphasis on connected semantic structures. More recently, Francisco Câmara Pereira presented an implementation of blending theory that employs ideas both from GOFAI and from genetic algorithms to realize some aspects of blending theory in a practical form; his example domains range from the linguistic to the visual, and the latter most notably includes the creation of mythical monsters by combining 3-D graphical models.

Linguistic Creativity

Language provides continuous opportunity for creativity, evident in the generation of novel sentences, phrasings, puns, neologisms, rhymes, allusions, sarcasm, irony, similes, metaphors, analogies, witticisms, and jokes. Native speakers of morphologically rich languages (including all Slavic languages) frequently create new word-forms that are easily understood, although they will never find their way to the dictionary. The area of natural language generation has been well studied, but these creative aspects of everyday language have yet to be incorporated with any robustness or scale.

Story Generation

Substantial work has been conducted in this area of linguistic creation since the 1970s, with the development of James Meehan's TALE-SPIN system. TALE-SPIN viewed stories as narrative descriptions of a problem-solving effort, and created stories by first establishing a goal for the story's characters so that their search for a solution could be tracked and recorded. The MINSTREL system represents a complex elaboration of this basis approach, distinguishing a range of character-level goals in the story from a range of author-level goals for the story. Systems like Bringsjord's BRUTUS elaborate these ideas further to create stories with complex inter-personal themes like betrayal. Nonetheless, MINSTREL explicitly models the creative process with a set of Transform Recall Adapt Methods (TRAMs) to create novel scenes from old. The MEXICA model of Rafael Pérez y Pérez and Mike Sharples is more explicitly interested in the creative process of storytelling, and implements a version of the engagement-reflection cognitive model of creative writing.

The company Narrative Science makes computer generated news and reports commercially available, including summarizing team sporting events based on statistical data from the game. It also creates financial reports and real estate analyses.

Metaphor and Simile

Example of a metaphor: "She was an ape."

Example of a simile: "Felt like a tiger-fur blanket." The computational study of these phenomena has mainly focused on interpretation as a knowledge-based process. Computationalists such as Yorick Wilks, James Martin, Dan Fass, John Barnden, and Mark Lee have developed knowledge-based approaches to the processing of metaphors, either at a linguistic level or a logical level. Tony Veale and Yanfen Hao have developed a system, called Sardonicus, that acquires a comprehensive database of explicit similes from the web; these similes are then tagged as bona-fide (e.g., "as hard as steel") or ironic (e.g., "as hairy as a bowling ball", "as pleasant as a root canal"); similes of either type can be retrieved on demand for any given adjective. They use these similes as the basis of an on-line metaphor generation system called Aristotle that can suggest lexical metaphors for a given descriptive goal (e.g., to describe a supermodel as skinny, the source terms "pencil", "whip", "whippet", "rope", "stick-insect" and "snake" are suggested).

Analogy

The process of analogical reasoning has been studied from both a mapping and a retrieval perspective, the latter being key to the generation of novel analogies. The dominant school of research, as advanced by Dedre Gentner. Views analogy as a structure-preserving process; this view has been implemented in the structure mapping engine or SME, the MAC/FAC retrieval engine (Many Are Called, Few Are Chosen), ACME (Analogical Constraint Mapping Engine) and ARCS (Analogical Retrieval Constraint System). Other mapping-based approaches include Sapper, which situates the mapping process in a semantic-network model of memory. Analogy is a very active sub-area of creative computation and creative cognition; active figures in this sub-area include Douglas Hofstadter, Paul Thagard, and Keith Holyoak. Also worthy of note here is Peter Turney and Michael Littman's machine learning approach to the solving of SAT-style analogy problems; their approach achieves a score that compares well with average scores achieved by humans on these tests.

Joke Generation

Humour is an especially knowledge-hungry process, and the most successful joke-generation systems to date have focussed on pun-generation, as exemplified by the work of Kim Binsted and Graeme Ritchie. This work includes the JAPE system, which can generate a wide range of puns that are consistently evaluated as novel and humorous by young children. An improved version of JAPE has been developed in the guise of the STANDUP system, which has been experimentally deployed as a means of enhancing linguistic interaction with children with communication disabilities. Some limited progress has been made in generating humour that involves other aspects of natural language, such as the deliberate misunderstanding of pronominal reference (in the work of Hans Wim Tinholt and Anton Nijholt), as well as in the generation of humorous acronyms in the HAHAcronym system of Oliviero Stock and Carlo Strapparava.

Neologisms

The blending of multiple word forms is a dominant force for new word creation in language; these new words are commonly called "blends" or "portmanteau words" (after Lewis Carroll). Tony Veale has developed a system called ZeitGeist that harvests neological headwords from Wikipedia and interprets them relative to their local context in Wikipedia and relative to specific word senses in WordNet. ZeitGeist has been extended to generate neologisms of its own; the approach combines elements from an inventory of word parts that are harvested from WordNet, and simultaneously determines likely glosses for these new words (e.g., "food traveller" for "gastronaut" and "time traveller" for "chrononaut"). It then uses Web search to determine which glosses are meaningful and which neologisms have not been used before; this search identifies the subset of generated words that are both novel ("H-creative") and useful. Neurolinguistic inspirations have been used to analyse the process of novel word creation in the brain, understand neurocognitive processes responsible for intuition, insight, imagination and creativity and to create a server that invents novel names for products, based on their description.

Poetry

Like jokes, poems involve a complex interaction of different constraints, and no general-purpose poem generator adequately combines the meaning, phrasing, structure and rhyme aspects of poetry. Nonetheless, Pablo Gervás has developed a noteworthy system called ASPERA that employs a case-based reasoning (CBR) approach to generating poetic formulations of a given input text via a composition of poetic fragments that are retrieved from a case-base of existing poems. Each poem fragment in the ASPERA case-base is annotated with a prose string that expresses the meaning of the fragment, and this prose string is used as the retrieval key for each fragment.

Metrical rules are then used to combine these fragments into a well-formed poetic structure. Example software projects include:

- Racter
- Flowerewolf automatic poetry generator.

And poetry collections include:

- The Policeman's Beard Is Half Constructed.

Musical Creativity

Computational creativity in the music domain has focused both on the generation of musical scores for use by human musicians, and on the generation of music for performance by computers. The domain of generation has included classical music (with software that generates music in the style of Mozartand Bach) and jazz. Most notably, David Cope has written a software system called "Experiments in Musical Intelligence" (or "EMI") that is capable of analysing and generalising from existing music by a human composer to generate novel musical compositions in the same style. EMI's output is convincing enough to persuade human listeners that its music is human-generated to a high level of competence.

Creativity research in jazz has focused on the process of improvisation and the cognitive demands that this places on a musical agent: reasoning about time, remembering and conceptualizing what has already been played, and planning ahead for what might be played next. The robot Shimon, developed by Gil Weinberg of Georgia Tech, has demonstrated jazz improvisation.

In the field of musical composition, the patented works by René-Louis Baron allowed to make a robot that can create and play a multitude of orchestrated melodies so-called "coherent" in any musical style. All outdoor physical parameter associated with one or more specific musical parameters, can influence and develop each of these songs. The patented invention Medal-Composerraises problems of copyright.

Visual and Artistic Creativity

Computational creativity in the generation of visual art has had some notable successes in the creation of both abstract art and representational art. The most famous program in this domain is Harold Cohen's AARON, which has been continuously developed and augmented since 1973. Though formulaic, Aaron exhibits a range of outputs, generating black-and-white drawings or colour paintings that incorporate human figures (such as dancers), potted plants, rocks, and other elements of background imagery. These images are of a sufficiently high quality to be displayed in reputable galleries.

Other software artists of note include the NEvAr system (for "Neuro-Evolutionary Art") of Penousal Machado. NEvAr uses a genetic algorithm to derive a mathematical function that is then used to generate a coloured three-dimensional surface. A human user is allowed to select the best pictures after each phase of the genetic algorithm, and these preferences are used to guide successive phases, thereby pushing NEvAr's search into pockets of the search space that are considered most appealing to the user.

The Painting Fool, developed by Simon Colton originated as a system for overpainting digital images of a given scene in a choice of different painting styles, colour palettes and brush types. Given its dependence on an input source image to work with, the earliest iterations of the Painting Fool raised as questions about the extent of, or lack of, creativity in a computational art system. Nonetheless, in more recent work, The Painting Fool has been extended to create novel images, much as AARON does, from its own limited imagination. Images in this vein include cityscapes and forests, which are generated by a process of constraint satisfaction from some basic scenarios provided by the user (e.g., these scenarios allow the system to infer that objects closer to the viewing plane should be larger and more colour-saturated, while those further away should be less saturated and appear smaller). Artistically, the images now created by the Painting Fool appear on a par with those created by Aaron, though the extensible mechanisms employed by the former (constraint satisfaction, etc.) may well allow it to develop into a more elaborate and sophisticated painter.

Creativity in Problem Solving

Creativity is also useful in allowing for unusual solutions in problem solving. In psychology and cognitive science, this research area is called creative problem solving. The Explicit-Implicit Interaction (EII) theory of creativity has recently been implemented using a CLARION-based computational model that allows for the simulation of incubation and insight in problem solving. The emphasis of this computational creativity project is not on performance per se (as in artificial intelligence projects) but rather on the explanation of the psychological processes leading to human creativity and the reproduction of data collected in psychology experiments. So far, this project has been successful in providing an explanation for incubation effects in simple memory experiments, insight in problem solving, and reproducing the overshadowing effect in problem solving

Bioinformatics

Bioinformatics is the application of computer science and information technology to the field of biology and medicine. Bioinformatics deals with algorithms, databases and information systems, web technologies, artificial intelligence and soft computing, information and computation theory, software engineering, data mining, image processing, modelling and simulation, signal processing, discrete mathematics, control and system theory, circuit theory, and statistics, for generating new knowledge of biology and medicine, and improving & discovering new models of computation (e.g. DNA computing, neural computing, evolutionary computing, immuno-computing, swarm-computing, cellular-computing).

Commonly used software tools and technologies in this field include Java, XML, Perl, C, C++, Python, R, SQL,CUDA and MATLAB.

Bioinformatics was applied in the creation and maintenance of a database to store biological information at the beginning of the "genomic revolution", such as nucleotide sequences and amino acid sequences. Development of this type of database involved not only design issues but the development of complex interfaces whereby researchers could both access existing data as well as submit new or revised data.

In order to study how normal cellular activities are altered in different disease states, the biological data must be combined to form a comprehensive picture of these activities. Therefore, the field of bioinformatics has evolved such that the most pressing task now involves the analysis and interpretation of various types of data, including nucleotide and amino acid sequences, protein domains, and protein structures. The actual process of analysing and interpreting data is referred to as computational biology. Important sub-disciplines within bioinformatics and computational biology include:

- the development and implementation of tools that enable efficient access to, and use and management of, various types of information.

- the development of new algorithms (mathematical formulas) and statistics with which to assess relationships among members of large data sets, such as methods to locate a gene within a sequence, predict protein structure and/or function, and cluster protein sequences into families of related sequences.

The primary goal of bioinformatics is to increase the understanding of biological processes. What sets it apart from other approaches, however, is its focus on developing and applying computationally intensive techniques (e.g., pattern recognition, data mining, machine learning algorithms, and visualization) to achieve this goal. Major research efforts in the field include sequence alignment, gene finding, genome assembly, drug design, drug discovery, protein structure alignment, protein structure prediction, prediction of gene expression and protein–protein interactions, genome-wide association studies and the modelling of evolution.

Interestingly, the term bioinformatics was coined before the "genomic revolution". Paulien Hogewegand Ben Hesper introduced the term in 1978 to refer to "the study of information processes in biotic systems"., a definition that placed bioinformatics as a field parallel to biophysics or biochemistry (e.g. biochemistry is the study of chemical processes in biological systems) . However, its primary use since at least the late 1980s has been to describe the application of computer science and information sciences to the analysis of biological data, particularly in those areas of genomics involving large-scale DNA sequencing.

Bioinformatics now entails the creation and advancement of databases, algorithms, computational and statistical techniques and theory to solve formal and practical problems arising from the management and analysis of biological data.

Over the past few decades rapid developments in genomic and other molecular research technologies and developments in information technologies have combined to produce a tremendous amount of information related to molecular biology. It is the name given to these mathematical and computing approaches used to glean understanding of biological processes.

Common activities in bioinformatics include mapping and analysing DNA and protein sequences, aligning different DNA and protein sequences to compare them and creating and viewing 3-D models of protein structures.

There are two fundamental ways of modelling a Biological system (e.g. living cell) both coming under Bioinformatic approaches.

- Static
- Sequences – Proteins, Nucleic acids and Peptides
- Structures – Proteins, Nucleic acids, Ligands (including metabolites and drugs) and Peptides
- Interaction data among the above entities including microarray data and Networks of proteins, metabolites
- Dynamic
- Systems Biology comes under this category including reaction fluxes and variable concentrations of metabolites
- Multi-Agent Based modelling approaches capturing cellular events such as signalling, transcription and reaction dynamics

A broad sub-category under bioinformatics is structural bioinformatics.

Major Research Areas

Sequence Analysis

Since the Phage Φ-X174 was sequenced in 1977, the DNA sequences of thousands of organisms have been decoded and stored in databases. This sequence information is analysed to determine genes that encode polypeptides (proteins), RNA genes, regulatory sequences, structural motifs, and repetitive sequences.

A comparison of genes within a species or between different species can show similarities between protein functions, or relations between species (the use of molecular systematics to construct phylogenetic trees). With the growing amount of data, it long ago became impractical to analyse DNA sequences manually.

Today, computer programs such as BLAST are used daily to search sequences from more than 260 000 organisms, containing over 190 billion nucleotides. These programs can compensate for mutations (exchanged, deleted or inserted bases) in the DNA sequence, to identify sequences that are related, but not identical. A variant of this sequence alignment is used in the sequencing process itself. The so-called shotgun sequencing technique (which was used, for example, by The

Institute for Genomic Research to sequence the first bacterial genome, Haemophilus influenzae) does not produce entire chromosomes, but instead generates the sequences of many thousands of small DNA fragments (ranging from 35 to 900 nucleotides long, depending on the sequencing technology). The ends of these fragments overlap and, when aligned properly by a genome assembly program, can be used to reconstruct the complete genome. Shotgun sequencing yields sequence data quickly, but the task of assembling the fragments can be quite complicated for larger genomes.

For a genome as large as the human genome, it may take many days of CPU time on large-memory, multiprocessor computers to assemble the fragments, and the resulting assembly will usually contain numerous gaps that have to be filled in later. Shotgun sequencing is the method of choice for virtually all genomes sequenced today, and genome assembly algorithms are a critical area of bioinformatics research.

Another aspect of bioinformatics in sequence analysis is annotation, which involves computational gene finding to search for protein-coding genes, RNA genes, and other functional sequences within a genome. Not all of the nucleotides within a genome are part of genes. Within the genome of higher organisms, large parts of the DNA do not serve any obvious purpose. This so-called junk DNA may, however, contain unrecognized functional elements. Bioinformatics helps to bridge the gap between genome and proteome projects — for example, in the use of DNA sequences for protein identification.

Genome Annotation

In the context of genomics, annotation is the process of marking the genes and other biological features in a DNA sequence. The first genome annotation software system was designed in 1995 by Dr. Owen White, who was part of the team at The Institute for Genomic Research that sequenced and analysed the first genome of a free-living organism to be decoded, the bacterium Haemophilus influenzae. Dr. White built a software system to find the genes (places in the DNA sequence that encode a protein), the transfer RNA, and other features, and to make initial assignments of function to those genes. Most current genome annotation systems work similarly, but the programs available for analysis of genomic DNA are constantly changing and improving.

Computational Evolutionary Biology

Evolutionary biology is the study of the origin and descent of species, as well as their change over time. Informatics has assisted evolutionary biologists in several key ways; it has enabled researchers to:

- trace the evolution of a large number of organisms by measuring changes in their DNA, rather than through physical taxonomy or physiological observations alone,
- more recently, compare entire genomes, which permits the study of more complex evolutionary events, such as gene duplication, horizontal gene transfer, and the prediction of factors important in bacterial speciation,
- build complex computational models of populations to predict the outcome of the system over time
- track and share information on an increasingly large number of species and organisms

Future work endeavours to reconstruct the now more complex tree of life. The area of research within computer science that uses genetic algorithms is sometimes confused with computational evolutionary biology, but the two areas are not necessarily related.

Literature Analysis

The growth in the number of published literature makes it virtually impossible to read every paper, resulting in disjointed subfields of research. Literature analysis aims to employ computational and statistical linguistics to mine this growing library of text resources. For example:

- abbreviation recognition - identify the long-form and abbreviation of biological terms,
- named entity recognition - recognizing biological terms such as gene names
- protein-protein interaction - identify which proteins interact with which proteins from text

The area of research draws from statistics and computational linguistics.

Analysis of Gene Expression

The expression of many genes can be determined by measuring mRNA levels with multiple techniques including microarrays, expressed cDNA sequence tag (EST) sequencing, serial analysis of gene expression (SAGE) tag sequencing, massively parallel signature sequencing (MPSS), RNA-Seq, also known as "Whole Transcriptome Shotgun Sequencing" (WTSS), or various applications of multiplexed in-situ hybridization. All of these techniques are extremely noise-prone and/or subject to bias in the biological measurement, and a major research area in computational biology involves developing statistical tools to separate signal from noise in high-throughput gene expression studies. Such studies are often used to determine the genes implicated in a disorder: one might compare microarray data from cancerous epithelial cells to data from non-cancerous cells to determine the transcripts that are up-regulated and down-regulated in a particular population of cancer cells.

Analysis of Regulation

Regulation is the complex orchestration of events starting with an extracellular signal such as a hormone and leading to an increase or decrease in the activity of one or more proteins. Bioinformatics techniques have been applied to explore various steps in this process. For example, promoter analysis involves the identification and study of sequence motifs in the DNA surrounding the coding region of a gene. These motifs influence the extent to which that region is transcribed into mRNA. Expression data can be used to infer gene regulation: one might compare microarray data from a wide variety of states of an organism to form hypotheses about the genes involved in each state. In a single-cell organism, one might compare stages of the cell cycle, along with various stress conditions (heat shock, starvation, etc.). One can then apply clustering algorithms to that expression data to determine which genes are co-expressed. For example, the upstream regions (promoters) of co-expressed genes can be searched for over-represented regulatory elements.

Analysis of Protein Expression

Protein microarrays and high throughput (HT) mass spectrometry (MS) can provide a snapshot of the proteins present in a biological sample. Bioinformatics is very much involved in making sense of protein microarray and HT MS data; the former approach faces similar problems as with microarrays targeted at mRNA, the latter involves the problem of matching large amounts of mass data against predicted masses from protein sequence databases, and the complicated statistical analysis of samples where multiple, but incomplete peptides from each protein are detected.

Analysis of Mutations in Cancer

In cancer, the genomes of affected cells are rearranged in complex or even unpredictable ways. Massive sequencing efforts are used to identify previously unknown point mutations in a variety of genes in cancer. Bioinformaticians continue to produce specialized automated systems to manage the sheer volume of sequence data produced, and they create new algorithms and software to compare the sequencing results to the growing collection of human genome sequences and germline polymorphisms. New physical detection technologies are employed, such as oligonucleotidem icroarrays to identify chromosomal gains and losses (called comparative genomic hybridization), and single-nucleotide polymorphism arrays to detect known point mutations. These detection methods simultaneously measure several hundred thousand sites throughout the genome, and when used in high-throughput to measure thousands of samples, generate terabytes of data per experiment. Again the massive amounts and new types of data generate new opportunities for bioinformaticians. The data is often found to contain considerable variability, or noise, and thus Hidden Markov model and change-point analysis methods are being developed to infer real copy number changes.

Another type of data that requires novel informatics development is the analysis of lesions found to be recurrent among many tumors.

Comparative Genomics

The core of comparative genome analysis is the establishment of the correspondence between genes (orthology analysis) or other genomic features in different organisms. It is these intergenomic maps that make it possible to trace the evolutionary processes responsible for the divergence of two genomes. A multitude of evolutionary events acting at various organizational levels shape genome evolution. At the lowest level, point mutations affect individual nucleotides. At a higher level, large chromosomal segments undergo duplication, lateral transfer, inversion, transposition, deletion and insertion. Ultimately, whole genomes are involved in processes of hybridization, polyploidization and endosymbiosis, often leading to rapid speciation. The complexity of genome evolution poses many exciting challenges to developers of mathematical models and algorithms, who have recourse to a spectra of algorithmic, statistical and mathematical techniques, ranging from exact, heuristics, fixed parameter and approximation algorithms for problems based on parsimony models to Markov Chain Monte Carlo algorithms for Bayesian analysis of problems based on probabilistic models.

Many of these studies are based on the homology detection and protein families computation.

Modelling Biological Systems

Systems biology involves the use of computer simulations of cellular subsystems (such as the networks of metabolites and enzymes which comprise metabolism, signal transduction pathways and gene regulatory networks) to both analyse and visualize the complex connections of these cellular processes. Artificial life or virtual evolution attempts to understand evolutionary processes via the computer simulation of simple (artificial) life forms.

High-throughput Image Analysis

Computational technologies are used to accelerate or fully automate the processing, quantification and analysis of large amounts of high-information-content biomedical imagery. Modern image analysis systems augment an observer's ability to make measurements from a large or complex set of images, by improving accuracy, objectivity, or speed. A fully developed analysis system may completely replace the observer. Although these systems are not unique to biomedical imagery, biomedical imaging is becoming more important for both diagnostics and research. Some examples are:

- high-throughput and high-fidelity quantification and subcellular localization (high-content screening, cytohistopathology, Bioimage informatics)
- morphometrics
- clinical image analysis and visualization
- determining the real-time air-flow patterns in breathing lungs of living animals
- quantifying occlusion size in real-time imagery from the development of and recovery during arterial injury
- making behavioural observations from extended video recordings of laboratory animals

- infrared measurements for metabolic activity determination
- inferring clone overlaps in DNA mapping, e.g. the Sulston score

Structural Bioinformatic Approaches

Prediction of Protein Structure

Protein structure prediction is another important application of bioinformatics. The amino acid sequence of a protein, the so-called primary structure, can be easily determined from the sequence on the gene that codes for it. In the vast majority of cases, this primary structure uniquely determines a structure in its native environment. (Of course, there are exceptions, such as the bovine spongi form encephalopathy – a.k.a. Mad Cow Disease – prion.) Knowledge of this structure is vital in understanding the function of the protein. For lack of better terms, structural information is usually classified as one of secondary, tertiary and quaternary structure. A viable general solution to such predictions remains an open problem. As of now, most efforts have been directed towards heuristics that work most of the time.

One of the key ideas in bioinformatics is the notion of homology. In the genomic branch of bioinformatics, homology is used to predict the function of a gene: if the sequence of gene A, whose function is known, is homologous to the sequence of gene B, whose function is unknown, one could infer that B may share A's function. In the structural branch of bioinformatics, homology is used to determine which parts of a protein are important in structure formation and interaction with other proteins. In a technique called homology modelling, this information is used to predict the structure of a protein once the structure of a homologous protein is known. This currently remains the only way to predict protein structures reliably.

One example of this is the similar protein homology between hemoglobin in humans and the hemoglobin in legumes (leghemoglobin). Both serve the same purpose of transporting oxygen in the organism. Though both of these proteins have completely different amino acid sequences, their protein structures are virtually identical, which reflects their near identical purposes.

Other techniques for predicting protein structure include protein threading and de novo (from scratch) physics-based modelling.

Molecular Interaction

Efficient software is available today for studying interactions among proteins, ligands and peptides. Types of interactions most often encountered in the field include – Protein–ligand (including drug), protein–protein and protein–peptide.

Molecular dynamic simulation of movement of atoms about rotatable bonds is the fundamental principle behind computational algorithms, termed docking algorithms for studying molecular interactions.

Docking Algorithms

In the last two decades, tens of thousands of protein three-dimensional structures have been determined by X-ray crystallography and Protein nuclear magnetic resonance spectroscopy (protein NMR). One central question for the biological scientist is whether it is practical to predict possible protein–protein interactions only based on these 3D shapes, without doing protein–protein interaction experiments. A variety of methods have been developed to tackle the Protein–protein docking problem, though it seems that there is still much work to be done in this field.

Software and Tools

Software tools for bioinformatics range from simple command-line tools, to more complex graphical programs and standalone web-services available from various bioinformatics companies or public institutions.

Open Source Bioinformatics Software

Many free and open source software tools have existed and continued to grow since the 1980s. The combination of a continued need for new algorithms for the analysis of emerging types of biological readouts, the potential for innovative in silico experiments, and freely available open code bases have helped to create opportunities for all research groups to contribute to both bioinformatics and the range of open source software available, regardless of their funding arrangements. The open source tools often act as incubators of ideas, or community-supported plug-ins in commercial applications. They may also provide de facto standards and shared object models for assisting with the challenge of bioinformation integration.

The range of open source software packages includes titles such as Bioconductor, BioPerl, BioJava,BioRuby, Bioclipse, EMBOSS, Taverna workbench, and UGENE. In order to maintain this tradition and create further opportunities, the non-profit Open Bioinformatics Foundation have supported the annual Bioinformatics Open Source Conference (BOSC) since 2000.

Web Services in Bioinformatics

SOAP and REST-based interfaces have been developed for a wide variety of bioinformatics applications allowing an application running on one computer in one part of the world to use algorithms, data and computing resources on servers in other parts of the world. The main advantages derive from the fact that end users do not have to deal with software and database maintenance overheads.

Basic bioinformatics services are classified by the EBI into three categories: SSS (Sequence Search Services), MSA (Multiple Sequence Alignment) and BSA (Biological Sequence Analysis). The availability of these service-oriented bioinformatics resources demonstrate the applicability of web based bioinformatics solutions, and range from a collection of standalone tools with a common data format under a single, standalone or web-based interface, to integrative, distributed and extensible bioinformatics workflow management systems.

Cryptanalysis

Figure: Close-up of the rotors in a Fialka cipher machine

Cryptanalysis (from the Greek kryptós, "hidden", andanalýein, "to loosen" or "to untie") is the study of methods for obtaining the meaning of encrypted information, without access to the secret information that is normally required to do so. Typically, this involves knowing how the system works and finding a secret key. In non-technical language, this is the practice of codebreaking or cracking the code, although these phrases also have a specialised technical meaning.

Cryptanalysis is also used to refer to any attempt to circumvent the security of other types of cryptographic algorithms and protocols in general, and not justencryption. However, cryptanalysis usually excludes methods of attack that do not primarily target weaknesses in the actual cryptography, such as bribery, physical coercion, burglary, keystroke logging, and social engineering, although these types of attack are an important concern and are often more effective than traditional cryptanalysis.

Even though the goal has been the same, the methods and techniques of cryptanalysis have changed drastically through the history of cryptography, adapting to increasing cryptographic complexity, ranging from the pen-and-paper methods of the past, through machines like Bombes and Colossus computers at Bletchley Park in World War II, to the computer-based schemes of the present. The results of cryptanalysis have also changed — it is no longer possible to have unlimited success in codebreaking, and there is a hierarchical classification of what constitutes an attack. In the mid-1970s, a new class of cryptography was introduced: asymmetric cryptography. Methods for breaking these cryptosystems are typically radically different from before, and usually involve solving carefully constructed problems in pure mathematics, the best-known being integer factorization.

History of Cryptanalysis

Cryptanalysis has coevolved together with cryptography, and the contest can be traced through the history of cryptography—new ciphers being designed to replace old broken designs, and new cryptanalytic techniques invented to crack the improved schemes. In practice, they are viewed as two sides of the same coin: in order to create secure cryptography, you have to design against possible cryptanalysis.

Classical Cryptanalysis

Although the actual word "cryptanalysis" is relatively recent (it was coined by William Friedman in 1920), methods for breaking codes and ciphers are much older. The first known recorded explanation of cryptanalysis was given by 9th-century Arabian polymath, Al-Kindi (also known as "Alkindus" in Europe), in A Manuscript on Deciphering

Cryptographic Messages. This treatise includes a description of the method of frequency analysis (Ibrahim Al-Kadi, 1992- ref-3). Italian scholar Giambattista della Porta was author of a seminal work on cryptanalysis "De Furtivis Literarum Notis".

Frequency analysis is the basic tool for breaking mostclassical ciphers. In natural languages, certain letters of the alphabet appear more frequently than others; in English, "E" is likely to be the most common letter in any sample of plaintext. Similarly, the digraph "TH" is the most likely pair of letters in English, and so on. Frequency analysis relies on a cipher failing to hide these statistics.

For example, in a simple substitution cipher (where each letter is simply replaced with another), the most frequent letter in the ciphertext would be a likely candidate for "E". Frequency analysis of such a cipher is therefore relatively easy, provided that the ciphertext is long enough to give a reasonably representative count of the letters of the alphabet that it contains.

In Europe during the 15th and 16th centuries, the idea of a polyalphabetic substitution cipher was developed, among others by the French diplomat Blaise de Vigenère (1523–96). For some three centuries, the Vigenère cipher, which uses a repeating key to select different encryption alphabets in rotation, was considered to be completely secure (le chiffre indéchiffrable—"the indecipherable cipher"). Nevertheless, Charles Babbage (1791–1871) and later, independently, Friedrich Kasiski(1805–81) succeeded in breaking this cipher. During World War I, inventors in several countries developed rotor cipher machines such as Arthur Scherbius' Enigma, in an attempt to minimise the repetition that had been exploited to break the Vigenère system.

In practice, frequency analysis relies as much on linguistic knowledge as it does on statistics, but as ciphers became more complex, mathematics became more important in cryptanalysis. This change was particularly evident before and during World War II, where efforts to crack Axis ciphers required new levels of mathematical sophistication. Moreover, automation was first applied to cryptanalysis in that era with the Polish Bomba device, the British Bombe development of it, the use of punched card equipment, and in the Colossus computers — the first electronic digital computers to be controlled by a program.

Depth

Sending two or more messages with the same key is an insecure process. To a cryptanalyst the messages are then said to be "in depth". This may be detected by the messages having the same indicator by which the sending operator informs the receiving operator about the key generator initial settings for the message.

In a symmetrical cipher, the same key that was applied to the plaintext to produce the ciphertext is applied to the ciphertext to recover the plaintext. A simple example of such a system is the Vernam cipher in which a long key is bit-for-bit combined with the plaintext or ciphertext using the "XOR" operator (symbolized by $\otimes$):

$$Plaintext \oplus Key = Ciphertext \text{ at each bit position}$$

and

$$Ciphertext \oplus Key = Plaintext \text{ at each bit position}$$

When the ciphertexts are in depth, combining them eliminates the common key, leaving just a combination of the two plaintexts:

$Ciphertext1 \oplus Ciphertext2 = \alpha = Plaintext1 \oplus Plaintext2$ at each bit position.

The individual plaintexts can then be worked out by trying probable words (or phrases) at various locations; when the corresponding section of á is XORed with a correct guess at the probable word, a stretch of the other plaintext is revealed, which can be recognized and (quite often) extended at each end, working back and forth between the plaintexts to recover much or all of them.

When a recovered plaintext is then combined with its ciphertext, the key is revealed:

$$Plaintext1 \oplus Ciphertext1 = Key \text{ at each bit position}$$

Knowledge of keys from a cipher may allow cryptanalysts to work out the system used for constructing them.

Depth reading can be applied in more complicated contexts to eliminate some of a system's parameters, or to "stack" messages so that source language statistics become exploitable. One way to properly align multiple messages that use the same periodic key starting at different positions is by the kappa test.

Modern Cryptanalysis

Figure: The Bombe replicated the action of several Enigma machines wired together. Each of the rapidly rotating drums, pictured above in a Bletchley Park museum mockup, simulated the action of an Enigma rotor.

Even though computation was used to great effect in cryptanalysis of the Enigma and other systems during World War II, it also made possible new methods of cryptography orders of magnitude more complex than ever before. Taken as a whole, modern cryptography has become much more impervious to cryptanalysis than the pen-and-paper systems of the past, and now seems to have the upper hand against pure cryptanalysis. The historian David Kahn notes,

"Many are the cryptosystems offered by the hundreds of commercial vendors today that cannot be broken by any known methods of cryptanalysis. Indeed, in such systems even a chosen plaintext attack, in which a selected plaintext is matched against its ciphertext, cannot yield the key that unlock[s] other messages. In a sense, then, cryptanalysis is dead. But that is not the end of the story. Cryptanalysis may be dead, but there is - to mix my metaphors - more than one way to skin a cat.". Kahn goes on to mention increased opportunities for interception, bugging, side channel attacks, and quantum computers as replacements for the traditional means of cryptanalysis. In 2010, former NSA technical director Brian Snow said that both academic and government cryptographers are "moving very slowly forward in a mature field."

However, any postmortems for cryptanalysis may be premature. While the effectiveness of cryptanalytic methods employed by intelligence agencies remains unknown, many serious attacks against both academic and practical cryptographic primitives have been published in the modern era of computer cryptography:

- The block cipher Madryga, proposed in 1984 but not widely used, was found to be susceptible to ciphertext-only attacks in 1998.
- FEAL-4, proposed as a replacement for the DES standard encryption algorithm but not widely used, was demolished by a spate of attacks from the academic community, many of which are entirely practical.
- The A5/1, A5/2, CMEA, and DECT systems used in mobile and wireless phone technology can all be broken in hours, minutes or even in real-time using widely-available computing equipment.
- Brute-force keyspace search has broken some real-world ciphers and applications, including single-DES, 40-bit "export-strength" cryptography, and the DVD Content Scrambling System.
- In 2001, Wired Equivalent Privacy (WEP), a protocol used to secure Wi-Fi wireless networks, was shown to be breakable in practice because of a weakness in the RC4 cipher and aspects of the WEP design that made related-key attacks practical. WEP was later replaced by Wi-Fi Protected Access.
- In 2008, researchers conducted a proof-of-concept break of SSL using weaknesses in the MD5hash function and certificate issuer practices that made it possible to exploit collision attacks on hash functions. The certificate issuers involved changed their practices to prevent the attack from being repeated.

Thus, while the best modern ciphers may be far more resistant to cryptanalysis than the Enigma, cryptanalysis and the broader field of information security remain quite active.

The Results of Cryptanalysis

Successful cryptanalysis has undoubtedly influenced history; the ability to read the presumed-secret thoughts and plans of others can be a decisive advantage. For example, in England in 1587, Mary, Queen of Scots was tried and executed for treason for her involvement in three plots to assassinate Elizabeth I of England which were known about because her coded correspondence with fellow conspirators had been deciphered by Thomas Phelippes; in World War I, the breaking of the Zimmermann Telegram was instrumental in bringing the United States into the war; in World War II, the cryptanalysis of the German ciphers — including the Enigma machine and the Lorenz cipher —

has been credited with everything between shortening the end of the European war by a few months to determining the eventual result. The United States also benefited from the cryptanalysis of the Japanese Purple code.

Governments have long recognized the potential benefits of cryptanalysis for intelligence, both military and diplomatic, and established dedicated organizations devoted to breaking the codes and ciphers of other nations, for example, GCHQ and the NSA, organizations which are still very active today. In 2004, it was reported that the United States had broken Iranian ciphers. (It is unknown, however, whether this was pure cryptanalysis, or whether other factors were involved:).

Types of Cryptanalytic Attack

Cryptanalytic attacks vary in potency and how much of a threat they pose to real-world cryptosystems. A certificational weakness is a theoretical attack that is unlikely to be applicable in any real-world situation; the majority of results found in modern cryptanalytic research are of this type. Essentially, the practical importance of an attack is dependent on the answers to the following four questions:

1. What knowledge and capabilities does the attacker need?
2. How much additional secret information is deduced?
3. How much computation is required? (What is the computational complexity?)
4. Does the attack break the full cryptosystem, or only a weakened version?

Access Needed for the Attack

Cryptanalysis can be performed under a number of assumptions about how much access the attacker has to the system under attack. As a basic starting point it is normally assumed that, for the purposes of analysis, the general algorithm is known; this is Kerckhoffs' principle of "the enemy knows the system". This is a reasonable assumption in practice — throughout history, there are countless examples of secret algorithms falling into wider knowledge, variously through espionage, betrayal and reverse engineering. (On occasion, ciphers have been reconstructed through pure deduction; for example, the German Lorenz cipher and the Japanese Purple code, and a variety of classical schemes).

Other assumptions include:

- Ciphertext-only: the cryptanalyst has access only to a collection of ciphertexts or codetexts.
- Known-plaintext: the attacker has a set of ciphertexts to which he knows the corresponding plaintext.
- Chosen-plaintext (chosen-ciphertext): the attacker can obtain the ciphertexts (plaintexts) corresponding to an arbitrary set of plaintexts (ciphertexts) of his own choosing.
- Adaptive chosen-plaintext: like a chosen-plaintext attack, except the attacker can choose subsequent plaintexts based on information learned from previous encryptions. Similarly Adaptive chosen ciphertext attack.
- Related-key attack: Like a chosen-plaintext attack, except the attacker can obtain ciphertexts encrypted under two different keys. The keys are unknown, but the relationship between them is known; for example, two keys that differ in the one bit.

These types of attack clearly differ in how plausible they would be to mount in practice. Although some are more likely than others, cryptographers will often take a conservative approach to security and assume the worst-case when designing algorithms, reasoning that if a scheme is secure even against unrealistic threats, then it should also resist real-world cryptanalysis as well. The assumptions are often more realistic than they might seem upon first glance. For a known-plaintext attack, the cryptanalyst might well know or be able to guess at a likely part of the plaintext, such as an encrypted letter beginning with "Dear Sir", or a computer session starting with "LOGIN:". A chosen-plaintext attack is less likely, but it is sometimes plausible: for example, you could convince someone to forward a message you have given them, but in encrypted form. Related-key attacks are mostly theoretical, although they can be realistic in certain situations, for example, when constructing cryptographic hash functions using a block cipher.

Usefulness of Attack Results

The results of cryptanalysis can also vary in usefulness. For example, cryptographer Lars Knudsen(1998) classified various types of attack on block ciphers according to the amount and quality of secret information that was discovered:

- Total break — the attacker deduces the secret key.
- Global deduction — the attacker discovers a functionally equivalent algorithm for encryption and decryption, but without learning the key.
- Instance (local) deduction — the attacker discovers additional plaintexts (or ciphertexts) not previously known.
- Information deduction — the attacker gains some Shannon information about plaintexts (or ciphertexts) not previously known.
- Distinguishing algorithm — the attacker can distinguish the cipher from a random permutation.

Similar considerations apply to attacks on other types of cryptographic algorithm.

Computational Resources Required

Attacks can also be characterised by the resources they require. Those resources include:

- Time — the number of computation steps (like encryptions) which must be performed.
- Memory — the amount of storage required to perform the attack.
- Data — the quantity of plaintexts and ciphertexts required.

It's sometimes difficult to predict these quantities precisely, especially when the attack isn't practical to actually implement for testing. But academic cryptanalysts tend to provide at least the estimated order of magnitude of their attacks' difficulty, saying, for example, "SHA-1 collisions now 2". Bruce Schneier notes that even computationally impractical attacks can be considered breaks: "Breaking a cipher simply means finding a weakness in the cipher that can be exploited with a complexity less than brute force. Never mind that brute-force might require 2 encryptions; an attack requiring 2 encryptions would be considered a break...simply put, a break can just be a certificational weakness: evidence that the cipher does not perform as advertised."

Partial Breaks

Academic attacks are often against weakened versions of a cryptosystem, such as a block cipher or hash function with some rounds removed. Many, but not all, attacks become exponentially more difficult to execute as rounds are added to a cryptosystem, so it's possible for the full cryptosystem to be strong even though reduced-round variants are weak. Nonetheless, partial breaks that come close to breaking the original cryptosystem may mean that a full break will follow; the successful attacks on DES, MD5, and SHA-1 were all preceded by attacks on weakened versions.

Academic Weakness versus Practical Weakness

In academic cryptography, a weakness or a break in a scheme is usually defined quite conservatively: it might require impractical amounts of time, memory, or known plaintexts. It also might require the attacker be able to do things many real-world attackers can't: for example, the attacker may need to choose particular plaintexts to be encrypted or even to ask for plaintexts to be encrypted using several keys related to the secret key. Furthermore, it might only reveal a small amount of information, enough to prove the cryptosystem imperfect but too little to be useful to real-world attackers. Finally, an attack might only apply to a weakened version of cryptographic tools, like a reduced-round block cipher, as a step towards breaking of the full system.

Cryptanalysis of Asymmetric Cryptography

Asymmetric cryptography (or public key cryptography) is cryptography that relies on using two keys; one private, and one public. Such ciphers invariably rely on "hard" mathematical problems as the basis of their security, so an obvious point of attack is to develop methods for solving the problem. The security of two-key cryptography depends on mathematical questions in a way that single-key cryptography generally does not, and conversely links cryptanalysis to wider mathematical research in a new way.

Asymmetric schemes are designed around the (conjectured) difficulty of solving various mathematical problems. If an improved algorithm can be found to solve the problem, then the system is weakened. For example, the security of the Diffie-Hellman key exchange scheme depends on the difficulty of calculating the discrete logarithm. In 1983, Don Coppersmith found a faster way to find discrete logarithms (in certain groups), and thereby requiring cryptographers to use larger groups (or different types of groups). RSA's security depends (in part) upon the difficulty of integer factorization — a breakthrough in factoring would impact the security of RSA. In 1980, one could factor a difficult 50-digit number at an expense of 10 elementary computer operations. By 1984 the state of the art in factoring algorithms had advanced to a point where a 75-digit number could be factored in 10 operations. Advances in computing technology also meant that the operations could be performed much faster, too. Moore's law predicts that computer speeds will continue to increase.

Factoring techniques may continue to do so as well, but will most likely depend on mathematical insight and creativity, neither of which has ever been successfully predictable. 150-digit numbers of the kind once used in RSA have been factored. The effort was greater than above, but was not unreasonable on fast modern computers. By the start of the 21st century, 150-digit numbers were no longer considered a large enough key size for RSA. Numbers with several hundred digits were still considered too hard to factor in 2005, though methods will probably continue to improve over time, requiring key size to keep pace or other methods such as elliptic curve cryptography to be used.

Another distinguishing feature of asymmetric schemes is that, unlike attacks on symmetric cryptosystems, any cryptanalysis has the opportunity to make use of knowledge gained from the public key.

Quantum Computing Applications for Cryptanalysis

Quantum computers, which are still in the early phases of research, have potential use in cryptanalysis. For example, Shor's Algorithm could factor large numbers in polynomial time, in effect breaking some commonly used forms of public-key encryption. By using Grover's algorithm on a quantum computer, brute-force key search can be made quadratically faster. However, this could be countered by doubling the key length.

Pop Music

Pop music (a term that originally derives from an abbreviation of "popular") is usually understood to be commercially recorded music, often oriented toward a youth market, usually consisting of relatively short, simple songs utilizing technological innovations to produce new variations on existing themes.

Definitions

David Hatch and Stephen Millward define pop music as "a body of music which is distinguishable from popular, jazz and folk musics". Although pop music is often seen as oriented towards the singles charts it is not the sum of all chart music, which has always contained songs from a variety of sources, including classical, jazz, rock, and novelty songs, while pop music as a genre is usually seen as existing and developing separately. Thus "pop music" may be used to describe a distinct genre, aimed at a youth market, often characterized as a softer alternative to rock and roll.

Origin of the Term

The term "pop song" is first recorded as being used in 1926, in the sense of a piece of music "having popular appeal". Hatch and Millward indicate that many events in the history of recording in the 1920s can be seen as the birth of the modern pop music industry, including in country, blues and hillbilly music. According to Grove Music Online, the term "pop music" "originated in Britain in the mid-1950s as a description for Rock and roll and the new youth music styles that it influenced...". The Oxford Dictionary of Music states that while pop's "earlier meaning meant concerts appealing to a wide audience...[,] since the late 1950s, however, pop has had the special meaning of non-classical music, usually in the form of songs, performed by such artists as the Beatles, the Rolling Stones, ABBA, etc." Grove Music Online also states that "... in the early 1960s [the term] 'pop music' competed terminologically with Beat music [in England], while in the USA its coverage overlapped (as it still does) with that of 'rock and roll'." Chambers' Dictionary mentions the contemporary usage of the term "pop art"; Grove Music Online states that the "term pop music... seems to have been a spin-off from the terms pop art and pop culture, coined slightly earlier, and referring to a whole range of new, often American, media-culture products".

From about 1967 the term was increasingly used in opposition to the term rock music, a division that gave generic significance to both terms. Whereas rock aspired to authenticity and an expansion of the possibilities of popular music, pop was more commercial, ephemeral and accessible. According to Simon Frith pop music is produced "as a matter of enterprise not art", is "designed to appeal to everyone" and "doesn't come from any particular place or mark off any particular taste". It is "not driven by any significant ambition except profit and commercial reward... and, in musical terms, it is essentially conservative". It is, "provided from on high (by record companies, radio programmers and concert promoters) rather than being made from below... Pop is not a do-it-yourself music but is professionally produced and packaged".

Influences and Development

Throughout its development, pop music has absorbed influences from most other genres of popular music. Early pop music drew on the sentimental ballad for its form, gained its use of vocal harmonies from gospel and soul music, instrumentation from jazz, country, and rock music, orchestration from classical music, tempo from dance music, backing from electronic music, rhythmic elements from hip-hop music, and has recently appropriated spoken passages from rap. It has also made use of technological innovation. In the 1940s improved microphone design allowed a more intimate singing style and ten or twenty years later inexpensive and more durable 45 r.p.m. records for singles "revolutionized the manner in which pop has been disseminated" and helped to move pop music to 'a record/radio/film star system'. Another technological change was the widespread availability of television in the 1950s; with televised performances, "pop stars had to have a visual presence". In the 1960s, the introduction of inexpensive, portable transistor radios meant that teenagers could listen to music outside of the home. Multi-track recording (from the 1960s); and digital sampling (from the 1980s) have also been utilized as methods for the creation and elaboration of pop music. By the early 1980s, the promotion of pop music had been greatly affected by the rise of Music Television channels like MTV, which "favoured those artists such as Michael Jackson andMadonna who had a strong visual appeal".

Pop music has been dominated by the American and (from the mid-1960s) British music industries, whose influence has made pop music something of an international monoculture, but most regions and countries have their own form of pop music, sometimes producing local versions of wider trends, and lending them local characteristics. Some of these trends (for example Europop) have had a significant impact of the development of the genre.

According to Grove Music Online, "Western-derived pop styles, whether coexisting with or marginalizing distinctively local genres, have spread throughout the world and have come to constitute stylistic common denominators in global commercial music cultures". Some non-Western countries, such as Japan, have developed a thriving pop music industry, most of which is devoted to Western-style pop, has for several years has produced a greater quantity of music of everywhere except the USA. The spread of Western-style pop music has been interpreted variously as representing processes of Americanization, homogenization, modernization, creative appropriation, cultural imperialism, and/or a more general process of globalization.

Characteristics

Musicologists often identify the following characteristics as typical of the pop music genre:

- an aim of appealing to a general audience, rather than to a particular subculture or ideology
- an emphasis on craftsmanship rather than formal "artistic" qualities
- an emphasis on recording, production, and technology, over live performance
- a tendency to reflect existing trends rather than progressive developments
- much pop music is intended to encourage dancing, or it uses dance-oriented beats or rhythms

The main medium of pop music is the song, often between two and a half and three and a half minutes in length, generally marked by a consistent and noticeable rhythmic element, a mainstream style and a simple traditional structure. Common variants include the verse-chorus form and the thirty-two-bar form, with a focus on melodies and catchy hooks, and a chorus that contrasts melodically, rhythmically and harmonically with the verse. The beat and the melodies tend to be simple, with limited harmonic accompaniment. The lyrics of modern pop songs typically focus on simple themes – often love and romantic relationships – although there are notable exceptions.

Harmony in pop music is often "that of classical European tonality, only more simple-minded. "Clichés include the barbershop harmony (i.e. moving from a secondary dominant harmony to a dominant harmony, and then to the tonic) and blues scale-influenced harmony. "The influence of the circle-of-fifths paradigm has declined since the mid-1950s.

The harmonic languages of rock and soul have moved away from the all-encompassing influence of the dominant function....There are other tendencies (perhaps also traceable to the use of a guitar as a composing instrument) – pedal-pointharmonies, root motion by diatonic step, modal harmonic and melodic organization – that point away from functional tonality and toward a tonal sense that is less directional, more free-floating."

Travelling Salesman Problem

The travelling salesman problem (TSP) is an NP-hard problem in combinatorial optimisation studied in operations research and theoretical computer science. Given a list of cities and their pairwise distances, the task is to find the shortest possible tour that visits each city exactly once. It is a special case of the Travelling purchaser problem. The problem was first formulated as a mathematical problem in 1930 and is one of the most intensively studied problems in optimisation. It is used as a benchmark for many optimisation methods. Even though the problem is computationally difficult, a large number of heuristics and exact methods are known, so that some instances with tens of thousands of cities can be solved.

The TSP has several applications even in its purest formulation, such as planning, logistics, and the manufacture of microchips. Slightly modified, it appears as a sub-problem in many areas, such as DNA sequencing. In these applications, the concept city represents, for example, customers, soldering points, or DNA fragments, and the concept distance represents travelling times or cost, or a similarity measure between DNA fragments. In many applications, additional constraints such as limited resources or time windows make the problem considerably harder. In the theory of computational complexity, the decision version of the TSP (where, given a length L, the task is to decide whether any tour is shorter than L) belongs to the class of NP-complete problems. Thus, it is likely that the worst case running time for any algorithm for the TSP increases exponentially with the number of cities.

History

The origins of the travelling salesman problem are unclear. A handbook for travelling salesmen from 1832 mentions the problem and includes example tours through Germany and Switzerland, but contains no mathematical treatment.

The travelling salesman problem was defined in the 1800s by the Irish mathematician W. R. Hamilton and by the British mathematician Thomas Kirkman. Hamilton's Icosian Game was a recreational puzzle based on finding a Hamiltonian cycle. The general form of the TSP appears to have been first studied by mathematicians during the 1930s in Vienna and at Harvard, notably by Karl Menger, who defines the problem, considers the obvious brute-force algorithm, and observes the non-optimality of the nearest neighbour heuristic:

We denote by messenger problem (since in practice this question should be solved by each postman, anyway also by many travelers) the task to find, for finitely many points whose pairwise distances are known, the shortest route connecting the points. Of course, this problem is solvable by finitely many trials. Rules which would push the number of trials below the number of permutations of the given points, are not known. The rule that one first should go from the starting point to the closest point, then to the point closest to this, etc., in general does not yield the shortest route.

Hassler Whitney at Princeton University introduced the name travelling salesman problem soon after.

In the 1950s and 1960s, the problem became increasingly popular in scientific circles in Europe and the USA. Notable contributions were made by George Dantzig, Delbert Ray Fulkerson and Selmer M. Johnson at the RAND Corporation in Santa Monica, who expressed the problem as an integer linear program and developed the cutting plane method for its solution.

With these new methods they solved an instance with 49 cities to optimality by constructing a tour and proving that no other tour could be shorter. In the following decades, the problem was studied by many researchers from mathematics, computer science, chemistry, physics, and other sciences.

Richard M. Karp showed in 1972 that the Hamiltonian cycle problem was NP-complete, which implies the NP-hardness of TSP. This supplied a mathematical explanation for the apparent computational difficulty of finding optimal tours.

Great progress was made in the late 1970s and 1980, when Grötschel, Padberg, Rinaldi and others managed to exactly solve instances with up to 2392 cities, using cutting planes and branch-and-bound.

In the 1990s, Applegate, Bixby, Chvátal, and Cook developed the program Concorde that has been used in many recent record solutions. Gerhard Reinelt published the TSPLIB in 1991, a collection of benchmark instances of varying difficulty, which has been used by many research groups for comparing results. In 2005, Cook and others computed an optimal tour through a 33,810-city instance given by a microchip layout problem, currently the largest solved TSPLIB instance. For many other instances with millions of cities, solutions can be found that are guaranteed to be within 1% of an optimal tour.

Description

As a graph problem:

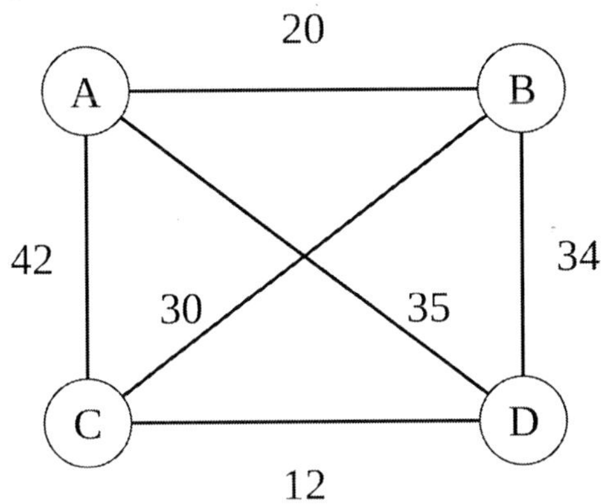

Figure: Symmetric TSP with four cities

TSP can be modelled as an undirected weighted graph, such that cities are the graph's vertices, paths are the graph's edges, and a path's distance is the edge's length. A TSP tour becomes a Hamiltonian cycle if and only if every edge has the same distance. Often, the model is a complete graph (i.e., an edge connects each pair of vertices). If no path exists between two cities, adding an arbitrarily long edge will complete the graph without affecting the optimal tour.

Asymmetric and Symmetric

In the symmetric TSP, the distance between two cities is the same in each opposite direction, forming an undirected graph. This symmetry halves the number of possible solutions. In the asymmetric TSP, paths may not exist in both directions or the distances might be different, forming a directed graph.

Traffic collisions, one-way streets, and airfares for cities with different departure and arrival fees are examples of how this symmetry could break down.

Related Problems

- An equivalent formulation in terms of graph theory is: Given a complete weighted graph (where the vertices would represent the cities, the edges would represent the roads, and the weights would be the cost or distance of that road), find a Hamiltonian cycle with the least weight.
- The requirement of returning to the starting city does not change the computational complexity of the problem.

- Another related problem is the bottleneck travelling salesman problem (bottleneck TSP): Find a Hamiltonian cycle in a weighted graph with the minimal weight of the weightiest edge. The problem is of considerable practical importance, apart from evident transportation and logistics areas. A classic example is in printed circuit manufacturing: scheduling of a route of the drill machine to drill holes in a PCB. In robotic machining or drilling applications, the "cities" are parts to machine or holes (of different sizes) to drill, and the "cost of travel" includes time for retooling the robot (single machine job sequencing problem).
- The generalised travelling salesman problem deals with "states" that have (one or more) "cities" and the salesman has to visit exactly one "city" from each "state". Also known as the "travelling politician problem". One application is encountered in ordering a solution to the cutting stock problem in order to minimise knife changes. Another is concerned with drilling in semiconductor manufacturing. Surprisingly, Behzad and Modarres demonstrated that the generalised travelling salesman problem can be transformed into a standard travelling salesman problem with the same number of cities, but a modified distance matrix.
- The sequential ordering problem deals with the problem of visiting a set of cities where precedence relations between the cities exist.
- The travelling purchaser problem deals with a purchaser who is charged with purchasing a set of products. He can purchase these products in several cities, but at different prices and not all cities offer the same products. The objective is to find a route between a subset of the cities, which minimizes total cost (travel cost + purchasing cost) and which enables the purchase of all required products.

Computing a Solution

The traditional lines of attack for the NP-hard problems are the following:

- Devising algorithms for finding exact solutions (they will work reasonably fast only for small problem sizes).
- Devising "suboptimal" or heuristic algorithms, i.e., algorithms that deliver either seemingly or probably good solutions, but which could not be proved to be optimal.

- Finding special cases for the problem ("subproblems") for which either better or exact heuristics are possible.

Computational Complexity

The problem has been shown to be NP-hard (more precisely, it is complete for the complexity class FP), and the decision problem version ("given the costs and a number x, decide whether there is a round-trip route cheaper than x") is NP-complete. The bottleneck travelling salesman problem is also NP-hard. The problem remains NP-hard even for the case when the cities are in the plane with Euclidean distances, as well as in a number of other restrictive cases. Removing the condition of visiting each city "only once" does not remove the NP-hardness, since it is easily seen that in the planar case there is an optimal tour that visits each city only once (otherwise, by the triangle inequality, a shortcut that skips a repeated visit would not increase the tour length).

Complexity of Approximation

In the general case, finding a shortest travelling salesman tour is NPO-complete. If the distance measure is a metric and symmetric, the problem becomes APX-complete and Christofides's algorithm approximates it within 1.5. If the distances are restricted to 1 and 2 (but still are a metric) the approximation ratio becomes 7/6. In the asymmetric, metric case, only logarithmic performance guarantees are known, the best current algorithm achieves performance ratio 0.814 log n; it is an open question if a constant factor approximation exists. The corresponding maximization problem of finding the longest travelling salesman tour is approximable within 63/38. If the distance function is symmetric, the longest tour can be approximated within 4/3 by a deterministic algorithm and within by a randomised algorithm.

Exact Algorithms

The most direct solution would be to try all permutations (ordered combinations) and see which one is cheapest (using brute force search). The running time for this approach lies within a polynomial factor of O(n!), the factorial of the number of cities, so this solution becomes impractical even for only 20 cities. One of the earliest applications of dynamic programming is the Held–Karp algorithm that solves the problem in time O(n2). The dynamic programming solution requires exponential space. Using inclusion–exclusion, the problem can be solved in time within a polynomial factor of 2 and polynomial space. Improving these time bounds seems to be difficult. For example, it has not been determined whether an exact algorithm for TSP that runs in time O(1.9999) exists. Other approaches include:

- Various branch-and-bound algorithms, which can be used to process TSPs containing 40–60 cities.
- Progressive improvement algorithms which use techniques reminiscent of linear programming. Works well for up to 200 cities.
- Implementations of branch-and-bound and problem-specific cut generation; this is the method of choice for solving large instances. This approach holds the current record, solving an instance with 85,900 cities.

An exact solution for 15,112 German towns from TSPLIB was found in 2001 using the cutting-plane method proposed by George Dantzig, Ray Fulkerson, and Selmer M. Johnson in 1954, based on linear programming. The computations were performed on a network of 110 processors located at Rice University and Princeton University. The total computation time was equivalent to 22.6 years on a single 500 MHz Alpha processor. In May 2004, the travelling salesman problem of visiting all 24,978 towns in Sweden was solved: a tour of length approximately 72,500 kilometres was found and it was proven that no shorter tour exists. In March 2005, the travelling salesman problem of visiting all 33,810 points in a circuit board was solved using Concorde TSP Solver: a tour of length 66,048,945 units was found and it was proven that no shorter tour exists. The computation took approximately 15.7 CPU-years (Cook et al. 2006). In April 2006 an instance with 85,900 points was solved using Concorde TSP Solver, taking over 136 CPU-years.

Heuristic and Approximation Algorithms

Various heuristics and approximation algorithms, which quickly yield good solutions have been devised. Modern methods can find solutions for extremely large problems (millions of cities) within a reasonable time which are with a high probability just 2–3% away from the optimal solution.

Several categories of heuristics are recognized.

Constructive Heuristics

The nearest neighbour (NN) algorithm (or so-called greedy algorithm) lets the salesman choose the nearest unvisited city as his next move. This algorithm quickly yields an effectively short route.

For N cities randomly distributed on a plane, the algorithm on average yields a path 25% longer than the shortest possible path. However, there exist many specially arranged city distributions which make the NN algorithm give the worst route (Gutin, Yeo, and Zverovich, 2002). This is true for both asymmetric and symmetric TSPs (Gutin and Yeo, 2007). Rosenkrantz et al. [1977] showed that the NN algorithm has the approximation factor $\Theta(\log |V|)$ for instances satisfying the triangle inequality. Constructions based on a minimum spanning tree have an approximation ratio of 2. The Christofides algorithm achieves a ratio of 1.5. The bitonic tour of a set of points is the minimum-perimetre monotone polygon that has the points as its vertices; it can be computed efficiently by dynamic programming.

Another constructive heuristic, Match Twice and Stitch (MTS) (Kahng, Reda 2004), performs two sequential matchings, where the second matching is executed after deleting all the edges of the first matching, to yield a set of cycles. The cycles are then stitched to produce the final tour.

Iterative Improvement

Pairwise Exchange, or Lin–Kernighan Heuristics

The pairwise exchange or 2-opt technique involves iteratively removing two edges and replacing these with two different edges that reconnect the fragments created by edge removal into a new and shorter tour. This is a special case of the k-opt method. Note that the label Lin–Kernighan is an often heard misnomer for 2-opt. Lin–Kernighan is actually a more general method.

k-opt Heuristic

Take a given tour and delete k mutually disjoint edges. Reassemble the remaining fragments into a tour, leaving no disjoint subtours (that is, don't connect a fragment's endpoints together). This in effect simplifies the TSP under consideration into a much simpler problem. Each fragment endpoint can be connected to 2k " 2 other possibilities: of 2k total fragment endpoints available, the two endpoints of the fragment under consideration are disallowed.

Such a constrained 2k-city TSP can then be solved with brute force methods to find the least-cost recombination of the original fragments. The k-opt technique is a special case of the V-opt or variable-opt technique. The most popular of the k-opt methods are 3-opt, and these were introduced by Shen Lin of Bell Labs in 1965. There is a special case of 3-opt where the edges are not disjoint (two of the edges are adjacent to one another).

In practice, it is often possible to achieve substantial improvement over 2-opt without the combinatorial cost of the general 3-opt by restricting the 3-changes to this special subset where two of the removed edges are adjacent. This so-called two-and-a-half-opt typically falls roughly midway between 2-opt and 3-opt, both in terms of the quality of tours achieved and the time required to achieve those tours.

V-opt Heuristic

The variable-opt method is related to, and a generalisation of the k-opt method. Whereas the k-opt methods remove a fixed number (k) of edges from the original tour, the variable-opt methods do not fix the size of the edge set to remove. Instead they grow the set as the search process continues. The best known method in this family is the Lin–Kernighan method (mentioned above as a misnomer for 2-opt). Shen Lin and Brian Kernighan first published their method in 1972, and it was the most reliable heuristic for solving travelling salesman problems for nearly two decades. More advanced variable-opt methods were developed at Bell Labs in the late 1980s by David Johnson and his research team. These methods (sometimes called Lin–Kernighan–Johnson) build on the Lin–Kernighan method, adding ideas from tabu search and evolutionary computing. The basic Lin–Kernighan technique gives results that are guaranteed to be at least 3-opt. The Lin–Kernighan–Johnson methods compute a Lin–Kernighan tour, and then perturb the tour by what has been described as a mutation that removes at least four edges and reconnecting the tour in a different way, then v-opting the new tour. The mutation is often enough to move the tour from the local minimum identified by Lin–Kernighan. V-opt methods are widely considered the most powerful heuristics for the problem, and are able to address special cases, such as the Hamilton Cycle Problem and other non-metric TSPs that other heuristics fail on. For many years Lin–Kernighan–Johnson had identified optimal solutions for all TSPs where an optimal solution was known and had identified the best known solutions for all other TSPs on which the method had been tried.

Randomised Improvement

Optimised Markov chain algorithms which use local searching heuristic sub-algorithms can find a route extremely close to the optimal route for 700 to 800 cities.

TSP is a touchstone for many general heuristics devised for combinatorial optimisation such as genetic algorithms, simulated annealing, Tabu search, ant colony optimisation, river formation dynamics and the cross entropy method.

Ant Colony Optimisation

Artificial intelligence researcher Marco Dorigo described in 1997 a method of heuristically generating "good solutions" to the TSP using a simulation of an ant colony called ACS (Ant Colony System). It models behaviour observed in real ants to find short paths between food sources and their nest, an emergent behaviour resulting from each ant's preference to follow trail pheromones deposited by other ants. ACS sends out a large number of virtual ant agents to explore many possible routes on the map. Each ant probabilistically chooses the next city to visit based on a heuristic combining the distance to the city and the amount of virtual pheromone deposited on the edge to the city. The ants explore, depositing pheromone on each edge that they cross, until they have all completed a tour. At this point the ant which completed the shortest tour deposits virtual pheromone along its complete tour route (global trail updating). The amount of pheromone deposited is inversely proportional to the tour length: the shorter the tour, the more it deposits.

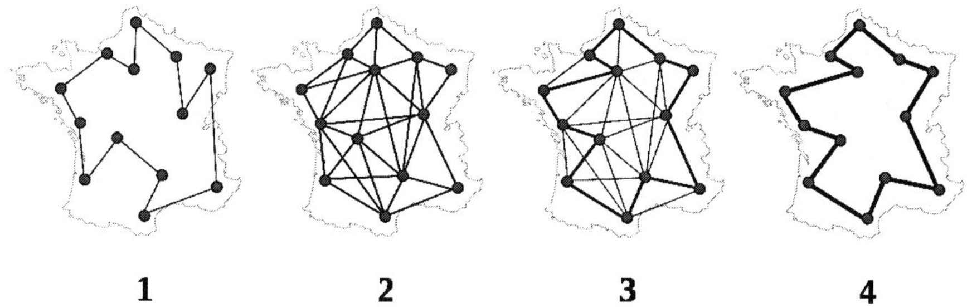

1 2 3 4

Special Cases

Metric TSP

In the metric TSP, also known as delta-TSP or Ä-TSP, the intercity distances satisfy the triangle inequality. A very natural restriction of the TSP is to require that the distances between cities form a metric, i.e., they satisfy the triangle inequality. This can be understood as the absence of "shortcuts", in the sense that the direct connection from A to B is never longer than the route via intermediate C:

$$d_{AB} \leq d_{AC} + d_{CB}$$

The edge lengths then form a metric on the set of vertices. When the cities are viewed as points in the plane, many natural distance functions are metrics, and so many natural instances of TSP satisfy this constraint. The following are some examples of metric TSPs for various metrics.

- In the Euclidean TSP the distance between two cities is the Euclidean distance between the corresponding points.
- In the rectilinear TSP the distance between two cities is the sum of the differences of their x- and y-coordinates. This metric is often called the Manhattan distance or city-block metric.
- In the maximum metric, the distance between two points is the maximum of the absolute values of differences of their x- and y-coordinates.

The last two metrics appear for example in routing a machine that drills a given set of holes in a printed circuit board. The Manhattan metric corresponds to a machine that adjusts first one co-ordinate, and then the other, so the time to move to a new point is the sum of both movements. The maximum metric corresponds to a machine that adjusts both co-ordinates simultaneously, so the time to move to a new point is the slower of the two movements. In its definition, the TSP does not allow cities to be visited twice, but many applications do not need this constraint. In such cases, a symmetric, non-metric instance can be reduced to a metric one. This replaces the original graph with a complete graph in which the inter-city distance d_{AB} is replaced by the shortest path between A and B in the original graph.

There is a constant-factor approximation algorithm for the metric TSP due to Christofides that always finds a tour of length at most 1.5 times the shortest tour. In the next paragraphs, we explain a weaker (but simpler) algorithm which finds a tour of length at most twice the shortest tour. The length of the minimum spanning tree of the network is a natural lower bound for the length of the optimal route. In the TSP with triangle inequality case it is possible to prove upper bounds in terms of the minimum spanning tree and design an algorithm that has a provable upper bound on the length of the route. The first published (and the simplest) example follows:

1. Construct the minimum spanning tree.
2. Duplicate all its edges. That is, wherever there is an edge from u to v, add a second edge from u to v. This gives us an Eulerian graph.

3. Find a Eulerian cycle in it. Clearly, its length is twice the length of the tree.
4. Convert the Eulerian cycle into the Hamiltonian one in the following way: walk along the Eulerian cycle, and each time you are about to come into an already visited vertex, skip it and try to go to the next one (along the Eulerian cycle).

It is easy to prove that the last step works. Moreover, thanks to the triangle inequality, each skipping at Step 4 is in fact a shortcut; i.e., the length of the cycle does not increase. Hence it gives us a TSP tour no more than twice as long as the optimal one.

The Christofides algorithm follows a similar outline but combines the minimum spanning tree with a solution of another problem, minimum-weight perfect matching. This gives a TSP tour which is at most 1.5 times the optimal. The Christofides algorithm was one of the first approximation algorithms, and was in part responsible for drawing attention to approximation algorithms as a practical approach to intractable problems. As a matter of fact, the term "algorithm" was not commonly extended to approximation algorithms until later; the Christofides algorithm was initially referred to as the Christofides heuristic.

In the special case that distances between cities are all either one or two (and thus the triangle inequality is necessarily satisfied), there is a polynomial-time approximation algorithm that finds a tour of length at most 8/7 times the optimal tour length. However, it is a long-standing (since 1975) open problem to improve the Christofides approximation factor of 1.5 for general metric TSP to a smaller constant. It is known that, unless P = NP, there is no polynomial-time algorithm that finds a tour of length at most 220/219=1.00456... times the optimal tour's length. In the case of bounded metrics it is known that there is no polynomial time algorithm that constructs a tour of length at most 321/320 times the optimal tour's length, unless P = NP.

Euclidean TSP

The Euclidean TSP, or planar TSP, is the TSP with the distance being the ordinary Euclidean distance.

The Euclidean TSP is a particular case of the metric TSP, since distances in a plane obey the triangle inequality.

Like the general TSP, the Euclidean TSP (and therefore the general metric TSP) is NP-complete. However, in some respects it seems to be easier than the general metric TSP. For example, the minimum spanning tree of the graph associated with an instance of the Euclidean TSP is a Euclidean minimum spanning tree, and so can be computed in expected O(n log n) time for n points (considerably less than the number of edges). This enables the simple 2-approximation algorithm for TSP with triangle inequality above to operate more quickly.

In general, for any c > 0, where d is the number of dimensions in the Euclidean space, there is a polynomial-time algorithm that finds a tour of length at most (1 + 1/c) times the optimal for geometric instances of TSP in time; this is called a polynomial-time approximation scheme (PTAS). Sanjeev Arora and Joseph S. B. Mitchell were awarded the Gödel Prize for their concurrent discovery of a PTAS for the Euclidean TSP in 2010. In practice, heuristics with weaker guarantees continue to be used.

Asymmetric TSP

In most cases, the distance between two nodes in the TSP network is the same in both directions. The case where the distance from A to B is not equal to the distance from B to A is called asymmetric TSP. A practical application of an asymmetric TSP is route optimisation using street-level routing (which is made asymmetric by one-way streets, slip-roads, motorways, etc.).

Solving by Conversion to Symmetric TSP

Solving an asymmetric TSP graph can be somewhat complex. The following is a 3×3 matrix containing all possible path weights between the nodes A, B and C. One option is to turn an asymmetric matrix of size N into a symmetric matrix of size 2N.

Asymmetric path Weights

	A	B	C
A		1	2
B	6		3
C	5	4	

To double the size, each of the nodes in the graph is duplicated, creating a second ghost node. Using duplicate points with very low weights, such as □”, provides a cheap route “linking” back to the real node and allowing symmetric evaluation to continue. The original 3×3 matrix shown above is visible in the bottom left and the inverse of the original in the top-right. Both copies of the matrix have had their diagonals replaced by the low-cost hop paths, represented by $-\infty$.

Symmetric path Weights						
	A	B	C	A′	B′	C′
A				$-\infty$	6	5
B				1	$-\infty$	4
C				2	3	$-\infty$
A′	$-\infty$	1	2			
B′	6	$-\infty$	3			
C′	5	4	$-\infty$			

The original 3×3 matrix would produce two Hamiltonian cycles (a path that visits every node once), namely A-B-C-A [score 9] and A-C-B-A [score 12]. Evaluating the 6×6 symmetric version of the same problem now produces many paths, including A-A2 -B-B2 -C-C2 -A, A-B2 -C-A2 -A, A-A2 -B-C2 -A [all score 9 $-\infty$]. The important thing about each new sequence is that there will be an alternation between dashed (A2,B2,C2) and undashed nodes (A, B, C) and that the link to "jump" between any related pair (A-A2) is effectively free. A version of the algorithm could use any weight for the A-A2 path, as long as that weight is lower than all other path weights present in the graph. As the path weight to "jump" must effectively be "free", the value zero (0) could be used to represent this cost—if zero is not being used for another purpose already (such as designating invalid paths). In the two examples above, non-existent paths between nodes are shown as a blank square.

Benchmarks

For benchmarking of TSP algorithms, TSPLIB is a library of sample instances of the TSP and related problems is maintained. Many of them are lists of actual cities and layouts of actual printed circuits.

Human Performance on TSP

The TSP, in particular the Euclidean variant of the problem, has attracted the attention of researchers in cognitive psychology. It is observed that humans are able to produce good quality solutions quickly. The first issue of the Journal of Problem Solving is devoted to the topic of human performance on TSP.

TSP path length for random pointset in a square: Suppose N points are randomly distributed in a 1 x 1 square with N>>1. Consider many such squares. Suppose we want to know the average of the shortest path length (i.e. TSP solution) of each square.

Lower Bound

$\frac{1}{2}\sqrt{N}$ is a lower bound obtained by assuming i be a point in the tour sequence and i has its nearest neighbour as its next in the path.

$\left(\frac{1}{4}+\frac{3}{8}\right)\sqrt{N}$ is a better lower bound obtained by assuming is next nearest, and is previous second nearest.

$\sqrt{\frac{N}{2}}$ is an even better lower bound obtained by dividing the path sequence into two parts as before_i and after_i with each part containing N/2 points, and then deleting the before_i part to form a diluted pointset.

- David S. Johnson obtained a lower bound by computer experiment: $0.7080\sqrt{N}+0.522$, where 0.522 comes from the points near square boundary which have fewer neighbours.
- Christine L. Valenzuela and Antonia J. Jones obtained another lower bound by computer experiment: $0.7078\sqrt{N}+0.551$,

Upper Bound

By applying Simulated Annealing method on samples of N=40000, computer analysis shows an upper bound of

$\left(\frac{\sqrt{N}}{2}+0.72\right)\cdot 1.015$, where 0.72 comes from the boundary effect.

Because the actual solution is only the shortest path, for the purposes of programmatic search another upper bound is the length of any previously discovered approximation.

Analyst's Travelling Salesman Problem

There is an analogous problem in geometric measure theory which asks the following: under what conditions may a subset E of Euclidean space be contained in a rectifiable curve (that is, when is there a continuous curve that visits every point in E)? This problem is known as the analyst's travelling salesman problem or the geometric travelling salesman problem.

Bibliography

Amirthavalli, M. : *Fuzzy Logic And Neural Networks*, Scitech Pub, Delhi, 2010.

Bezdec, J.C.: *Pattern Recognition with Fuzzy Objective Function Algorithms,* Plenum Press, New York, 1981.

Bhaskar, C. Naga and G. Vijay Kumar: *Neural Networks and Fuzzy Logic*, BS Publications, Delhi, 2011.

David R and Alla H : *Petri Nets and Grafcet: Tools for Modeling Discrete Event Systems.* Prentice Hall, New York, 1992.

Dubois, D. and H. Prade: *Fuzzy Sets and Systems: Theory and Applications*, Academic Press, New York, 1980.

Fogel, David B: *Evolutionary Computation: Toward a New Philosophy of Machine Intelligence,* IEEE Press, Piscataway, NJ. 2006.

Goldberg, David E: *Genetic Algorithms in Search, Optimization and Machine Learning,* Kluwer Academic Publishers, Boston, 1989.

Hájek, Petr: *Metamathematics of Fuzzy Logic*, Dordrecht: Kluwer, 1998.

Haykin, S.: *Neural Networks: A Comprehensive Foundation*, Prentice Hall, 1999.

Hertz, J., Palmer, R.G., Krogh. A.S.: *Introduction to the Theory of Neural Computation*, Perseus Books, 1990.

Holland, John H: *Adaptation in Natural and Artificial Systems*, University of Michigan Press, 1975.

Ibrahim, Ahmad M.: *Introduction to Applied Fuzzy Electronics.* Englewood Cliffs, N.J: Prentice Hall, 1997.

Jang, J.-S. R. and C.-T. Sun: *Neuro-Fuzzy and Soft Computing: A Computational Approach to Learning and Machine Intelligence*, Prentice Hall, 1997.

Kaufmann, A. and M.M. Gupta: *Introduction to Fuzzy Arithmetic*, V.N. Reinhold, 1985.

Klir, George J.; Folger, Tina A.: *Fuzzy Sets, Uncertainty, and Information.* Englewood Cliffs, N.J: Prentice Hall, 1988. ISBN 0-13-345984-5.

Kosko B: *Neural Networks and Fuzzy Systems. A Dynamical Systems Approach to Machine Intelligence.* Prentice Hall, New York, 1992.

Koza, John: *Genetic Programming: On the Programming of Computers by Means of Natural Selection*, MIT Press, Cambridge, 1992.

Kumar, Rajesh: *Fundamental of Artificial Neural Network and Fuzzy Logic*, Laxmi Pub, Delhi, 2009.

Lamba, V.K.: *Neuro Fuzzy Systems*, Laxmi Publications, Delhi, 2008.

Lawrence, Jeanette: *Introduction to Neural Networks*, California Scientific Software Press, 1994.

Lin CT and Lee CSG : *Neural Fuzzy Systems: A Neuro-Fuzzy Synergism to Intelligent Systems*. Prentice Hall PTR, London, 1996.

Masters, Timothy: *Signal and Image Processing with Neural Networks*, John Wiley & Sons, 1994.

Mitchell, Melanie: *An Introduction to Genetic Algorithms*, MIT Press, Cambridge, 1996.

Palm R, Driankov D and Hellendoorn H : *Model Based Fuzzy Control*. Springer, Delhi, 1997.

Passino, Kevin M.; Yurkovich, Stephen: *Fuzzy Control*. Boston: Addison-Wesley, 1998.

Pedrycz W : *Fuzzy Control and Fuzzy Systems*, John Wiley & Sons, London, 1993.

Pedrycz, Witold; Gomide, Fernando: *Fuzzy Systems Engineering: Toward Human-Centerd Computing*. Hoboken: Wiley-Interscience, 2007.

Ripley, Brian D.: *Pattern Recognition and Neural Networks*, Cambridge, London, 1996.

Ross T : *Fuzzy Logic with Engineering Applications*. McGraw-Hill, New York, 1995.

Stoll RR : *Set Theory and Logic*, Dover Publications, New York, 1979.

Sugeno, M.: *Industrial Applications of Fuzzy Control*, Elsevier Science Pub. Co., 1985.

Von Altrock, Constantin: *Fuzzy Logic and NeuroFuzzy Applications Explained*. Upper Saddle River, NJ: Prentice Hall, 1995.

Vose, Michael D: *The Simple Genetic Algorithm: Foundations and Theory*, MIT Press, Cambridge, 1999.

Wang, L.-X.: *Adaptive Fuzzy Systems and Control: Design and Stability analysis*, Prentice Hall, New York, 1994.

Zimmermann HJ : *Fuzzy Set Theory – and its Applications*, Kluwer Academic Publishers, Boston, 1993.